MODERN HUMOR
for
EFFECTIVE SPEAKING

MODERN HUMOR

for

EFFECTIVE SPEAKING

Edited by

EDWARD FRANK ALLEN

NEW YORK

THE CITADEL PRESS

ACKNOWLEDGMENTS

The Editor is indebted to the following publishers for permission to quote copyrighted material: The Viking Press for excerpts from *The Portable Dorothy Parker* (copyright 1944 by Dorothy Parker); Doubleday, Doran and Company, Inc., for an excerpt from *Not for Children* by Roland Young (copyright 1930 by Doubleday, Doran and Company, Inc); Little, Brown & Company for excerpts from poems by Ogden Nash; Simon & Schuster for a passage from *I Never Left Home* by Bob Hope.

PRINTED IN THE UNITED STATES OF AMERICA
BY THE VAIL-BALLOU PRESS, INC., BINGHAMTON, N. Y.

TO VERA

WHO

EXCEPT FOR A SENSE OF HUMOR,

WOULD HAVE MADE ME A GRASS WIDOWER

YEARS AGO

INTRODUCTION

How to Use Humor in Your Speech

There are few tools of the speaker so effective as humor in establishing audience rapport, for presenting ideas vividly and convincingly, or for combatting opposing points of view without arousing unnecessary antagonism. But humor is like dynamite. It can accomplish great feats when used judiciously and can also cause catastrophes when employed without special care and knowledge.

Contrary to many overcautious opinions, there is nothing mysterious or elusive about this special knowledge. Most speakers with an innate sense of humor can successfully introduce an occasional joke into their speeches without fear of having their sallies drop dolefully at their feet. Today's audiences have come to expect a certain amount of wit in every speech. They are willing and eager to meet you more than half way if you select your humorous material with the same care and attention that you give to your diction and grammar. You will find that the success of the humor in your speech depends largely on the following qualities, all of which I have conscientiously attempted to incorporate in this book.

Don't use a humorous story unless it is clearly appropriate and directly illustrates the point you want to make. There are few things more difficult to do than to tell a humorous story purely as a humorous story, out of all context. This is a skill peculiar to a few (and very few) professional comedians. On the other hand, if the joke or witticism is pertinent and an integral part of the ideas presented, it is almost certain to win easy audience acceptance.

So that you may have an instant choice of a number of relevant anecdotes relating to many common subjects, special care has been taken in the arrangement and indexing of this book. Broad general groupings such as "Business & Trade" are used because anecdotes common to the insurance business may be equally applicable to the food seller, etc. References to specific subjects such as Friendship, Pharmacy, Labor, Cleanliness, Radio, etc., will be found in the index.*

Although the anecdotes and epigrams in this book may be used successfully without drastic adaptation, the more you alter them to tie in with the interests of your audience, the more effective they will be. To accomplish this, make a point of using poetic license in retelling your stories. The same story told about General Eisenhower today was told about General Pershing during the last war, and about General Grant during the Civil War. Your stories will seem funnier and more pointed if their leading characters are familiar to your audience. For instance, your audience will be very happy if you have Jack Benny (or your good-natured club treasurer) instead of the usual "Scotchman" say: "The girl I escorted to the dance was so pretty that I could hardly keep my eyes on the taxi meter." Don't talk about "the main street in a small town." Talk about a specific street in *your* city or town. Don't talk about "a grocer" or "a bank president." Build the story around a grocer or bank president in your own locality. In theory it may sound a little threadbare to preface a story with the remark that ". . . as I walked into the lobby of this hall, I met our chairman's little daughter Jane and she said . . ." Actually this technique remains surprisingly effective. Don't fear that you'll be accused of perjury. Your audience will accept your "white lies" in a spirit of good fellowship.

Don't attempt to cram a laugh into every paragraph of your speech. You can achieve a very satisfactory audience connection with the use of only one or two well-chosen remarks of a humorous nature.

* The numbering of each entry is not consecutive between sections and subsections in order to (1) allow for later revisions and additions in future editions, and (2) make convenient the addition of your own material within the framework of the book.

Beware of the "off-color" story, or the story that depreciates religion, political beliefs, etc. Never take the risk of offending any part of your audience.

But the most painstaking care in selecting your anecdotes will serve no good purpose unless you rehearse every joke completely. Learn the story point by point. Memorize the exact phraseology of the punch line—and don't repeat or fumble it. Make an effort to maintain a conversational, slightly amused or straightfaced manner. Don't anticipate or follow the climax of your tale with gales of self-admiring laughter.

Keep your humorous material short, succinct, clearly phrased, free of literary verbiage which is difficult to understand at speaking speed. Don't elaborate and stretch your story. Even a bad joke can be forgiven if it is mercifully short.

Dialect stories are to be shunned like a plague. Too often you will not only appear ridiculous but will also mutilate your story beyond the understanding of the audience. Any really good anecdote will stand on its own legs, without the crutch of dialect.

Should your witty attempt fold its wings and die amidst melancholy silence, don't halt and grieve, or wait for the stillborn roars of laughter. Pass along into the next section of your speech and pretend that the joke never happened.

In compiling this book the author has kept in mind that the audience of today will not accept ready-made jokes any more than it will accept a ready-made or "canned" speech. The book has been designed to provide you with a ready reservoir of all the available raw material of modern humor. It will save you hours of research, but you must use your own discretion in selecting and adapting material that tells *your* story and appeals to *your* audience.

—The Editor.

TABLE OF CONTENTS

PAGE

INTRODUCTION: How to Use Humor in Your Speech . . . vii

1. AGRICULTURE . . . 1
2. ANIMALS . . . 7
3. ART AND MUSIC . . . 13
   Art . . . 13
   Music . . . 18
4. BEHAVIOR AND MANNERS . . . 27
   Advice and Criticism . . . 27
   Bravery and Cowardice . . . 29
   Caution . . . 31
   Cleanliness . . . 31
   Desires . . . 32
   Experience . . . 33
   Friendship and Enmity . . . 35
   Humor . . . 38
   Imagination . . . 39
   Ingenuity . . . 39
   Insult . . . 41
   Laziness . . . 45
   Luck and Accidents . . . 47
   Meanness . . . 47
   Memory and Absentmindedness . . . 48
   Modesty and Conceit . . . 49
   Morals . . . 52
   Optimism and Pessimism . . . 54
   Perseverance and Self-Reliance . . . 55
   Prejudice . . . 56
   Principles and Ideals . . . 58
   Simplicity . . . 59
   Social Graces . . . 62

PAGE

Stinginess 74
Stupidity 76
Success and Fame 77
Truth and Dishonesty 78
General Observations 81

5. Birth, Death, Ancestry and Age 87
6. Business and Trades 99
7. Children 125
8. Climate and Places 139
9. Clothing and Appearance 143
10. Eating and Drinking 149
Eating 149
Drinking 159
11. Education 177
12. Fighting Forces 195
13. Journalism 219
14. Law and Lawyers 225
15. Love 239
16. Marriage and Married Life 253
17. Medicine, Illness and Health 299
18. Money and Finance 315
19. Politics 323
20. Religion 335
21. Science and Psychology 365
22. Speaking, Writing and Language 369
23. Sports 393
24. The Theatre and the Movies 405
25. Travel 417
26. Writers and Books 423
27. Woman 431
Index 445

Section 1

AGRICULTURE

1

Every season out in Pomona, California, they hold a county fair that is attended from far and wide. A farmer from up in the valley attended the fair particularly because he wanted to see the grand champion bull. And he brought his whole family.

When he arrived at the entrance, he found that he and his wife and the two eldest children would have to pay fifty cents each and the other seven children twenty-five cents. Being a cattle-minded man, he kicked like a steer. The manager was going by and asked what was the matter. Said the farmer:

"I and the wife and the children have traveled nigh on to 200 miles to see that champion bull, but I'm danged if I can afford to pay $3.75 to get in."

"Are all those children yours?" the manager asked.

"They certainly are," said the farmer.

"Let 'em in free," the manager instructed the gatekeeper. Then, turning to the farmer, he said, "We want that bull to see you."

2

Believe it or not, one day a tenderfoot asked for food and lodging at a sheep ranch. The ranchman told him it was okay if he would go out and drive the sheep into the corral. So the man from the East set out, and he was gone a long, long time. When he returned, he said:

"I thought I never would get through. I drove the sheep in all right, but the lambs were a definite problem."

"Lambs?" the rancher exclaimed; "we don't have any lambs this time of year."

So he went out to the corral to investigate. He found that the tenderfoot had rounded up eighteen jackrabbits.

3

During a serious labor shortage a young woman got herself a job on a farm. At the end of the first day she returned to the house with an empty milk pail, and the farmer said:

"What's the idea? Didn't the old cow give anything?"

"Sure she did," the girl replied; "she gave nine quarts and one kick."

4

"Why do prices go up?" repeated the farmer when a city man asked the question. "I'll tell ye. When the farmer has to know the botanical name of what he grows, the entomological name of the pests that try to destroy it, and the pharmaceutical name of the stuff to spray it with, then, gol durn it, somebody's got to pay for it."

5

A farmer whose homestead was on the Polish-Russian border was in the position of not being certain whether his farm was in Poland or Russia. He got the advice of everybody he knew, but he still couldn't be sure. Finally he raised enough money to engage the services of a surveyor, and he waited nervously for the authoritative word. At length the report came through. His farm lay in Poland.

"Thank God," the farmer cried. "Now I won't have to endure another of those terrible Russian winters!"

6

It developed that the man who claimed to be a Southern planter was only a New Orleans undertaker.

7

Definition of *Farmer:* A handy man with a sense of humus.

8

"How do you figger it, Bill?" asked the farmer of his neighbor. "You paid three dollars for the shoat, then five dollars more for his feed. Then you sold him for eight dollars."

"Well," said Bill, "I had the company of the pig all summer, didn't I?"

9

A farmer told his hired man that both his clocks had run down and he wanted him to ride over to town and get the right time.

"Yes, sir," the hired man agreed, "but I ain't got a watch. Will you lend me yours?"

"Why the heck do you want a watch," asked the farmer. "Can't you write the time down on a piece of paper?"

10

Idaho potatoes are a reality that make one inclined to believe the stories they tell about Paul Bunyan, and so it is easy to credit this story. A Civilian Conservation Camp was established out in the Snake River country, and one day the foreman walked up to a potato farmer's house and asked if he could buy a hundred pounds. The farmer looked puzzled.

"Only a hundred pounds?" he echoed. The foreman nodded.

"No sir!" the farmer exclaimed. "I wouldn't cut a spud in half for nobody."

11

An old Negro cotton picker from the south, was asked what time he went to work in the morning. To which he replied:

"Boss, Ah doan go to work in the mawnin'; Ah's surrounded with it when Ah gits up."

12

No race can prosper till it learns that there is as much dignity in tilling a field as in writing a poem.

Booker T. Washington

13

During apple harvest time the new hired hand, preparing to pack a barrel, asked his employer:

"Large on top and small at the bottom?"

"Absolutely not," was the quick and virtuous answer. "Honesty, as you may have heard, is the best policy. The little apples go at the top and the large ones at the bottom."

The hired man thought it didn't make sense, but did as he was told. When the barrel was full according to specifications, the employer said:

"Now turn the barrel upside down and label it."

14

A Yankee farmer went to town one day and happened in a hardware store where an enterprising salesman tried to sell him a bicycle. The farmer considered all the arguments that were offered, and then he said:

"Guess I'll buy a cow instead."

"But," said the salesman, "think what a fool you would look riding around on a cow."

"Humph," the farmer returned; "I wouldn't look like half such a fool as if I tried to milk a bicycle."

15

If you tickle the earth with a hoe she laughs with a harvest.

Douglas Jerrold

16

A worm, coming out of the ground and meeting another worm, became enthusiastic, and said:

"Gosh, but you're a knockout; I'd like to marry you."

"Don't be a sap," was the bored reply; "I'm your other end."

17

A prize heifer belonging to a New Hampshire farmer was chewing her cud in a pasture when a stranger happened along and admired her. So he drove over to the farmer's house to see if he could buy the handsome animal.

"What'll you take for your cow?" he said to the Yankee.

The owner narrowed his eyes, ejected a squirt of tobacco juice, and wiped off his mouth before he answered:

"First-off I wanter know if you're the tax assessor or has the cow been killed by a railroad train?"

Section 2

ANIMALS

25

In the deep South a mule had been shipped on a train to a farmer in another country. Around his neck the shipper had tied a tag indicating his destination, but in the course of the journey the mule chewed up both the tag and the rope that bound him. A Negro brakeman on the train discovered the loss and was greatly exercised. He rushed back to the conductor and exclaimed:

"Boss, for de Lawd's sake, where we goin' to put off that fool mule? He done ate up where he's gwine."

26

The kangaroo was weeping bitterly.

"Why do you weep?" asked a passer-by.

"My little son," she said, "ran away from me and left me holding the bag."

27

Great fleas have little fleas upon their backs to bite 'em,
And little fleas have lesser fleas, and so ad infinitum.
The great fleas themselves in turn have greater fleas to go on,
While these again have greater still, and greater still,
and so on.

28

A smart young show-off from the city
Met what he opined was a kitty.

He gave it a pat
And said, "Nice little cat!"
They buried his clothes—out of pity.

29

The Sultan was peeved with his harem,
And cooked up a scheme for to scare 'em.
He caught a big mouse
Which he loosed in the house.
(Such confusion is called harem-scarem).

30

Behold the duck.
It does not cluck.
A cluck it lacks.
It quacks.
It is specially fond
Of a puddle or pond.
When it dines or sups,
It bottoms ups.

Ogden Nash

31

A cheerful old bear at the Zoo
Could always find something to do.
When it bored him, you know,
To walk to and fro,
He reversed it, and walked fro and to.

32

Cat: (Pussy). A pigmy lion who loves mice, hates dogs and patronizes human beings.

Oliver Herford

33

If you pick up a starving dog and make him prosperous he will not bite you. This is the principal difference between a dog and a man.

Mark Twain

34

On New York's 42nd Street there used to be a flea circus. One evening while the show was in progress, the insect that acted as driver of the flea coach jumped off the box and lit on a stout lady near by. This was serious for the owner of the show, who had spent a great deal of time training the fleas, so he asked the dame if she would look for the missing performer. She therefore retired to a private room and presently returned with the captive, which she handed triumphantly to the owner. He received it with thanks. Then he exclaimed:

"But, madam, this is not my flea."

35

A cockroach was running at great speed across the top of an unopened cracker box, and another one was trying to keep up with him.

"Why are we in such a hurry?" the second one asked.

"Can't you see the sign?" said the other. "It says, 'Tear along the dotted line.' "

36

Add this one to the kid questions that won't be answered. An eight-year-old said to his mother:

"I see in the paper that a single fly can lay 7,992 eggs."

"Isn't that wonderful," Mother commented.

"Yes," said the boy, "but if that's the case, how many could a married one lay?"

37

Zoo: A place devised for animals to study the habits of human beings.

Oliver Herford

38

A flea and a fly in a flue
Were imprisoned, so what could they do?
  Said the fly, "Let us flee."
  "Let us fly," said the flea,
And they flew through a flaw in the flue.

39

Protect the birds. The dove brings peace and the stork brings tax exemptions.

40

"Now it all comes back to me," as the skunk said when the wind changed.

41

A big tom-cat was rushing hither and thither, over back fences, through alleys, across streets, down cellar steps and into hidden corners. A neighbor who recognized the cat reported its goings-on to its owner.

"Oh, yes," said the owner, "I know. Tom's just been sterilized and he's rushing around cancelling engagements."

42

The most ingenious person who emerged from World War II was the fellow who crossed a homing pigeon with a woodpecker and produced a bird that not only delivered the message but knocked on the door.

43

"Papa," Willie asked, "is it right to say you water a horse when he is thirsty?"

"Sure it is," said his father; "why?"

"All right," said the boy as he picked up a bowl; "I'm going to milk the cat."

44

The lightning bug is brilliant, but hasn't any mind;
He flutters through existence with his headlight on behind.

45

The flea is always a pessimist. He knows that his children will more than likely go to the dogs.

46

"The most useful animal on earth," said a Negro recently, "is the chicken. You can eat him before he is born and after he is dead."

47

No wonder there were fewer accidents in the old horse-and-buggy days; the driver didn't have to depend wholly on his own intelligence.

A man walking along a country road saw a farmer having trouble with his horse. The animal would start, walk for a short distance, and then stop. Then he would repeat the performance.

The traveler said to the farmer:

"What's wrong with your horse? Is he sick?"

"Nope, he ain't sick."

"Is he balky?"

"Nope, he ain't balky."

"Then what the devil is the matter with him?"

"Heck, nothin'," the farmer replied. "But he's so tarnation afraid I'll say 'Whoa' and he won't hear me that he stops every once in a while to make sure I'm not talkin' to him."

48

Nobody will believe this story anyway, so you may as well tell it on any friend of yours who has a dog.

You dropped in unexpectedly one evening and found Bill Smith playing chess with his Airedale. You watched for a little while without saying a word. Then you exclaimed:

"That's the most wonderful dog I ever saw!"

"Oh, he isn't too good," Bill Smith said; "I've beaten him three games out of four."

49

Said an envious erudite ermine,
"There's one thing I cannot determine:
When a dame wears my coat,
She's a person of note;
When I wear it, I'm called only vermin."

50

The man was explaining where the mule kicked him. "If," he said, "my head was in New York and my feet in San Francisco, he would have kicked me in Omaha."

Section 3

ART AND MUSIC

Art

59

John Singer Sargent defined a portrait as a picture of someone with something wrong with the mouth.

60

Samuel Goldwyn was inordinately proud of his wife's hands.

A visitor to Hollywood made mention of their beauty, to which Mr. Goldwyn replied:

"Yes, she has such beautiful hands, I'm thinking of having a bust made of them."

61

James McNeill Whistler despised gushers, especially of the female persuasion. One day a woman said to him:

"Dear Mr. Whistler, this morning I came up from the country along the Thames, and there was such an exquisite haze in the atmosphere that I was constrained to think that the views were a perfect series of Whistlers."

"No doubt," the artist replied in his most serious manner; "Nature is creeping up."

62

One afternoon Mark Twain called at Whistler's studio and looked at some of his paintings. Presently he ran his finger over one of them.

"Be careful," Whistler exclaimed. "Don't you see it isn't dry?"

"Oh that's all right," Mark answered; "I have gloves on."

63

Mark Twain's impression of J. M. W. Turner's impressionistic painting *The Slave Ship* was "a tortoise-shell cat having a fit in a platter of tomatoes."

64

The artist Whistler was well qualified to write a book on "The Gentle Art of Making Enemies." When he had finished painting a portrait of a London celebrity he asked the man if he liked it.

"No, Mr. Whistler," was the reply; "I can't say that I do. You'll have to admit it's a bad work of art."

Whistler adjusted his monocle and looked at his sitter. Then he said:

"Yes, but then you must admit that you're a bad work of nature."

65

Whistler's landlady once offended him, and he went to a good deal of trouble to get revenge. The woman lived on the floor below his apartment and had a bowl of goldfish on her window sill. Whistler got a hook and line and from his window caught all the fish. Then he fried them to a turn and skillfully dropped them back into the bowl.

66

Dilettante: A philanderer who seduces the several Arts and deserts each in turn for another.

Oliver Herford

67

Mr. and Mrs. Wortle returned from abroad and were telling their friends of their visit to Paris. Mr. Wortle mentioned especially a painting in the Louvre of Adam and Eve and the serpent, when Mrs. Wortle chimed in:

"Oh yes, it was most interesting to us, because"—and she beamed in a superior way—"you see, we knew the anecdote."

68

GERTRUDE, JACOB, AND ALBERT

There's a wonderful family called Stein,
There's Gert, and there's Ep, and there's Ein.
  Gert's poems are bunk,
  Ep's statues are junk,
And no one can understand Ein.

69

Charles M. Schwab, steel magnate, was known personally by many of his older employees, who regarded him as a "regular guy." One day he went into the open-hearth room of one of his mills and saw a big hairy-chested workman with the glow of the furnaces reflected in his sweat.

"Sam," Schwab said, "you look like an old Rembrandt."

"Well," was the reply, "you don't look so good yourself, Charlie."

70

James McNeill Whistler used to take pleasure in baiting Oscar Wilde, but occasionally Oscar got back at him. At one time he wrote:

"Whistler is indeed one of the greatest masters of painting in my opinion. And I may add that in this opinion Mr. Whistler himself entirely concurs."

71

A tourist, who, we are afraid, was an American, was scornful of what he saw in a London art gallery, and told the guide what he thought.

"Sir," the guide replied, "these pictures are no longer on trial; the spectators are."

72

When Ralph Waldo Emerson was sitting to the sculptor Daniel Chester French for his bust, he observed:

"The trouble is, the more it resembles me, the worse it looks."

73

Samuel F. B. Morse would be remembered for his paintings even if he had not invented the Morse telegraph. At one time he painted a picture of a man in the agony of death and asked a doctor friend to look at it. The doctor gave it one glance and without hesitation said:

"Malaria."

74

As an art critic, James McNeill Whistler was sometimes politely devastating, but he was always devastating. On one occasion he was painting a portrait of Lady Eden, who told him of a Turner that someone wanted her to purchase. She said that she was not sure whether it was a real Turner or a fake Turner, and asked Whistler to come and give his opinion.

"Quite impossible, my dear Lady Eden," he replied; "and, after all, isn't the distinction a very subtle one?"

75

I cannot spare the luxury of believing that all things beautiful are what they seem.

Fitz-Greene Halleck

76

What garlic is to salad, insanity is to art.

Homer Saint-Gaudens

77

Art is limitation; the essence of every picture is the frame.

Gilbert K. Chesterton

78

Dun Phares, who works for The Associated Press, comes from Texas, where his name does not seem an unusual one. But according to a story they tell on him, he was introduced to a man who seemed curious about it.

"Phares, Phares," he repeated. "What a strange name. How long have you lived in this country? Where were you born? You certainly speak good English."

The newspaper man answered the questions politely, but after the stranger had gone he asked:

"Who was that bird who seemed to think I had a curious name?"

"That," his friend said, "was Gutzon Borglum."

79

Poetry is vocal painting, as painting is silent poetry.

Simonides

80

Note from a newspaper art critic's column: They couldn't find the artist, so they hung his picture.

81

Along with G. Bernard Shaw's, shall we say, critical perspicacity, he packs a real sense of humor. Listen to what he said on the subject of pictures:

"A photograph is 80 per cent sitter, 20 per cent photographer. A painting is 75 per cent artist, and only 25 per cent sitter. Caricatures? Bah! Child's play! Caricatures are never like me. One day I went into a friend's flat and I did at last see a caricature of me that seemed to be good. It was cruel, of course, but still it was what a caricature should be. Then it moved, and I saw it was a mirror."

Music

90

A promising young violinist was sent to Eugene Ormandy with an impressive letter of introduction from an old and respected friend of the famous conductor.

"I'm sorry," said Ormandy, "but there is no opening for you now in the orchestra, but if you care to stay in town for awhile, I'll be glad to place you at the first opportunity."

The opportunity came a week later, when the second violinist was taken to the hospital for an appendectomy.

In the opening passage of the Seventh Symphony that night, the conductor listened intently for the strains of the second violin and was pleased that he was doing well. Glancing at him, he was surprised to see an expression of pain on the violinist's face. "Heavens," he thought, "is he ill, too?"

As the symphony progressed, the second violinist appeared in great agony. During the intermission, Ormandy went to the musician's dressing room and asked, "Are you sick?"

"No, sir," said the young man.

"Is there anything paining you?"

"Not at all."

"Then," shouted Ormandy angrily, "you must not approve of my conducting."

"On the contrary," said the musician, "I consider it a great privilege to play under you, sir."

"Then why in heaven's name were you making such hideous faces?"

"Oh, that—" said the young man. "You see, sir, I just don't like music."

91

Mark Twain was invited to be the guest of a box-holder at the Metropolitan Opera House to hear "Aida," a favorite of the humorist. All through the performance his hostess talked so much that no one could follow the music. As the last curtain descended, she turned to Mark and said effusively:

"Dear Mr. Clemens, I hope you can join us again next Thursday evening. The opera is 'Tosca,' and I know you'll enjoy it."

"I'll be delighted," Mark rejoined, "I've never heard you in that."

92

During a war boom Mr. Stonestein made ten million dollars and began to "go to town." Among other extravagances, he decided that his son should take violin lessons. And nothing but the most expensive instrument would do for the boy. The dealer showed him a real Stradivarius.

"This," he said, "was made in 1748. The price is fifty thousand dollars."

Stonestein nearly took the count, but he remembered his immense fortune and recovered his poise.

"So," he said. " 'Made in 1748. Price fifty thousand dollars. . . .' Tell me, is the factory that made this fiddle still in existence?"

"Oh no, sir," the dealer said.

"Well," concluded Stonestein, "I won't take it then. What would I do about spare parts?"

93

Two men were discussing a mutual acquaintance. Said one:

"He talks interminably about his ills—heart, liver, kidneys, lungs, etc."

"Sounds to me like an organ recital—without stops."

94

The composer Mozart was once asked by a young man how to write a symphony.

"You're still very young," Mozart objected; "why don't you begin with ballads?"

"But," urged the young man, "you composed symphonies when you were only ten years old."

"True enough," the composer said, "but I didn't ask how."

95

Jascha Elman and Mischa Heifetz were eating lunch together in one of New York's swanky restaurants when the head waiter brought to their table an envelope addressed: "To the World's Greatest Violinist."

Heifetz picked it up from the tray, smiled, and passed it over to Elman, who, always the gentleman, said:

"No, Mahster, it is for you."

So, protesting modestly, Heifetz opened it. The note began:

"Dear Fritz. . . ."

96

This doesn't sound like the kindly Fritz Kreisler, but he's the man they tell it on, so it must be true. The master violinist was walking with a friend one afternoon and passed a fish shop with a windowful of cod with staring eyes and open mouths.

Kreisler suddenly grasped his friend by the arm.

"Mein Gott!" he exclaimed. "That reminds me; I am playing at a concert this afternoon."

97

Dr. Samuel Johnson, who lived chiefly through having a good biographer, was doubtless a very stuffy person, but he had an engaging way of being offensive. Some woman at a party asked him if he liked music, and he replied:

"No, madam, but of all noises, I think that music is the least disagreeable."

98

Alec Templeton, the blind piano virtuoso, is credited with having the last word in the following story.

A woman waylaid him after the radio broadcast and gushed:

"Oh, Mr. Templeton, that last selection you played was divine. May I ask who was the composer?"

"Bach, madam," Templeton replied.

"Wonderful," the lady burbled, "and is he composing at present?"

"No," the pianist answered, "he is decomposing."

99

Lullaby: A Rotarian's account of his trip around the world.

Oliver Herford

100

Song: The licensed medium for bawling in public things too silly or too sacred to be uttered in ordinary speech.

Oliver Herford

101

Definition of a *Piccolo:* An ill wood-wind that nobody blows good.

102

A newspaper reporter who covered a recital made his story short with:

"An amateur string quartette played Brahms here last evening. Brahms lost."

103

There was an old person of Tring
Who, when somebody asked her to sing,
  Replied, "Ain't it odd?
  I can never tell 'God
Save the Weasel' from 'Pop Goes the King.' "

104

In the latter part of his career Giuseppe Verdi became popular and his townsfolk would listen at doors and win

when he was rehearsing a new opera. The result was that before the opera was produced the whole town would be humming the score. This so annoyed Verdi that he vowed that he would compose an aria that no one would hear before its presentation.

The first two acts of the next opera went over big. At the beginning of the fourth act, Verdi himself sat down at the piano, placed a manuscript before him, and played six or eight measures. Then he paused, turned, and thumbed his nose at the audience. He resumed playing, the curtain rose, and the tenor brought down the house with the thrilling *La Donna E Mobile,* which Verdi had composed just an hour before the debut of *Rigoletto*.

105

A small boy was taken to a concert of classical music for children. The conductor took the trouble to explain various musical forms to his young audience. Among these forms was swing, which he defined as an unconventional and irregular movement from bar to bar. Whereat the small boy was heard to exclaim, "My pop calls that a bender."

106

The scene was Heaven. Into its radiance strutted the great opera singer. Heaven was properly impressed, and asked him to name his greatest wish. He would like, he said, to organize the greatest chorus of all time.

"Give me ten thousand sopranos, ten thousand tenors and, say, a thousand altos."

"Magnificent," said one of the heavenly attendants, "but what about basso voices?"

"Oh," replied the distinguished artist, "I'll sing bass myself."

107

Swans sing before they die; 'twere no bad thing
Should certain persons die before they sing.

Samuel Coleridge

108

This story is told about Grace Moore—although it has also been credited to Caruso, Gladys Swarthout, etc. A wealthy profiteer's wife decided to make a big splurge at her mansion-warming by hiring the famous singer to entertain. When a fee of $5,000 was quoted for a single evening she caught her breath sharply but agreed at last.

"However," she said regally, "you must remember that you are not expected to associate with my guests."

"In that event, my charge drops to only $2,000," said the singer.

109

A Park Avenue nabob invited his nephew to spend a week with him in New York, and the young man from the middle West accepted. He was lavishly entertained, and the culminating event was a visit to the "diamond horseshoe" of the Metropolitan Opera. The lad was entranced, and his uncle was pleased at his appreciation. Catching the enthusiasm, the older man said:

"Did you ever see anything like it?"

"No," the boy answered; "I didn't, for a fact—leastwise not since I was weaned."

110

A girl called one day on the pianist-composer Rubinstein to play for him. When she had finished, she asked him:

"What do you think I should do now?"

"Get married," said Rubinstein.

111

Johnnie sat patiently through the first number of the San Francisco Symphony concert. Next, the coloratura soprano was featured with orchestral accompaniment.

"Mother," Johnnie exclaimed, "why is that man shaking his stick at the lady?"

"Shush! He's not shaking his stick at her," said the parent.

"Then what," queried Johnny, "is she screaming about?"

112

Noise: A stench in the ear. Undomesticated music. The chief product and authenticating sign of civilization.

Ambrose Bierce

113

At the first performance of George Antheil's modernistic Ballet Mécanique, the orchestra contained ten grand pianos, six xylophones, a fire-alarm siren, an airplane propeller, and several automobile horns. As the music mounted in volume, the audience became restless and continued to grow more excitable. Finally, after eight minutes of the composition, a man in one of the front rows raised a white handkerchief tied to his cane, and the entire audience burst into laughter.

114

The musicians who invented swing ought to.

O. O. McIntyre

115

Millions of dollars are spent on the opera which could be used in abolishing it.

116

Bernard Shaw went into a London restaurant for lunch one day, ordered a mess of vegetables, and began to eat. Presently an orchestra struck up a particularly noisy tune, and without any intermission, followed it with another. Shaw called the head waiter and asked:

"Does the orchestra play anything on request?"

"Yes, sir," the man replied; "is there something you would like them to play?"

"There is," said Shaw; "ask them to play dominoes until I have finished eating."

117

No doubt this has been told on every famous conductor over a period of many centuries, so when you tell it, you can pick out the appropriate one.

At a certain point during a symphony, a soloist began his cadenza with a flourish, but he soon ran into heavy weather and got further and further off the key. The conductor (call him Bodansky, Stowkowski, or Toscanini, or even make up a name) was definitely worried.

But just before the orchestra's cue to begin playing again, the soloist got back on the beam and finished on the original key. The great conductor bowed, and said:

"Welcome home, Mr. Lipschutz!"

118

This is another story that may be told on different celebrities.

A well known composer of popular music approached a top-flight conductor of a big symphony orchestra and asked:

"How much would you charge to give me lessons in orchestration?"

"How much do you make in a year?" the maestro inquired.

"About $150,000," the song writer replied.

"Gosh," said the maestro; "how about your giving *me* lessons?"

Section 4

BEHAVIOR AND MANNERS

Advice and Criticism

145

As a critic, Matthew Arnold was, in a word, critical. When he died, someone remarked:

"Poor Matthew, he won't like God!"

146

A nervous old lady went to the captain of a steamship on its way to Europe by a northern route. She asked him:

"What would happen if we struck an iceberg?"

"Calm your fears, Madam," the captain replied; "the iceberg would continue on its way as if nothing had happened."

And the old lady was reassured.

147

A teacher once said this to me:
"Be sure you're right—then go ahead:"
But she didn't take in account the fact
That sometimes a nut has a left-hand thread.

Ned Allen

148

Up in Maine last summer I asked a native if he knew where Samuel Stevens lived.

"Do you know Stevens?" I asked.

"Yep."

"Do you know where he lives?"

"Yep."

"Do you think he's at home now?"

"Nope."

"Well, where can I find him?"

"Here. I'm Sam Stevens."

"Why didn't you tell me in the first place?"

"You didn't ask me."

149

Advice: One thing that is more blessed to give than to receive.

150

The Department of Agriculture receives thousands of requests for advice from homeowners with small lawns and gardens.

One man wrote that he was having a losing fight trying to keep the dandelions out of his lawn. He asked the department to suggest some way of ridding the lawn of the weeds, for he loved his lawn and wanted to save it.

After the usual lapse of time, the Department of Agriculture answered his appeal with the practical suggestion that he learn to love the dandelions too.

151

The feller that sets on a store box with his mouth full of scrap terbacker while his wife is at home sewin' fer a livin' knows jist exactly how t' regulate th' railroads.

Kin Hubbard

152

Don't cross the bridge until you come to it, and then be sure there's a bridge.

153

On the palisades at Santa Monica, California, a man was walking up and down shouting, "No, no, no, no!" He attracted the attention of a little old lady, and she asked a policeman what was the matter.

"He's all right, lady," the officer said, "he's just a Hollywood yes-man on vacation."

154

Yesman: A fellow who hangs around the man that nobody noes.

Bravery and Cowardice

160

This was away back in the 'sixties when the first train was crossing the plains of Texas. Charging down the track headed straight for the locomotive, the engineer saw a shaggy monster of a buffalo coming full tilt. And the man at the throttle observed:

"Old boy, I sure admire your nerve; but damn your judgment."

161

It was in Arizona and Cactus Pete was telling some tourists one of his experiences.

"Just the other day," he said, "I fell asleeep under a mesquite bush. A little later I felt a pressure on my chest. When I opened my eyes I was looking straight at a rattlesnake, coiled and all ready for business. If I'd 'a made a move, he'd 'a struck quickern grease."

One of the tourists spoke up and asked:

"What did you do?"

And Pete replied:

"There wasn't nothin' I *could* do; so I just went back to sleep."

162

It is open to debate as to whether men have more courage than women, but one thing is certain: they don't have as many opportunities to show their backbone.

163

Coward: One who, in a perilous emergency, thinks with his legs.

Ambrose Bierce

164

A German and a Frenchman had a quarrel, and arranged to fight a duel with pistols. Both of them being cowards, they arranged to fight in a pitch dark room. Lots were drawn and the German won the right to fire first. When the signal was given, he fumbled his way to the fireplace and shot up the chimney—and brought down the Frenchman.

165

An old-time whaler, was harpooning a big sperm whale when the monster turned, crushed the boat and tossed the crew in the sea. For a deadly moment the whaler was in the monster's great jaws, but managed to pull himself out and was rescued by his mates.

"Captain," said a friend, "what did you think when you found yourself in the whale's jaws?"

"I thought," replied the captain, "the whale would make 100 barrels—and by the prophets, he did!"

166

"It was at this base that Captain Bud Ross (I understand he's now a major) took me up in a P-38. They're made for only one person, so I kind of rode piggy-back. Those things really travel. Just for fun I decided to spit down at the ground. Ross should have told me we were flying upside down.

"He went into a dive so steep the instruments couldn't record our speed. It's the only dive I was ever anxious to get out of. On top of that he started stunting with me, but we got our signals crossed. Ross did an inside turn while my stomach was doing an outside loop. Things didn't seem to be going right after that. I've done enough flying to know when a pilot's in trouble. I didn't want to show my nervousness, but I couldn't help saying, 'Do you mind if I bite my nails?' Ross said, 'No! Go right ahead. Anything to make you stop biting mine.' "

Bob Hope in "I Never Left Home,"
Published by Simon & Schuster

Caution

170

Zeke Daniel would never commit himself by a positive statement. He was the most careful man that way in six counties. Finally one of his friends made a bet with another that he would make him be definite on at least one occasion. One day not long afterward Zeke and the two friends were driving along a country road, on one side of which was a pasture in which there was a flock of sheep that without doubt had recently given up their wool. Said one of the men:

"Those sheep have certainly been sheared close, haven't they, Zeke?"

And Zeke replied:

"It looks so from this side."

171

"Is that man careful?" echoed a gossiper. "Why he's as careful as a nudist going through a barbed wire fence."

Cleanliness

174

Small boys don't look in the glass after washing to see if their faces are clean. They look at the towel.

175

If dirt was trumps, what hands you would hold!

Charles Lamb

176

Frederick had reached the new and colorful necktie stage and occasionally he combed his hair, but he still hated to wash behind his ears.

"Cleanliness is next to godliness," his mother said in despair.

"Oh sure, Mater, maybe in the Bible it's next to godliness, but in Pittsburgh it's next to impossible."

Desires

179

A mountaineer who came into town saw a bunch of bananas for the first time. He asked the dealer what they were.

"Bananas," he said; and then he good-naturedly added, "Try one."

"No, I reckon not," the man from the mountains replied. "I've got so many tastes now I can't satisfy, I ain't aimin' to take on any more."

180

Of Franklin D. Roosevelt it was said: "He is a man of simple tastes; all he wants is the best of everything."

181

A small boy was chided by his mother for always wishing for what he didn't have.

"But Mother," he said, "what else can I wish for?"

182

Fanatic: One who redoubles his energies after he has forgotten his aim.

183

Oliver Herford was seated next to a very serious and awesome young woman at a dinner party.

"Mr. Herford," she asked, "have you no other ambition than to make people laugh?"

In the same solemn vein, Mr. Herford replied, "Yes, I have. And some day I hope to gratify it."

Flattered upon being taken into his confidence, she begged, "Please tell me. What is it?"

"I want," replied Mr. Herford, "to throw an egg into an electric fan."

184

Wit is current change, but humor is priceless.

One of Abraham Lincoln's neighbors in Springfield, Illinois, told the following:

One day, arrested by the cries of children, I looked out the door and saw Mr. Lincoln stalking by with two of his boys. Both of them were weeping out loud.

"What's the matter with the boys, Mr. Lincoln?" I asked.

The future president looked at me, smiled, and answered:

"Just what's the matter with the whole world. I've got three walnuts and each wants two."

185

Desire: There are two tragedies in life. One is not to get your heart's desire. The other is to get it.

George Bernard Shaw

186

I would rather be able to appreciate things I cannot have than to have things I am not able to appreciate.

Elbert Hubbard

Experience

190

I am an old man and have known a great many troubles, but most of them never happened.

Mark Twain

191

He jests at scars that never felt a wound.

Shakespeare

192

An Asiatic prince raised his little son with an eye to preparing him for the cruel realities of life. As an object lesson he put the child on a high ledge and urged him to jump into his arms. The boy did this repeatedly until he was no longer afraid. On the last jump the father stepped aside and the child fell to the ground. Lifting the whimpering little son of his heart, he said, "Let this be a lesson to you. Never trust anyone—not even your own father."

193

I had rather have a fool to make me merry than experience to make me sad.

Shakespeare

194

Life is like playing a violin solo in public and learning the instrument as one goes on.

Bulwer-Lytton

195

We came into this world naked and bare,
We go through this world full of sorrow and care;
We go out of this world we know not where,
But if we're good fellows here we'll be thoroughbreds there.

196

Razors pain you;
Rivers are damp;
Acids stain you;
And drugs cause cramp.

Guns aren't lawful;
Nooses give;
Gas smells awful;
You might as well live.

Dorothy Parker

197

In the School of Experience there has never been but one class yell: "Ouch!"

198

It is said that an Eastern monarch once charged his wise men to invent a sentence to be ever in view, and which should be true and appropriate in all times and situations. They presented him these words: "And this, too, shall pass away."

Elbert Hubbard

Friendship and Enmity

200

There is a pathetic note as well as the usual wry humor in the statement Whistler wrote in his later years:

"I'm lonesome. They are all dying. I have hardly a warm personal enemy left."

201

Artistry in cursing a hated person reached the zenith when a well-known entomologist exploded with:

"May you turn into a centipede with ingrown toenails!"

202

One wise mother tells her children to divide all people into two classes—friends and strangers. Friends we love too well to gossip about; strangers we know too little.

Heywood Broun

203

I choose my friends for their good looks, my acquaintances for their good characters, and my enemies for their good intellects. A man cannot be too careful in the choice of his enemies.

Oscar Wilde

204

It's easy enough to stand up to your enemies; it's another matter to stand up to your friends.

205

Friends: People with the same enemies.

206

When you're down and out, something always turns up—and it's usually the noses of your friends.

Orson Welles

207

An acquaintance, says Ambrose Bierce in "The Devil's Dictionary," is "a person whom we know well enough to borrow from but not well enough to lend to."

208

The chances are when a man slaps you on the back he is trying to make you cough up something.

209

Defend me from my friends; I can defend myself from my enemies.

Voltaire

210

The only way to have a friend is to be one.

Emerson

211

A city dweller had been listening to his friend extolling the advantages of suburban life: green trees and flowers, sunlight, space, quiet, and a lovely back yard.

"But how," asked the skeptical city man, "do you make your next door neighbor keep his hens in his own yard?"

"Oh, I fixed that all right," said the suburbanite. "One dark evening I hid a few eggs under a bush in my garden. Then the next day, when my neighbor was looking our way, I took pains to have him see me find them. After that I wasn't bothered at all."

212

Among the many stories that may be adapted to almost any pair of well known people is another one on Wilson Mizner. Someone asked him what he thought of Frank Case, the genial manager of New York's Algonquin Hotel.

"He's a prince," Mizner exclaimed; "he'd give you the—" Then he opened his coat, looked down, and blurted, "Mercy, this *is* his shirt!"

213

The best way to keep your friends is not to give them away.

Wilson Mizner

214

He makes no friends who never made a foe.

Tennyson

215

A motorist stopped his car in front of a cabin in the Kentucky mountains and asked if Jim Mudge lived in the neighborhood.

"No," the native replied.

"Over in town they told me he lived near here. Do you know Bill Podd?"

"I'm Bill Podd," came the answer.

"Well," the motorist persisted, "they said Mudge lived within gunshot of you."

Bill Podd expectorated, and said, "He did."

216

A friend that ain't in need is a friend indeed.

Abe Martin

Humor

217

It is related that George M. Cohan once said that he would rather play to an English audience than an American audience. When he was asked to tell the difference between these two audiences, he replied:

"It's this way: an Englishman first laughs out of courtesy; then he laughs when the rest of the audience gets the joke; and again when he gets it himself."

"How about the American?" came the question.

"He doesn't laugh," said Mr. Cohan; "he's heard the joke before."

218

Facetious: Funny without being vulgar and vice versa.

Oliver Herford

219

Lincoln's sense of humor began to develop at an early age. When he was fourteen years old he wrote in his copy-book:

" 'Tis Abraham Lincoln holds the pen;
He will be good, but God knows when."

Imagination

221

In the war against Reality, man has but one weapon—Imagination.

Jules de Gaultier

222

Were it not for imagination, Sir, a man would be as happy in the arms of a chambermaid as of a Duchess.

Samuel Johnson

Ingenuity

225

Conan Doyle taxied from the station to his hotel in Paris. As he left his cab the driver said, "Merci, Monsieur Conan Doyle."

"How did you know my name?" asked Doyle curiously.

"There was a notice in the paper that you were arriving in Paris from the South of France this evening," explained the driver. "I knew from your general appearance that you were an Englishman. It is evident that the barber has cut your hair within the week, and that a barber from the South of France cut it. By these indications I knew you."

"This is amazing. You had no other evidence to go upon?" queried Doyle.

"Nothing," said the taxi man, "except the fact that your name is on your luggage."

226

Ingenuity: The different things you can do with Spam.

Bob Hope

227

Strategy: It's when you keep on firing after you're out of ammunition.

228

Horse sense is what keeps horses from betting on what people will do.

229

Nobody Home

You beat your pate, and fancy wit will come.
Knock as you please—there's nobody at home.

Alexander Pope

230

The Life of the Party was telling about his invitation to a nudist dinner.

"When I rang the doorbell," he said, "the door was opened by a nudist butler."

"How on earth did you know it was the butler?" inquired a listener.

"Well anyway," the man replied, "I knew it wasn't the maid."

231

A man sat by the window of a Pullman smoking compartment figuring with a pencil and paper. Occasionally he looked intently out of the window and then figured vigorously. The curiosity of a fellow passenger was aroused and he said:

"May I ask what you are doing?"

"Sure," answered the man by the window; "I'm counting the cows that we pass."

Since the train was making fully eighty miles an hour, the questioner was skeptical.

"How on earth can you do it at the speed we're going?" he asked.

"It's quite easy," was the reply. "I simply count the legs and divide by four."

232

Maybe the boy was playing dumb, but if he was, he was a consummate actor. He hung around the shop of the village blacksmith until the horse-shoer couldn't stand it any more. Finally the smith held a red-hot horse shoe under the boy's nose.

"Give me half a dollar and I'll lick it," said the simple-minded one.

This was too good. The smith passed him a fifty-cent piece, and the boy took it, licked it, and stuck it in his pocket. He was on his way before the blacksmith could do anything.

233

Mark Twain was fond of feats of heroism and ingenuity and often bragged of his own.

"Once there was a fire in Hannibal," he related, "and an old man was trapped on the fourth floor of a burning house. We all thought he was a goner. There wasn't a ladder in town long enough to reach his window. The crowd gaped at one another, but no one could think of any way to help.

"All of a sudden, I got an idea. 'Bring me a long rope,' I yelled, and, with great presence of mind, I flung the end of it to the old man. 'Tie it around your waist,' I yelled. The old man did, and I pulled him down."

234

Idea: Something that begins in a brain cell and ends in a skyscraper.

Oliver Herford

Insult

237

Two friends met, one of them much excited.

"Hello, Smith; I just met Wilson, and he insulted you. He said that you weren't fit to sleep with pigs."

"Oh," replied Smith with a rising inflection; "and I suppose you pulled the old gag that I *was* fit to sleep with pigs."

"No indeed," came the answer; "I stuck up for the pigs."

238

The cattiest remark on record was made about the woman who didn't show up at the bridge club. Between hands one of the girls said:

"I don't know how old she is, but a good cup of tea rests her. Besides, she has stopped patting herself on the back and is patting herself under the chin."

239

Those two outstanding 19th century British statesmen, Gladstone and Disraeli, were political opponents on many occasions. One day in the House of Commons they had had a much more violent battle than usual, and as he left the floor, Gladstone was trembling with rage. As he passed Disraeli he burst out:

"Sir, you will come to your end either on the gallows or of a venereal disease!"

"That," said Disraeli, adjusting his monocle, "depends on whether I embrace your principles or your mistress."

240

Congressman Maury Maverick received a five-page letter from a very angry and caustic voter. His reply was succinct:

"My dear Sir: Ph-f-f-ft. Yours very truly, Maury Maverick."

241

John Barrymore has had as many stories hung on him as Henry Ford or Mae West, but this one has the ring of authenticity.

One day he was rehearsing a play, and his leading lady irritated him. Barrymore made cutting and personal remarks to her, whereupon she drew herself up to her full height (and possibly a couple of inches more) and said:

"You will please remember that I am a lady."

As always, John had a ready reply.

"Madam," he barked, "I will respect your secret."

242

Wit may be described as humor with a barb, such as the statement that Calvin Coolidge looked as if he had been weaned on a pickle; also the comment attributed to Dorothy Parker when she was told that Coolidge was dead—"How can they tell?"

243

It is said that someone asked Disraeli the difference between a misfortune and a calamity, and that the answer was:

"If Gladstone fell into the Thames, it would be a misfortune; if anyone pulled him out, that would be a calamity."

244

George Bernard Shaw, doing his duty at a benefit affair, asked a maiden lady to dance. As they waltzed, she simpered, "Oh, Mr. Shaw, whatever made you ask poor little me to dance?"

The gallant Mr. Shaw replied: "This is a charity ball, isn't it?"

245

Two well known American artists, James Montgomery Flagg and Arthur William Brown, were at a beach party one day and saw some refuse washed up on the shore.

"Well I declare," said Brown; "there's Blank." And he named another artist they both disliked.

"Yes," Flagg answered, "and I've never seen him looking better."

246

Alexander H. Stevens, who became Vice-President of the Confederate States of America, was five feet tall and weighed only about eighty pounds, but he had a dynamic personality and was fearless. One day a big westerner lost his temper over something Stevens had said, and burst forth at him:

"Why you—you—. Why, I could swallow you alive and never even know I'd et a thing!"

Stevens was unimpressed. He replied:

"In that case you would have more brains in your belly than you ever had in your head."

247

Henry Clay had a quarrel with John Randolph in the Senate, and for a week they did not speak. One day they met on a narrow sidewalk on Pennsylvania Avenue and it become apparent that one of them would have to turn out to let the other pass. As they met, Randolph looked Clay in the eye and said:

"I never turn out for a scoundrel."

"But I always do," returned Clay as he stepped politely aside.

248

Voltaire, the great French satirist, had just said some nice things about another writer. His companion was surprised, and commented:

"You are very kind to speak so pleasantly about Monsieur X when he always says such derogatory things about you."

"Ah, well," Voltaire replied, "perhaps we are both mistaken."

249

The slug, he is a gastropod of elongated form
Who crawls round on his belly when the weather's rather warm.
He is so low that he can go neath any garden gate,
But compared to you, you so-and-so, the slug's an Empire State.

Ned Allen

Laziness

255

The general storekeeper in a sleepy midwestern village was playing checkers with a pal in the back room of the shop.

Someone came in by the front door, and the other player said:

"Bill, there's a customer in the store."

"Just keep your mouth shet, and don't make any noise," Bill answered. "Maybe she'll go out again."

256

The prize for laziness should go to the fellow who tried to climb a barbed-wire fence without taking his hands out of his pockets.

257

In the backwoods of Kentucky there was a woman who never wore shoes. The soles of her bare feet were calloused and toughened by constant plodding about. One day she was standing in front of the cabin fireplace when her husband said:

"Maw, you'd better move your foot a leetle mite; you're standing on a live coal."

The woman lifted one eyebrow, and replied:

"Which foot, Paw?"

258

Mr. Jones kept himself in trim through the radio. Every morning at seven o'clock he leaped out of bed and turned on the physical exercise program. Then he flung open the window, took a deep breath of fresh air, and watched the girl opposite do the exercises.

259

I know a man so lazy that he crosses sword-grass with ordinary grass, and when the wind blows the grass on his lawn it cuts itself.

Michael W. Donaher

260

A Georgia hillbilly sat on a rail fence whittling. On the ground nearby a hound dog sat and howled mournfully and dismally. The man on the fence paid no attention to him whatever, but just went on whittling. Along the road came a stranger who looked as if he were on a walking tour. He greeted the hillbilly and then asked.

"What's the matter with your dog?"

"Ain't nothin' the matter."

"But he appears to be in pain," the man persisted.

"Nope, jest lazy. That damfool dawg is sittin' on a burr and he's too lazy to get off'n it."

261

Saint Francis of Assisi
Was incapable of taking things easy.
That is one of the advances
I have made upon Saint Francis.

262

Another of the topflight lazy men is the one who doesn't make coffee, but puts the ground bean on his mustache and drinks hot water.

263

Indolent Man: One who runs his car over a bump to knock the ashes off his cigar.

264

It was pay day in camp, and when evening came, one of the GI's had most of his pals' money. He felt so good about it that he sang out: "I've got a dollar for the laziest man here!"

Everybody but one man jumped to his feet and sprang forward to tell how lazy he was.

The exception didn't even stir. He merely drawled: "Just roll me over, Buddy, and slip the buck in my pocket."

Luck and Accidents

265

Luck: Something that enables another person to succeed where we have failed.

266

May Dame Fortune ever smile on you
But never her daughter—Miss Fortune.

267

"How on earth did you break your leg?" a solicitous friend asked the man on crutches.

"Well, you see it was this way;" was the answer, "I threw a cigarette butt in a manhole and stepped on it."

268

Two colored gentlemen were riding home on the bus one evening after a long day at the shipyard.

"Sam," said Rastus, who was reading in the paper of a number of fatal accidents, "if you was to take your choice 'twixt one or t'other, which would you ruther be in, a collision or an explosion?"

Sam scratched his head.

"Man—a collision," he said finally.

"How come, big boy?"

"Why man alive, if you's in a collision thar you is, but if you's in an explosion, whar is you?"

Meanness

270

A motorist in the New Hampshire countryside came across an old car that was stuck in a mud puddle. He stopped to see if he could help when he discovered the bucolic driver harnessing two kittens to the front axle.

"For the love of Mike," he gasped; "you're not going to try to haul the car out with those kittens, are you?"

"I don't know why not," the farmer replied; "I've got a whip, ain't I?"

271

Another record for meanness was established by the woman who bought an electric refrigerator and then had installed on it a whistle that blew every time the iceman went by.

272

Add this to your thesaurus of meanest men in the world: A fellow who would milk a cow without taking off his ring.

273

The worst tempered people I've ever met were people who knew they were wrong.

Wilson Mizner

274

"No, no, no," protested the agreeable fellow; "I wouldn't call her a sourpuss at all. All I know is that when she rubs cold cream on her face, it curdles."

Memory and Absentmindedness

276

A young sceptic went about trying to disprove all the commonly accepted beliefs. He made his first great demonstration when he gave the lie to the statement that "a watched pot never boils." He actually watched a pot until it did boil. It was equally difficult, but just as worth while, to prove that sometimes a rolling stone *does* gather moss. He kept on, however, until he amassed considerable data on the subject of popular misinformation.

Then he heard the statement that "an Indian never forgets" and he set out to disprove it. He went out to the Crow Reservation in Montana and became acquainted with a young buck. He asked him if he liked eggs, and the Indian replied:

"Yes."

Twenty-five years later the sceptic returned to the Crow Reservation and met his Indian friend. Raising his hand in salutation, he said to the redskin:

"How!"

"Fried," the Indian replied.

277

Tops in absentmindedness is the man who poured catsup on his shoelaces and tied bowknots in his spaghetti.

278

They tell a story about the late Dwight Morrow and his absentmindedness. He was on a train, immersed in a book, when the conductor asked for his ticket. He searched his pockets without finding it. So the conductor, who knew him, said:

"Don't bother, Mr. Morrow. When you find it, just mail it to the company. There's no doubt that you have it."

"I know blame well I have it," Morrow exclaimed; "but what I want to know is, where in the world am I going?"

Modesty and Conceit

280

Modesty: The gentle art of enhancing your charm by pretending not to be aware of it.

Oliver Herford

281

Even when he was old, the Duke of Wellington disliked being shown any marked politeness or given any assistance. Usually he said, "Can't you be good enough to mind your own business?"

One day at a London street crossing a man who was nearly as old as the Duke assisted him through the traffic. When Wellington, contrary to his custom, said, "I thank you, sir," the elderly gentleman took off his hat and said to him:

"My lord, I have passed a long and not uneventful life, but never did I hope to reach the day when I might be of the slightest assistance to the greatest man who ever lived."

"Don't be a damned fool," said the Duke, and walked on.

282

Elbert Hubbard went to the old Palmer House in Chicago to spend the night. The last entry before his on the hotel register was "Richard Harding Davis and Valet." Hubbard took the pen proffered by the clerk and wrote under it with a flourish: "Elbert Hubbard and Valise."

283

A purity league, or something, called on General Pershing during World War I and asked him to stop the soldiers in France singing a somewhat bawdy song called "I Wanna Go Home." The General heard the delegation and then promptly threw them out, bellowing:

"Who the h— don't?"

284

It is characteristic of certain bumptious individuals to want always to be in the spotlight. Of one of these it was said that when he went to a wedding he wanted to be the bridegroom, and when he went to a funeral he wanted to be the corpse.

285

I would rather sit on a pumpkin and have it all to myself than to be crowded on a velvet cushion.

Henry D. Thoreau

286

According to those in the know, the world's most conceited man was the fellow who celebrated his birthday by sending his mother a telegram of congratulation.

287

A newspaper correspondent visited Coolidge at Plymouth. Watching the automobiles rolling by, he said to Mr. Coolidge:

"It must make you very proud to see all these people coming by here, to look at you sitting here on the porch. It shows that although you are an ex-president, you are not forgotten. Just look at the number of cars passing."

"Not as many as yesterday," replied Mr. Coolidge. "There were 163 then."

288

Did the praise go to his head? Why, it swelled so that when he went through the Grand Canyon they had to pin his ears back.

289

Conceit: He was like the cock who thought the sun had risen to hear him crow.

George Eliot

290

The human body still remains the most wonderful mechanism in existence. For instance, if you pat a man on the back, his head will swell.

Morals

295

A man without an address is a vagabond.
A man with two addresses is a libertine.

G. B. Shaw

296

They say best men are moulded out of faults;
And, for the most, become much more the better
For being a little bad.

Shakespeare

297

A New England conscience doesn't keep you from doing anything; it just keeps you from enjoying it.

H. L. Mencken

298

What men call gallantry, and gods adultery,
Is much more common where the climate's sultry.

Byron

299

I can resist everything except temptation.

Oscar Wilde

300

The only way to get rid of a temptation is to yield to it.

Oscar Wilde

301

And what is a weed? A plant whose virtues have not been discovered.

Emerson

302

It has ever been my experience that folks who have no vices have very few virtues.

Lincoln

303

What is moral is what you feel good after, and what is immoral is what you feel bad after. . . .

Ernest Hemingway

304

Adolescence has been defined as the period between puberty and adultery.

305

Every vice was once a virtue, and may become respectable again, just as hatred becomes respectable in wartime.

Will Durant

306

Many wish not so much to be virtuous, as to seem to be.

Cicero

307

Young men going to the big city to carve out a career are usually more concerned with their comforts than their morals. A lad from the country applied to an employment agency and was offered a job at a salary of $15 a week.

"But," the boy remonstrated, "can I lead a good Christian life in the city on $15 a week?"

"Believe me," was the reply, "that's the only kind of a life you can lead."

308

What Adam and Eve didn't do in the Garden of Eden! Come to

think of it, they were responsible for the first case of juvenile delinquency.

Vera Allen

Optimism and Pessimism

310

MIND OVER MATTER

There was a faith-healer of Deal
Who said, "Although pain isn't real,
If I sit on a pin
And it punctures my skin,
I dislike what I fancy I feel."

311

"Mother," said a six-year-old, "does worry make wrinkles?"

"Yes, child," the mother replied, "it certainly does."

"Well, then," the child continued, "raisins must be worried grapes."

312

The optimist fell ten stories,
And at each window bar
He shouted to the people,
"I'm all right so far!"

313

The optimist proclaims that we live in the best of all possible worlds; and the pessimist fears this is true.

Branch Cabell

314

He seems
To have seen better days, as who has not
Who has seen yesterday?

Byron

315

Our idea of a contented man is the one, if any, who enjoys the scenery along the detour.

Perseverance and Self-Reliance

318

That fellow even started out by being self-reliant. When he was a baby, he walked the floor alone.

319

"Uncle Mose," said Oliver Gramling, the author, meeting an old Negro who was always cheerful in spite of his troubles, "how do you manage to keep so cheerful and serene?"

"Well, I'll tell yo, Boss," replied Uncle Mose. "I'se jus' learned to cooperate wid de inevitable."

320

It's easy enough to be pleasant
When life flows round and round,
But the man worth while
Is the one who can smile
When his garter drags the ground.

321

There was a young lady said, "Why
Can't I look in my ear with my eye?
I'm sure I can do it
If I put my mind to it.
You never can tell till you try."

322

It was the worst storm on record. Finally the dam burst and a raging torrent forced the townfolks to flee to higher ground.

From the hill, as they looked down on their flooded houses, they noticed a straw hat float slowly downstream for fifty feet or so. Then the hat stopped, turned around and made its way upstream a similar distance. When this performance was repeated, one of the group said:

"What makes that straw hat act so durn funny?" And a boy replied:

"Last night I heard Grandpa say that, come hell or high water, he was going to mow the lawn today."

Prejudice

325

On one of his trips to London, Eugene Field was invited to a dinner, and during the conversation the subject of lynching in the United States was brought up. Most of the Britishers present seemed to think that a large proportion of Yankees came to their end through this procedure. The genial hostess turned to Field and said:

"Of course you must have often seen these grewsome affairs."

"Hundreds of them," he replied with feeling. And four or five of the party clamored to hear about one of them. The American poet was nothing loath to tell.

"It happened," said Field, "the night before I left for England. I was giving a dinner party at a hotel to a group of intimate friends when a Negro waiter spilled a plate of soup on the dress of a lady at a nearby table. The dress was spoiled entirely, so the men of her party grabbed the waiter, put a rope around his neck, and hanged him."

"Perfectly ghastly!" exclaimed the hostess. "And you yourself saw all this?"

"As a matter of fact, I didn't," Field admitted. "At the time I was downstairs killing the Negro cook for putting pepper in the ice cream."

326

Asa Hancock is very proud of his England background and the fact that he has retained all his faculties though he has reached the venerable age of ninety-nine years. Every day, rain or shine, he walks down to the village, a distance of some two miles to "chew the rag" with his cronies who line up outside the post office. A summer visitor questioned him concerning his activities through the years.

"I guess you've seen many changes in your day, Asa!" he remarked, hoping the old codger would open up and tell him some interesting stories.

"Yep," Asa answered, "And I've been agin every one of 'em!"

327

PRIDE

Of all the lunacies earth can boast,
The one that must please the devil most
Is pride reduced to the whimsical terms
Of causing the slugs to despise the worms.

Robert Brough

328

It is with narrow-minded people as with narrow-necked bottles; the less they have in them, the more noise they make in pouring it out.

Alexander Pope

329

The following well known rhyme is attributed to Dr. John C. Bossidy, who is said to have written it for an alumni dinner of Holy Cross College, Boston:

Here's to our good old Boston,
The home of the bean and the cod,

Where the Lowells talk only to Cabots,
And the Cabots talk only to God.

Not long after it found its way into print a newspaper item told of how a newly naturalized Pole named Kabotchnik had successfully petitioned the court to have his name changed to Cabot.

Some wit on the Harvard *Lampoon* thereupon made this comment:

Here's to our good old Boston,
The home of the bean and the cod,
Where the Lowells talk only to Cabots,
And the Cabots speak Yiddish, by God!

330

Prejudice makes wars, political combats and horse races. Sometimes, it might be said, it makes fools out of people. Classify the following if you can.

A Southerner went to a convention in a northern city, and when he returned was asked whom he met.

"Well, suh," he said, "there was a distinguished gentleman from Kentucky, a very charming gentleman from Virginia, a fellow from Maine, a man from Michigan, a bounder from Chicago, and a dope from New York."

Principles and Ideals

333

Our differences, said President William McKinley, are politics; our agreements are principles.

334

Ideals are like the stars—we never reach them, but like the mariners of the sea, we chart our course by them.

Carl Schurz

335

It is easier to fight for one's principles than to live up to them.

Alfred Adler

336

To be positive: to be mistaken at the top of one's voice.

Ambrose Bierce

337

We would often be ashamed of our finest actions if the world understood all the motives that produced them.

La Rochefoucauld

338

Infidelity does not consist in believing or disbelieving; it consists in professing to believe what one does not believe.

Thomas Paine

Simplicity

340

A Bronx cafeteria was crowded at the noon hour. Suddenly above the clatter of dishes came the cry:

"Fire! Sweeney's house is on fire."

A man getting coffee let his tray of dishes crash to the floor, dashed out of the cafeteria, and made a bee line toward home.

Then when he had gone three blocks, he stopped short, clapped his hand to his head, groaned, and exclaimed:

"Oi gevalt! Why should I run? My name ain't Sweeney."

341

A sailor coming ashore in San Francisco, the city noted for parades that are bigger, better, and oftener, noticed crowds of people lining the Market Street curbs.

He stopped to see what kind of procession it would be. After he had waited some time, he asked the man in front of him what the people expected to see.

"Well," said the man, "the big feature of the parade will be a nude woman riding a white horse."

"Wow!" the sailor exclaimed. "I'm certainly going to stick around. Why, I haven't seen a white horse in years."

342

There was an old man of Tarentum
Who gnashed his false teeth till he bent 'em.
When asked of the cost
Of what he had lost,
He said, "I can't tell; I just rent 'em."

343

Two Italians, Tony and Beppo, kept a fruit and vegetable store on New York's lower East Side. Beppo, by sharp practice, cheated Tony out of his share of the business, and shortly afterward made off with Tony's young wife.

Tony then became enraged. When he met Beppo on the street, he shook his fist in his face and shouted:

"Somma time you go too far!"

344

One morning Hiram Dobbs awoke at the usual time, stretched, and got out of bed. As was his wont, he then went over to the dresser and looked into the mirror. He was surprised, not to say alarmed, to find that a red tulip was growing out of the crown of his head.

"Most unusual," he exclaimed. "I don't quite like it."

In fact, it worried him considerably. So, after he had tubbed, shaved and dressed, he went directly to see his physician, in whom he had implicit faith. But the good doctor was quite as flabbergasted as Dobbs was.

"Really," he said, "this is most unusual—a tulip in full bloom growing out of the top of a man's head. It's unheard of."

"But what shall I do?" Dobbs cried in anguish.

"Really I don't know," said the doctor, "unless—unless you go to see 'Believe It or Not' Ripley."

Dobbs thought that might be an excellent idea. So he went right down to the Ripley headquarters. When he arrived he was shown into an oak-paneled room where a young blond woman was seated at a desk.

Dobbs walked over to her and with a flourish removed his hat. The tulip blossom snapped upright on his head. Said he:

"I would like to see Mr. Ripley."

The receptionist raised her eyes, looked him over in a bored manner, and replied:

"What's it about?"

345

Mrs. Calvin Coolidge is a modest, retiring woman, avoiding ostentation, preferring to remain in the background. When she went abroad after her husband's death, she feared she would be given unnecessary homage, being the wife of an ex-President.

The good friend with whom she was traveling allayed her fears somewhat by assuring her that in the little out-of-the-way places where they would stop the people wouldn't know one President of the United States from another; they would think she was just a tourist and let it go at that.

Mrs. Coolidge traveled through several European countries and no one recognized her. However, in a small Italian town she and her friend received word that reservations had been made for them in the next village. When they reached the designated hotel, they were received with great deference by the manager, who bowed graciously, and said, "We are proud to welcome the wife of the great President of the United States. Will you register, Mrs. Lincoln?"

346

Two old fishermen on the way to the Grand Banks had a discussion as to who was the better mathematician. They took their argument to the captain, and he gave them a problem to work out:

"Suppose you sold two hundred and thirty-eight pounds of codfish at seven cents a pound, how much would you make?"

The two old salts worked with their pencils for a while, but they didn't get any particular results. Finally one of them said to the captain:

"Did you say it was codfish that was caught?"

"Yes," the captain replied.

"Heck," the fisherman replied; "no wonder I couldn't figger it out. I've been figgering on shad all the time."

Social Graces

350

In former days, when manners and living in general were more gracious, a gentleman would bow low and kiss a lady's hand. The pleasant custom went by the board when the men began burning their noses on lighted cigarettes.

351

A small Southern boy and his father were walking one day on their plantation when an old Negro came along and doffed his hat to the master. The gentleman in turn raised his, whereat the boy said:

"Papa, why did you take off your hat to that Negro?"

"Because, Son," the man replied, "I will not be outdone in politeness by anyone."

352

The inveterate questioner may sometimes be an awful pest.

"How is it," asked one of them to an acquaintance, "that you were born in Massachusetts, while your brother was born in California?"

"I suppose," came the tired answer, "it was because my mother wanted me near her."

353

He was always late on principle, his principle being that punctuality is the thief of time.

Oscar Wilde

354

He gave her a look that you could have poured on a waffle.

Ring Lardner

355

A man gave a woman a seat on a street car. She promptly fainted. When she revived she thanked him. Then he fainted.

356

When Dr. Robert M. Hutchins was elected president of the University of Chicago, a dinner was given and attended by many educators. A visiting professor remarked to the lady who was seated beside him:

"So *that* is the new president!"

The lady rather perceptibly froze. She turned and said:

"Do you know who I am?"

"I'm afraid I do not," the professor replied.

"Well," observed the lady in a somewhat frigid tone of voice, "I am Mrs. Hutchins."

The professor at her side swallowed six or eight times. Then he said:

"So sorry; do you know who I am?"

Mrs. Hutchins said she didn't.

"Thank God!" the professor responded fervently.

357

Etiquette: The noise you don't make when you are eating soup.

358

Dorothy Parker once attended a party down in the Village at which most of the guests were a choice collection of Bohemians. Her companion said to her, "Where on earth do these people come from and where do they stay the rest of the time?"

"I think," Miss Parker said gravely, "that after it's over they crawl back into the woodwork."

359

John Barrymore, in his heyday, went into a smart haberdashery in Hollywood. He left an order and started to leave.

"Your name, please?" the clerk asked.

The Barrymore brows did a high dive. "Barrymore," he informed the clerk coldly.

"Which Barrymore, please?"

Coolness turned to ice.

"Ethel," he said.

360

One of the younger members of a staid and conservative New York club returned from several years' absence in South America and stopped in to have a friendly chat with one or more of the men he had known. After being admitted by the door man, he ambled through several deserted rooms without seeing any sign of life.

At length he came upon an old fellow seated beside a window in the extreme rear of the building.

"Hello," he said jovially. "My name's Winters; come have a drink with me."

The man looked up from the copy of the Saturday Review of Literature he was reading, and said:

"Thanks. I don't drink. Tried it once; didn't like it."

Winters was rather amused at the old man's manner, but he said nothing, and as he had some time to kill, he continued his perambulations around the club. Then he went back to the old fellow with another idea.

"Have a cigar," he said as he held one out. He had no better success. The man replied:

"Thanks. I don't smoke. Tried it once; didn't like it."

After two rebuffs, Winters went into the library and looked at the pictures in half a dozen old copies of Life. Then he decided to try once more. He approached the old fellow and said:

"How about a game of billiards?"

"Thanks," came the reply. "I don't play billiards. Tried it once; didn't like it." There was a moment of hesitation, and then: "My son will be in here in a few minutes. No doubt he'll play with you."

Winters made only one comment. He said: "I'll bet a thousand dollars he's your only son."

361

I sneezed a sneeze into the air;
It fell to the ground I knew not where,
But hard and cold were the looks of those
In whose vicinity I snoze.

362

Snootiness was the last thing on earth that Abraham Lincoln could ever be accused of. He was even inclined to be embarrassed at being called "Mr. President." At one time he was called on by some old friends from Illinois who addressed him as such, and he said:

"Please, please call me Lincoln, and I'll promise not to divulge your breach of etiquette."

363

When he was in America a number of years ago, Wu Ting Fang, the great Chinese diplomat, met an American woman at a reception. She did not know who he was, and she asked him sweetly:

"What 'nese' are you—Japanese, Javanese, or Chinese?"

"I am Chinese," replied Dr. Wu; and then he continued: "What 'kee' are you—monkey, donkey, or Yankee?"

364

A man who was traveling out of Chicago on the Milwaukee Railroad ordered his dinner from the dining-car waiter.

"Also," he said, "for dessert bring me some plum pudding."

"Very sorry, gentleman," said the waiter; "we ain't got any plum pudding."

Whereupon the passenger lost his temper, and exclaimed to the waiter:

"What? No plum pudding? Ridiculous. Do you realize that I am one of this road's biggest customers? I ship thousands of tons of freight every week. And now you won't give me what I want to eat. I'll take this up with the president of the road."

Meanwhile the steward had overheard, and he called the waiter aside, saying:

"We'll be in Milwaukee in five minutes, and when we stop there, we'll pick up a plum pudding. Just get the chef to make some hard sauce and have some of that good brandy to go with it."

Orders were carried out, and as the train left Milwaukee the steward appeared at the diner's table and said with a smile:

"I am glad to tell you that we have your plum pudding, and the chef has made you a special sauce to go with it. Also, with the compliments of the road, we are serving you this fifty-year-old brandy."

The diner scowled, slammed his napkin on the table, and blurted:

"The devil with it. I'd rather be mad."

365

It was during a wartime era of prosperity in New York that a bum approached a man in Rockefeller Center and said:

"Would you give me $27.60 for a cup of coffee?"

"What!" the man exclaimed; "coffee is only a dime."

"Well, for cryin' out loud," said the bum; "you wouldn't expect me to go into a restaurant with *this* suit on."

366

To apologize, according to Ambrose Bierce, is to lay the foundation for a future offense.

367

Bill Jones was very meticulous. When he ran his car into a nudist colony, he stripped his gears.

368

Abash: To shock people, formerly done without difficulty, today an almost impossible feat.

Oliver Herford

369

A woman of the ultra sort, one of those too-too creatures who frequent artistic circles, ran into James McNeill Whistler at a studio party. Rushing up to him, she exclaimed:

"Oh, Mr. Whistler, I passed your studio today."

Whistler simply said, "Thank you," and turned on his heel.

370

That brilliant British statesman, Charles James Fox, in canvassing for parliament, asked a citizen for his vote. The man replied negatively, adding:

"Mr. Fox, I admire your head, but damn your heart."

"Sir, I admire your candor," said Fox; "but damn your manners."

371

The most perfect gentleman I ever saw: He turned his back on me—while I poured myself a drink from his own decanter.

372

You can't believe everything you hear, the Cynic said; but you can repeat it.

373

The wit of Oliver Herford was always pungent, but it seldom carried a sting, but once at the Players Club a man who was noted as a bore stopped him and said:

"Oliver, I've been grossly insulted. As I passed a group over there I heard a fellow say he would give me $50 if I would resign from the club."

"I don't blame you," Herford sympathized. "Hold out for a hundred; you'll get it."

374

There was a young fellow of Wheeling
Endowed with such delicate feeling,
When he read on the door,
"Don't spit on the floor,"
He jumped up and spat on the ceiling.

375

Mabel wanted her friend Clara to go apartment hunting with her.

"But why should you move, Mabel? You were perfectly delighted with this neighborhood when you came here a year ago."

"I know I was, but I'm tired of talking about the same old neighbors for a whole year," protested Mabel.

376

Good breeding consists in concealing how much we think of ourselves and how little we think of the other person.

Mark Twain

377

A gentleman is one who never hurts anyone's feelings unintentionally.

Oscar Wilde

378

Fashions exist for women with no taste, etiquette for people with no breeding.

379

Henry James, the novelist, lived next door to a retired jam manufacturer. His neighbor was married to an earl's daughter, and he tried to disguise the fact that he had amassed his fortune through the manufacture of jam.

One day he wrote Mr. James an insolent letter, protesting that the James's servants were trespassing on his grounds. Mr. James wrote back:

"Dear Sir: I am sorry to hear that my servants have been poaching on your preserves.

P.S.—You'll excuse my mentioning your preserves, won't you?"

380

The company of George Bernard Shaw has been much sought after by "lion hunters." One of these sent him an invitation as follows: "Lady Blank will be at home Friday between four and six." Shaw sent the card back. At the bottom he had written, "Mr. Bernard Shaw likewise."

381

A story is told of the poet Tennyson dining one night at his club with a party of friends. When dinner was over, the whiskered

Laureate leaned back in his chair and put his feet on the table. He was remonstrated with in vain. Finally his host said;

"Do put your feet down," and Tennyson replied:

"Why should I? I'm very comfortable as I am."

"Everyone is staring at you," said one of his friends.

"Let them stare," the poet said carelessly.

"Alfred," said another of the party, "people will think you are Longfellow."

Down came the feet from the table!

382

Pity now poor Mary Ames,
Blinded by her brother James.
Nails into her eyes he poked.
I never saw Mary more provoked.

383

Some people can stay longer in an hour than others can in a week.

W. D. Howells

384

Madame Recamier, famous French literary and political figure of the early 19th century, used two expressions that always made her guests feel good. When people arrived, she said to them, "At last!" When they departed, she said, "Already?"

385

A city slicker, pointing to a hillside cornfield up in New England, asked a farmer, "How do you plow that field? It looks very steep."

"Don't plow it; when the spring thaws come, the rocks rolling down hill tear it up."

"That's wonderful! But how do you plant it?"

"Don't plant it really. Just stand in my back doorway and shoot the seed in with a shotgun."

"Is that gospel truth?" asked the man from the big city.

"Mercy, no. That's conversation."

386

New York is the last city in the world where this would happen; the scene was London. A taxicab driver saw a pedestrian directly in his way, stopped his car, leaned out, and inquired politely:

"I say, sir, may I awsk what are your plans?"

387

Mrs. Patrick Campbell was one of the guests at a party given by a Hollywood movie magnate. When she was leaving, he asked her to sign the guest book. She wrote: " 'Quoth the Raven'—— Stella Campbell."

388

The reactionary members of an exclusive club had resorted to every underhand method to reject the application bid of John Riley because they looked down on the ex-bricklayer although he had become a millionaire.

However, he had sufficient friends in the organization to insure his admission. He soon became extremely popular and was prevailed upon to run for the club's presidency against a representative of the reactionary group.

Unfortunately, the vote was tied and both candidates agreed to pull a slip from a box which was to contain one card marked "winner" and one marked "loser."

The membership committee was controlled by his enemies who decided to mark both cards with the word "loser" and force him to draw first. At the last minute Riley was informed of the deception by a friend. "Aren't you going to make a complaint and have the election declared invalid?" he was asked.

"Sure, and I'll do nothing about it," he answered cheerfully.

At the drawing he pulled out a card, read it, tore it into tiny pieces and walked away chuckling.

"Hold on there," said the angry election chairman. "What was written on your card?"

"Don't bother about that," urged Riley. "Just read what's on the card that's left."

389

Ginsburg wanted his name changed to Sweeney, so he went to court about it. The judge asked him why, and Ginsburg said it was for business reasons. It was so ordered.

After a year or so, the man came back and, as it happened, appeared before the same judge. This time he said he wanted his name changed to Casey.

"Why?" asked the judge.

"Because," the man replied, "whenever I tell a fellow my name he takes a look at me and asks, 'What was it before it was Sweeney?' "

390

Two explorers were guests at a dinner given by the Adventurers Club. One of them brought an Eskimo from the North Pole, and the other brought a similar resident from the region of the South Pole. There was considerable curiosity as to how they would greet each other. It worked out quite simply, however, for the Northern Eskimo said:

"Glub-glub."

And the Southerner replied:

"Glub-glub, you-all!"

391

Given plenty of brass, a presentable young man with passable clothes and a clean shirt can go places. One of such crashed the gate at a large party on Manhattan's ultra East Side. When the hostess was bidding her guests good-night the fellow edged into the line to pay his respects.

"Good-bye," he said, "it's been a wonderful party."

"I am so glad you enjoyed it," the hostess replied with cordiality; "remind me to ask you next time."

392

Broadway is a place where people spend money they haven't earned to buy things they don't need to impress people they don't like.

Walter Winchell

393

The train going across Arizona stopped fifteen minutes for lunch at one of the old Fred Harvey eating places. One waitress had trouble with the rush, and by the time she had served a young woman her coffee, steaming hot, there wasn't time to drink it. But a chivalrous cowpuncher came over to her and said:

"Here, Miss, take mine; it's already been saucered and blowed."

394

An English woman who had appointed herself supervisor of public morals in her village accused a laborer of getting drunk simply because she had seen his wheelbarrow outside a public house. The workman didn't say anything in his defense, but that same evening he put his wheelbarrow outside the lady's door and left it there all night.

395

A woman got onto a crowded street car with a friend and said in a loud voice:

"I wish that good looking man would give me his seat."

Five men immediately got up.

396

Cynic: A man who knows the price of everything and the value of nothing.

Oscar Wilde

397

To be capable of respect is almost as rare as to be worthy of it.

Joubert

398

It is remarkable with what Christian fortitude and resignation we can bear the suffering of other folks.

Swift

399

No one is useless in this world who lightens the burden of it to anyone else.

Dickens

401

He reminds me of the man who murdered both his parents, and then, when sentence was about to be pronounced, pleaded for mercy on the grounds that he was an orphan.

Abraham Lincoln

Stinginess

404

What would have passed for a heavy swell in Scotland fell into a roaring torrent and was in great danger of being swept away to his doom. Suddenly a young fellow appeared and jumped into the stream, grabbed the man, and brought him to shore.

" 'Tis a brave man you are," said the Scotchman. "You have risked your life to save mine. Never fear; I will reward you. Do you happen to have change for a sixpence?"

405

It was necessary to give three blood transfusions to save a girl's life, and a healthy young Scot came forward. For the first pint of blood the patient gave him $50. For the second pint the lady who needed it gave $25. The third time, she had so much Scotch blood in her that she merely said, "Thank you."

406

Add this item to your case of Scotch: Sandy MacTavish found a box of corn plasters, so he went out and bought a pair of tight shoes.

407

One bitter cold day Harry Lauder played around the golf course. When he came off the green, he slipped something into the hand of his caddie, saying, "That's for a glass of hot whiskey, m' lad." The boy opened his hand and found a lump of sugar.

408

Drowning notice.—Three Scotchmen each bet a quarter that he could stay under water the longest; winner take all.

409

They do say that a Scotchman can drink any given quantity of whiskey.

410

A Scotchman was hurt while watching a baseball game, so he sued the teams that were playing. He fell out of a tree.

411

The man who invented slow-motion movies probably got his idea when he saw a Scotchman reach for a restaurant check.

412

One difference between a Scotchman and a canoe is that a canoe has the habit of tipping.

413

Then there was the Scotch anarchist who lit a bomb and just hated to let go of it.

Stupidity

417

The man was so dumb that he thought that Rex Beach and Veronica Lake were summer resorts.

418

Then there is the fellow who is so dumb he thinks a fjord is a Norwegian automobile.

419

Where ignorance is bliss 'tis wisdom to be foolish.

420

The fellow was so dumb that he couldn't count up to twenty without taking off his shoes and stockings.

421

The man was so dumb that he always thought a myth was a female moth, and that a goblet was a little gob.

422

The following verse was written, it is said, about a United States Congressman by a friend of his—or was he?

John Wesley Gaines,
John Wesley Gaines,
Thou monumental mass of brains!
Come in, John Wesley—
For it rains.

423

See the happy moron,
He doesn't give a damn;
I wish I were a moron—
My God! Perhaps I am!

424

There was a moron. He had a credit in cash, but a debit in brains. He received a catalog of prefabricated houses and became so interested that he ordered one. Here follows a lapse of time. Then he wrote a scathing letter to the manufacturer of the house. An investigator came to look into the cause of the trouble. He looked at the result and lost his temper. Said he:

"You blinking idiot! you put up the thing upside down."

"Humph," exclaimed the moron; "that explains why I kept falling off the porch."

Success and Fame

426

Prophets were twice stoned—first in anger; then, after their death, with a handsome slab in the graveyard.

Christopher Morley

427

When ye build yer triumphal arch to yer conquerin' hero, Hinnissey, build it out of bricks so the people will have somethin' convenient to throw at him as he passes through.

Finley Peter Dunne

428

Popularity? It is glory's small change.

Victor Hugo

429

A promising young man in our office refused the job of president of the company because, he explained, there was no chance for advancement in it.

430

Fortune advanced thee that all might aver
That nothing is impossible to her.

Richard Garnett

431

Selfmade Man: Usually a pathetic example of unskilled labor.

432

It was Horace Greeley who made the historic retort to the congressman who boasted that he was a self-made man.

"That," said Greeley, "relieves the Almighty of a great responsibility."

Truth and Dishonesty

433

Even before radio came into being, Mark Twain said, "A lie can travel around the world and back again while the truth is lacing up its boots."

434

A country weekly published a notice that read: "Anyone found near my chicken house at night will be found there next morning."

435

"So you are trying to suggest that I'm a thief," exclaimed an excited individual to the man standing beside him.

"I wouldn't say you're a thief," the other replied, "but if I were a chicken, I sure would roost high."

436

On the same principle that if a man steals a dollar he is a thief, but if he steals a million dollars he is a financier, a man who tells a big enough lie is rated as an artist. And maybe that covers Lem Wiggins, who boasted about the rainstorm out in Wyoming back in '76. "Rain?" he said. "Why there was a barrel layin' on the ground with both ends out, and it rained so hard that the water went in the bunghole faster than it could run out both ends."

437

He who sells what isn't his'n,
Must buy it back or go to prison.

Daniel Drew

438

If one tells the truth, one is sure sooner or later to be found out.

Oscar Wilde

439

A little blond hat-check girl at one of New York's night clubs combined great efficiency with the appearance of absolute innocence. She never issued checks but there was no record of her making a mistake in returning hats left with her.

One evening as a show-off type of diner was leaving, she handed him his headgear.

"Look, Babe," he ogled, "how do you know this is my hat?"

She turned her big blue eyes on him and looked as if she were going to cry.

"I don't know, sir. All I know is that it's the hat you left with me when you came in."

440

One of the striking differences between a cat and a lie is that a cat has only nine lives.

Mark Twain

441

One of Wilson Mizner's better characterizations was of a skillful and dextrous croupier in a gambling house. "That guy," he said, "would steal a red-hot stove and then come back for the smoke."

442

During Civil War days a boat-builder who was trying to get a gunboat contract sought to impress Abraham Lincoln by making extravagant claims about his product. He finally said that they would run in unbelievably shallow water.

"I have no doubt of it," the President replied. "I wouldn't be surprised if they'd run anywhere if only the ground's a little moist."

443

President Lincoln was visited by a deputation who urged emancipation before he was ready to proclaim it. He told them he couldn't enforce it even if he proclaimed it.

"How many legs will a cow have if you call the tail a leg?" asked the President.

"Why, five," they answered, with one accord.

"You are wrong, gentlemen," said Lincoln, "for calling a tail a leg doesn't make it so."

444

An irate woman called her grocer on the telephone, saying:

"I sent my little boy for three pounds of peaches and you sent me only two pounds."

"Madam," was the reply, "my scales are accurate. Have you weighed your little boy?"

445

At a county fair in eastern Texas a lad entered a razorback in the hog competition. The official in charge said to him:

"That hog won't be much good for pork or lard. What are you entering him for?"

"Speed, mister," the boy replied; "where I come from a hog won't last very long if he can't outrun the black folks."

446

Two chorus girls met on Broadway, and one said:

"Your ex-husband is going around telling lies about you."

"So what?" was the reply; "but if the lug begins telling the truth, so help me, I'll break his neck."

447

It is said that there are three kinds of lies: lies, damned lies, and statistics.

448

Then there is the man who changed his name to Ritz Carlton so it would be the same as the name on his towels.

449

The Right Honorable gentleman is indebted to his memory for his jests, and to his imagination for his facts.

Sheridan

General Observations

450

I Don't

My parents told me not to smoke;
  I don't.
Or listen to a naughty joke;
  I don't.
They made it plain I must not wink
At pretty girls or even think
About intoxicating drink;
  I don't.

To dance and flirt is very wrong;
  I don't.
Wild youth chase women, wine and song;
  I don't.
I kiss no girls, not even one;
I do not know how it is done;
You wouldn't think I'd have much fun . . .
  I don't.

451

WISHES OF AN ELDERLY MAN

I wish I loved the Human Race;
I wish I loved its silly face;
I wish I liked the way it walks;
I wish I liked the way it talks;
And when I'm introduced to one,
I wish I thought, "What jolly fun!"

Walter Raleigh

452

It may be that the race is not always to the swift, nor the battle to the strong—but that's the way to bet.

Damon Runyon

453

If you pick up a starving dog and make him prosperous, he will not bite you. That is the principal difference between a dog and a man.

Mark Twain

454

He who sleeps in continual noise is wakened by silence.

W. D. Howells

455

God made man a little lower than the angels, and he has been getting a little lower ever since.

Will Rogers

456

It's goin' t' be fun t' watch an' see how long th' meek kin keep the earth after they inherit it.

Kin Hubbard

457

The great human asset is man himself.

Anatole France

458

Man is the only animal that blushes. Or needs to.

Mark Twain

459

If you make people think they're thinking, they'll love you. If you really make them think, they'll hate you.

Don Marquis

460

A shipwrecked mariner had spent several years on a deserted South Sea island. Then one bright morning he was thrilled to see a ship offshore and a boat putting out for the isle. When the boat grounded on the beach the officer in charge threw the mariner a bundle of papers, saying:

"The Captain's compliments, and will you read through these and then let us know whether you still want to be rescued."

461

There was nothing doing at the police station. Officer Casey yawned and said:

"What a dull week! No robberies, no murders, no drunk and disorderlies, not even any traffic arrests. They'll be laying us off pretty soon."

"Oh, don't be a pessimist, Casey," said Chief Sweeney. "Something's bound to happen. I've still got faith in human nature."

462

A sufficient commentary on human nature is that a mob never rushes madly across town to do a needed kindness.

463

Ages and ages hence, no doubt it will give pain to those of orthodox belief when the assertion is made that the creatures of that period descended from Man.

464

There is a little island in the vast expanse of the South Seas where there are no taxes, no unemployment, no beggars, no crime, no swing orchestras, no radios—and no inhabitants.

465

The world of fools has such a store
That he who would not see an ass
Must bide at home and bolt his door—
And even break his looking-glass.

466

A man's actions are motion pictures of his beliefs.

467

Impatience, according to a knowing child, is waiting for something in a hurry.

468

An old goat is never the more reverend for his beard.

469

He too serves a purpose who only stands and cheers.

Henry Adams

470

Positive anything is better than negative nothing.

Elbert Hubbard

471

The same idea has been put over in different ways, but never better than by Leonard Lyons of the New York Post in his paragraph:

"New York's Museum of Natural History has boasted of the countless visitors who come to see its wonders. But when a comfort station was erected on a nearby corner, museum attendance fell off 100,000."

472

Even the British Government found that it could not kill superstition. A good many years ago there were so many seamen who would not sail on a Friday that they tried to prove this was a fallacy. In line with this aim, they laid the keel of a new ship on a Friday, launched her on Friday, christened her H.M.S. Friday, and sent her to sea on Friday.

There was only one drawback to the well-laid plan. Neither the vessel nor her crew was ever heard from again.

473

NOTHING

Nothing to do but work,
  Nothing to eat but food,
Nothing to wear but clothes
  To keep one from going nude.
Nothing to breathe but air,
  Quick as a flash 'tis gone;
Nothing to fall but off,
  Nowhere to stand but on.

Ben King

474

A hen is only an egg's way of making another egg.

Samuel Butler

475

Who lives without folly is not so wise as he thinks.

La Rochefoucauld

476

The greatest pleasure in life is to do a good deed in secret and have it discovered by accident.

Charles Lamb

477

I hate to be a kicker, I always long for peace,
But the wheel that squeaks the loudest
Is the one that gets the grease.

Josh Billings

478

Ours is a world where people don't know what they want and are willing to go through hell to get it.

Don Marquis

479

The trouble with the world is that the stupid are cocksure and the intelligent full of doubt.

Bertrand Russell

Section 5

BIRTH, DEATH, ANCESTRY AND AGE

500

That fellow was born with a silver spoon in his mouth; but it had somebody else's initials on it.

501

The man who was born on April second must go through life being reminded that it was a day too late.

502

A young naval officer went home on furlough only to find that his wife was expecting a baby momentarily. He wired to his superior officer requesting an extension of furlough and gave his reasons in full.

A few hours later the following cryptic telegram arrived. "U.S. Navy recognizes necessity for your presence at laying of keel. Considers your presence superfluous at launching."

503

Boy and girl were going in for a little autobiography. Said the girl:

"I was born in Vancouver, B. C. And how about you?"

"Oh," the boy replied, "I was born in New York, A. D."

504

Father-in-waiting saw a nurse appear in the doorway and asked, "Well, nurse, will it use a lipstick or razor in the sweet by and by?"

505

The new and very proud father was boasting of the baby.

"He's the spitting image of me," he said.

"Well, you don't have to worry about that," comforted his friend, "so long as the kid's healthy."

506

An expectant father received the glad tidings in a telegram.

"Claire gave birth to a little girl this morning; both well."

On the message was a sticker reading: "When you want a boy, call Western Union."

507

Adam and Eve had many advantages, but the principal one was that they escaped teething.

Mark Twain

508

THE MENDELIAN THEORY

There was a young fellow called Starky
Who had an affair with a darky.
The result of his sins
Was quadruplets, not twins:
One black and one white, and two khaki.

Anonymous

509

Little Julia was watching her mother weigh the baby.

"Mummy," she asked. "How much do you have to pay a pound for babies?"

"Babies are not sold by the pound, my dear," smiled the mother.

"Then why do they always weigh them as soon as they are born?"

511

I often pause and wonder
At fate's peculiar ways,
For nearly all our famous men
Were born on holidays.

512

"We have a new baby at our house," said Billy.

"Is it a boy or a girl?" asked his playmate, Dick.

"I don't know; they haven't put its clothes on yet."

513

A little boy arrived at the schoolhouse all out of breath with excitement.

"What's the matter, Charles?" asked the teacher.

"We've got a new baby at our house," he said, proudly. "Won't you come and see it?"

"Thank you," said the teacher. "But I think I had better wait until your mother is feeling better."

"It'll be all right," said the little boy. "You don't need to be afraid—it's not catching."

514

A wistful spinster was taking two little girls around the zoo. The old, long-legged stork seemed to intrigue them, so she told them the story about the bird—how it was instrumental in bringing babies to their mothers.

The girls looked at each other and giggled. Presently one whispered to the other:

"Don't you think we ought to tell the dear old thing the truth?"

515

Two men were passing one of New York's staid old clubs. A well-known member had recently died, and the club windows were hung with black crêpe. Whereat the younger man was heard to say: "It does liven up the old place, doesn't it!"

516

We wanted Li Wing
  But we winged Willie Wong,
A sad but excusable
  Slip of the Tong.

Keith Preston

517

His death, which happened in his berth,
  At forty-odd befell;
They went and told the sexton, and
  The sexton toll'd the bell.

Thomas Hood

518

A silly young chap from the Clyde
In a funeral procession was spied.
  When asked, "Who is dead?"
  He snickered and said,
"I don't know; I just came for the ride."

519

Old Thomas Mulvaney lies here;
His mouth ran from ear to ear.
Reader, tread lightly on this wonder,
For if he yawns, you're gone to thunder.

520

Erected to the memory of
John Phillips
Accidentally shot,
As a mark of affection by his Brother.

522

There once was a lady from Guam
Who said, "Now the ocean's so calm,
  I will swim for a lark."
  She encountered a shark.
Let us now sing the 90th Psalm.

523

Since I am so quickly done for,
I wonder what I was begun for.

On an infant three months old

524

When Angus McPherson died, his widow was prostrated for a week bewailing the loss of her mate. However, she dried her tears when the insurance company lawyer called and suppressed her sobs long enough to read the figures on the insurance check.

"Fifty thousand dollars," she said. "But I miss him so much that I'd be glad to return twenty thousand of it to have him alive again."

525

Here lie I, Martin Elginbrodde:
Ha'e mercy o' my soul, Lord God,
As I wad do, were I Lord God
And ye were Martin Elginbrodde.

526

Here ended my sad life, my tomb you see,
Ask not my name—on all my curses be!

Greek epitaph by the original die-hard

527

The shortest recorded epitaph is on a New York State tombstone: JOHN BURNS.

528

HIS OWN EPITAPH

Life is a jest, and all things show it;
I said so once, and now I know it.

John Gay

529

The Body
of
Benjamin Franklin, Printer
(Like the cover of an old book,
Its contents torn out,
And stript of its lettering and gilding,)
Lies food for worms.
Yet the work itself shall not be lost,
For it will (as he believed) appear once more,
In a new
And more beautiful edition,
Corrected and amended
by
The Author.

Franklin

530

Some of the newspapers head the column "Vital Statistics," but an editor in a small Pennsylvania town always made the heading for Births, Marriages, and Deaths read "Hatched, Matched, and Dispatched."

531

Epitaph: I expected this, but not so soon.

532

The height of delicacy was recently displayed by a flagpole sitter who, when his wife died, sat at half-mast.

533

The engineer of a big hotel rushed into the office and shouted: "A man hanged himself in the cellar!"

"Did you cut him down?" asked the manager.

"No," said the engineer, "he wasn't dead yet."

534

An inquisitive visitor in a small village of Maine stopped in a drugstore for a bottle of soda mints. He had plenty of time and thought the druggist had, so he began to ask questions. He wanted to know everything about the community, its elevation above sea level, politics, religious tendencies, bank clearances, and so on. Finally he asked:

"What is the death rate in this town?"

By this time the druggist didn't even look up. He just said: "About one to a person."

535

The old man had died, and one of the heirs was asked:

"Was your uncle's mind clear until the last?"

"I hardly know," the heir replied; "the will won't be read until tomorrow."

536

Forty is the old age of youth; fifty is the youth of old age.

Victor Hugo

537

Alexander Dumas was asked by an admirer how he grew old so gracefully.

"Madam," he answered, "I give all my time to it."

538

A man is not old until regrets take the place of dreams.

John Barrymore

539

I'm growing old and older,
Every year;
I can see my finish clearer,
Every year;
Hoary hairs are growing thicker,
Less capacity for liquor,
And I'm growing more a kicker,
Every year.

540

LONGEVITY

The horse and mule live thirty years
And nothing know of wines and beers;
The goat and sheep at twenty die
And never taste of Scotch or Rye;
The cow drinks water by the ton
And at eighteen is mostly done;
The dog at fifteen cashes in
Without the aid of rum or gin;
The cat in milk and water soaks
And then in twelve short years it croaks;
The modest, sober, bone-dry hen
Lays eggs for nogs, then dies at ten.
All animals are strictly dry;

They sinless live and swiftly die,
But sinful, ginful, rum-soaked men
Survive for three score years and ten.

541

Consistent stand-patters are liable to make themselves ridiculous, no matter on which side of the fence they take their position. In a debate on whether to abolish capital punishment, a man who had made up his mind said:

"Capital punishment was good enough for my ancestors, and it's good enough for me."

542

A woman from Chicago was seated next to Mrs. Cabot of Boston. They exchanged pleasantries and then launched into a lively discussion concerning the relative merits of their home towns.

Mrs. Cabot said, "In Boston, we place all our emphasis on breeding."

To which the lady from Chicago replied: "In Chicago, we think it's a lot of fun, but we do manage to foster a great many outside interests."

543

Mark Twain, whenever confronted by people who were boastful of their ancestry, was fond of saying, "My grandfather was cut down in the prime of his life. My grandmother always used to say that if he had been cut down fifteen minutes earlier, he could have been resuscitated."

544

The French novelist and critic Paul Bourget was discussing one thing and another with Mark Twain, and Bourget made the observation that:

"When an American has nothing else to do, he can always spend a few years trying to discover who his grandfather was."

"Quite right, Monsieur Bourget," Mark answered; "and when

all other interests fail for a Frenchman, he can always try to find out who his father was."

545

Heredity: Something Pop believes in until his son begins acting like a darn fool.

546

Said a monk as he swung by his tail,
To the little monks, female and male,
"From your offspring, my dears,
In a few million years,
May evolve a professor at Yale."

547

It is told that Isadora Duncan, the world-famous dancer, wrote a letter to Bernard Shaw saying:

"You and I should have a child, who would inherit my beauty and your brains."

And the whiskered playwright is reported to have replied:

"Miss Duncan, I am flattered, but just suppose the child should inherit your brains and my beauty."

548

It is indeed a desirable thing to be well descended, but the glory belongs to our ancestors.

Plutarch

549

The man who has not anything to boast of but his illustrious ancestors is like a potato—the only good belonging to him is under ground.

Thomas Overbury

550

Every man is an omnibus in which his ancestors ride.

Oliver Wendell Holmes

551

He that has no fools, knaves, or beggars in his family, was begot by a flash of lightning.

552

There is no king who has not had a slave among his ancestors, and no slave who has not had a king among his.

Helen Keller

553

To a man who had proudly said, "My ancestors came over in the Mayflower," Will Rogers, of Indian ancestry, retorted, "My ancestors were waiting on the beach."

554

I don't know who my grandfather was; I am much more concerned to know what his grandson will be.

Abraham Lincoln

555

Genealogy: Tracing yourself back to people better than you are.

John Garland Pollard

556

The great criminal lawyer Clarence Darrow was asked to say a few words at the funeral of a man whose many misfortunes culminated in suicide. So he rose, and spoke briefly, saying:

"My friend decided, in a moment of temporary sanity, that his life was no longer worth living."

557

Under the sod and beneath the trees
Lies the body of Jonathan Pease.
His soul isn't here, only his pod;
He's shelled his peas and gone to God.

558

When Uncle Eb White was the guest of honor at a party given on his 100th birthday, everybody was enthusiastic but Seth Higgins, the prize belittler of the village.

"Can't see any reason for it," he said. "All Eb's done is grow old, and he's taken a lot longer to do it than anybody else."

Section 6

BUSINESS AND TRADES

589

In the battle of existence, Talent is the punch; Tact is the clever footwork.

Wilson Mizner

590

I cannot afford to waste my time making money.

Agassiz, when offered large sums for a course of lectures

591

Simile: As likely to make a living as a pickpocket in a nudist colony.

592

You have to work hard if you want to make a living, but if you want to get rich, you have to attack the problem from an entirely different angle.

593

Add newly filed saws: All work and no play makes jack.

594

An expert is one who knows more and more about less and less.

Nicholas M. Butler

595

Sorrow is the mere rust of the soul. Activity will cleanse and brighten it.

Samuel Johnson

596

I am only an average man, said Theodore Roosevelt, but, by George, I work harder at it than the average man.

597

I never saw a cord of wood;
I never hope to see one;
But I can tell you anyhow,
I'd rather see than saw one.

598

The reason why our work is brittle
And shatters at the slightest touch
Is that we think so much about so little,
And think so little about so much.

599

An editorial assistant on a New York magazine, who was drawn for jury service, asked to be excused by the judge. "We're awfully busy, and I ought not to be away."

"Do you think," asked the judge, "that you are one of those people the magazine couldn't get along without?"

"No, Your Honor," the editor replied. "There's no doubt that they could get along without me, but I don't want them to find it out."

"Excused," said the judge.

600

Deciding to take advantage of the wartime price boom in second-hand goods of all kinds, a farmer's wife offered her old, discarded butter churn for sale.

"About how much you figure to ask for that old churn?" asked a prospective buyer.

"Oh, I guess about $20.00 or $30.00—not counting sales tax," she replied rather haughtily.

"But the stores down in town are still selling them new for only $9.50," the purchaser countered.

"I'm tired of this haggling over pennies. Pass over two fifty-cent pieces and the churn is yours."

601

The reason why men who mind their own business succeed is because they have so little competition.

602

Sales resistance is the triumph of mind over patter.

603

One morning at Asbury Park a man with a pail went down to the beach to get some water. A lifeguard was on duty, so the man thought he had better get his permission.

"May I take a pail of water?" he asked.

"Yes," the lifeguard replied, "but it'll cost you a quarter."

The man paid his quarter, scooped up a pail of water, and left. The same day, in the afternoon, he came back with his pail for more water. The tide was way out, and he gazed in astonishment. Then he went to the lifeguard and said:

"Gee, but you must have had a lot of customers."

604

An insurance agent asked a cowboy if he had ever had any accidents.

"No," replied the cowboy, "none to speak of; a bronc kicked in a couple of my ribs and busted my collar bone and a rattlesnake bit me last year."

"Good gracious," said the agent, "don't you call those accidents?"

"No," said the cowpuncher, "they done it a-purpose."

605

A Scotch baker tried to save money on doughnuts by trying every day to make the holes larger. But he finally had to give up because the larger he made the holes, the more dough it took to go around them.

606

A man went into a delicatessen store and said, "Gimme a turkey sandwich." The proprietor replied, "Sorry, we ain't got no turkey."

"Then gimme a chicken sandwich," the man said.

"Brother, don't be silly," said the owner; "if I had chicken, wouldn't I have given you a turkey sandwich?"

607

The gent who wakes up and finds himself a success hasn't been asleep.

Wilson Mizner

608

This was long before the days of the Good Neighbor policy. When the Southern Pacific was laying down its railroad through Texas, Greasewood Joe obtained the contract for furnishing the necessary wood. He made a deal with a group of Mexicans to do the cutting, specifying that he would give them half of what they cut. When they finished, they had many stacks of cordwood on their hands, but they didn't know what to do with it. But Greasewood Joe was magnanimous; he took it off their hands and didn't charge them a cent.

609

When the former pants manufacturer branched out as a cinema producer, he decided that the members of his executive staff must have college degrees. He said to the first suitable looking applicant:

"Are you a colletch man?"

"Yes," was the answer; "Princeton 1935."

"Then should you show me your diploma."

The man pointed out that it was unusual for a bachelor of arts to carry his diploma around with him. The producer, however, was not quite satisfied.

"So!" he exclaimed. "Vell then, say me a big word."

610

Probably the best commentary on American advertising that has ever been given is that of the late English essayist, Gilbert K. Chesterton, who, when he was taken on a tour of New York's Times Square at night, said:

"How beautiful all of this would be for someone who could not read!"

611

While browsing in a shabby secondhand furniture store, a collector came upon a valuable antique chair.

"I'm willing to give you $10.00 for this chair," he said.

"It's yours," moaned the owner, "but I'm taking a terrible beating because I paid $25.00 for it."

"But how can you stay in business if you take losses like this?" asked the sceptical buyer.

"Very easy. I enter it on the wrong side of the ledger and my accountant never finds out."

612

When Mark Twain was editor of a small Missouri newspaper, he got a letter from a subscriber, saying he had found a spider in his paper, and he wanted to know if it were a good omen or bad.

Twain replied: "Finding a spider in your paper is neither good luck nor bad. The spider was merely looking over our paper to see which merchant was not advertising so that he could go to that store, spin his web across the door, and lead a life of undisturbed peace ever afterward."

613

The tired business man had just signed up for another $25,000 on his life insurance. He turned to the smiling agent and said: "Young man, you may well feel proud of yourself. I've refused to see five insurance men today."

"I know," said the agent, "I'm them."

614

The antique furniture fan was being shown around by Mr. Woodhouse, whose wife was a sincere collector.

"Goodness me," exclaimed the visitor; "I wonder where Mrs. Woodhouse got that huge old chest."

"You've got me," the host replied, "but they say that her old woman was the same way."

615

There was an occasional exception to the rule that the artist Whistler always had the better of an argument. His account at a London club was long overdue, and when asked to settle it, he gave a flippant reply. But the treasurer was equal to the occasion and wrote:

"Dear Mr. Whistler:

It is not a Nocturne in Purple nor a Symphony in Blue and Gray that we are after, but An Arrangement in Gold and Silver."

And Whistler paid up.

616

It has been definitely proved that advertising brings quick results. Just the other day a firm advertised for a night watchman, and that evening their safe was robbed.

617

A great big strapping he-looking man was talking to a much-impressed looking girl at a party. Said the Tarzan:

"What I do for a living takes a lot of guts."

Just then a lad who knew them both passed by.

"The feller's right," said the newcomer; "he strings tennis racquets."

618

What was found to be an effective collection letter was sent out by a merchant in a small Iowa town some years ago. It read:

"If you don't pay me what you owe me, I'll tell your other creditors that you did."

619

A restaurant in the Middle West featured a half-dollar Hangover Breakfast made up of: One jumbo orange juice, toast, coffee, two aspirins and our sympathy.

620

A Jewish storekeeper was on his death bed, and his family were gathered around him. They were properly upset about the whole proceeding and their sobbings were highly appropriate to the occasion.

"Here we are, Poppa; all of us, praying for you."

"Is Hyman here?" the dying man asked.

"Yes, Poppa."

"Is Milton here?"

"Yes, Poppa."

"Is Shirley here?"

"Yes indeed, Poppa."

The dying man jerked to a sitting posture and shrieked:

"Then who in — is taking care of the store?"

621

We brought an efficiency expert into our organization, but he didn't last. One of the first things he did was to put nonbreakable glass in all the fire-alarm boxes.

622

Wilton Lackaye, one of the topflight actors of the early years of the century, once posted a notice on the bulletin board of the Lambs, New York's most famous club for members of the theatrical profession. The notice read as follows:

"LOST—One gold cuff link. Will buy—or sell."

623

I think that I shall never see
  A billboard lovely as a tree.
Perhaps, unless the billboards fall,
  I'll never see a tree at all.

Ogden Nash

624

Bargain Sale: An event at which a woman ruins one dress while she buys another.

625

An insurance adjuster after returning from the investigation of a fire, told his boss what had occasioned the blaze.

"Friction," the investigator informed him.

"Was it caused by something rubbing together?" asked his boss.

"That's the answer," the adjuster said tersely, "the fire was caused by rubbing a $3,000 insurance policy against a $2,000 house."

626

An elderly lady was in a department store looking for a hat. The saleswoman showed her a good many models that did not please the customer at all, though they were the latest styles. Finally the motherly person said:

"Look here, girl; I wear a corset and I wear drawers, and I want a hat to match."

627

The manager of a green grocery store hired a boy to be on hand every morning at 3 o'clock sharp, to deal with the fruit and vegetable farmers. The manager himself never appeared until opening time. To check up on the boy he came to the store one night, and at 3 o'clock the boy had not shown up; at 3.05 the boy had not yet come. A moment or two later, the boy hurried in.

"So," bellowed the manager, "banker's hours."

628

The following is an advertisement that was used by Ciro, the perfumer:

"Stop, look, linger . . . with perceptions quickened, eyes keener, breath just a little faster. For the scent of Danger is in the air! Ciro has a really new note in perfumery—a fragrance distinctive in its frank emotional appeal. If you dare be daring, test your mettle with Danger—*it's not for the timid!*"

629

Izzy and Sam were taking a much needed day of rest and relaxation. They were on their way to Manhattan Beach when Izzy said in alarm, "Oi, Sam, we forgot to close the safe!"

"What's the difference?" replied Sam. "We're both here, ain't we?"

630

A cafeteria in San Francisco pleased its many patrons by displaying a sign on the walls announcing "Courteous and Efficient Self-Service."

631

Two Jewish rivals in business tried to outdo each other in every possible way. They weren't friendly enemies either.

One night as the clock was striking twelve, a little fairy named Semiticus came to Shapiro's bedside and said:

"I can geef you ennytings what you want. Mek a vish, but I warn you that ennytings what you esk for, Ginsburg gets it double."

"Oi," exclaimed Shapiro. "Such a grand vish I mek. I vish I go blind in one eye."

632

When two men in business always agree, one of them is unnecessary.

William Wrigley, Jr.

633

Add the following to the story of the boy who had an operation for appendicitis and cashed in on it by exhibiting his scar to the other boys of the neighborhood at ten cents a view.

Hedy Lamarr gave her photograph to the 14-year-old son of one of her friends, signing it "To Johnny, with love from Hedy Lamarr." A few days later Hedy visited her friend and looked into Johnny's room. The photograph was gone. Hedy was surprised and disappointed, and she said so.

"Oh dear," said the mother, "I've just found out that Johnny rented your picture for two dollars over the weekend to another boy whose name is Johnny."

634

Well, at least the man who sold fly paper in the winter didn't run into much competition.

635

A stringy man with a rather haunted look in his eye drew up at a gas station and said:

"Gimme a gallon of gas."

The attendant sauntered over to the rear of his car and inquired:

"Watcha doin', weaning your car?"

636

"What's the matter, Harry?" asked the man meeting a friend on the street. "You look very much upset."

"I'll tell you," said Harry. "A bus driver just looked at me as if I hadn't paid my fare."

"What did you do?" his friend inquired. And Harry replied:

"Oh, I just looked back at him as if I had."

637

A disgruntled floorwalker threw up his job and joined the police force. When asked why he made the change, he replied, "Well, you see it's this way. The pay and the hours aren't too good, but the customer is always wrong."

638

A police car was cruising along Tenth Avenue when there came this radio call:

"Calling Car 13. Car 13, go to Third Avenue and 16th street. Nude woman running down the street. That is all."

There was a pause. Then came the afterthought:

"All other cars stay on your beats. That is all."

639

She may have been stenographer for all the big shots in town, but she's on her last lap now.

640

A teacher in a California city was swindled out of a thousand dollars by a handsome and charming fellow who was promoting a new kind of training school. So she went to the Better Business Bureau with a complaint, and they said:

"Why didn't you let us investigate first? You must have known about our service."

"Of course," she said. "I've heard of the Bureau for a long time; but I was afraid you'd tell me not to invest."

641

A top-flight English advertising man was delegated to attend a convention in New York. He was wined and dined and entertained thoroughly, and then one evening he was taken on a tour of New York by night.

One of the spots to which he was conducted was Times Square. At that time there was an electric sign a block long and extremely garish. The American pointed it out and told how many thousand dollars a month it cost to maintain it.

The Britisher was speechless. Finally his American guide burst out, "Well, what do you think of it?" And the Britisher replied:

"Well, isn't it frightfully conspicuous?"

642

A smart young man tried to sell a successful manufacturer on the desirability of hiring him as press agent. Said the manufacturer:

"Our company is the biggest in its field, and therefore what it does, and what I do, is news."

But the young man was not to be put off.

"Ever hear of Napoleon?" he asked.

"Of course," said the business man.

"How about Wellington?" continued the job-hunter.

"Let's see," was the answer; "didn't he have something to do with the Battle of Waterloo?"

"There you are," the young man came back. "Wellington was the man who didn't need a press agent. He beat the pants off Napoleon at the Battle of Waterloo, but it's Napoleon you always hear of. He had a press agent."

643

A real estate agent advertised a house for sale, with the usual embellishments. He got no results.

Finally he inserted this advertisement:

"Six tiny rooms, ratty decorations, leaky basement, muddy street, no bus, no furnace—$5,000."

Ten prospective customers appeared. He sold the house.

644

During the drear, drab days of the depression, many discussions were overheard of the direct cause of the slump. One battered, disheartened veteran of the crash, more honest and outspoken than the others, offered a good explanation to a friend's question.

"So you lost a lot of money? Were you a bull or a bear?"

"Neither, just a plain, simple jackass."

645

There was a For Sale sign hung around the neck of a mongrel pup on a Chicago corner beside a newsstand. A patron asked the newsboy:

"How much for the pooch?"

"Fifty thousand dollars," the boy answered seriously.

Naturally there was no sale, but a few days later the patron saw that the dog was missing.

"Well," he said, "I notice you've disposed of your dog. Did you get your price?"

"You bet I did," said the boy. "I took in a couple of twenty-five-thousand-dollar cats."

646

A woman, wearing an anxious expression, called at an insurance office one morning.

"I understand," she said, "that for $5 I can insure my house for $1,000."

"Yes," replied the agent, "that is right."

"And," continued the woman, anxiously, "do you make any inquiries as to the origin of the fire?"

"Certainly," was the prompt reply.

"Oh!" and she turned to leave the office. "I thought there was a catch in it somewhere."

647

The traveling salesman came downstairs in the hotel one morning and went to the manager.

"What do you stuff the mattresses on your beds with?" he asked in a slightly acid tone of voice.

"We stuff them with the best straw we can buy," the manager answered tartly.

The salesman rubbed his spine reflectively before he spoke.

"Then," he said, "it must be the straw that broke the camel's back."

648

The making of billiard tables is a highly specialized trade, and there are few who can qualify. There is one craftsman in this line who tells of a prosperous looking man who came to him one day with an unusual request. He said:

"I want you to build me a round billiard table. Wait a minute. You'll say it can't be done. I say it can. Here's a thousand dollars on account." And he laid ten one hundred-dollar bills on the table.

Before the billiard table expert could get his breath, the man continued:

"The table must be eighteen inches high and must have one pocket. "What'll it cost?"

"Five thousand dollars, and I'll have to take three months for the job."

The man was satisfied with the price and went away. A month later he returned and said:

"By the way, I neglected to mention that I want the table covered with leopard skin instead of the conventional green cloth. You can add another thousand dollars onto the price."

It was so arranged. But about three days before the agreed date of delivery the customer had a heart attack and died.

So if any of you gentlemen (or ladies) know of anyone who is looking for a circular billiard table, eighteen inches high, with one pocket and a leopard skin cover, I wish you'd let me know.

649

The son of a Jewish tradesman asked his father to give him a definition of ethics.

"Ethics is this way, Abie," he said. "A man comes into the store and buys plenty of goods. When he goes out he leaves ten dollars too much money. Ethics is the question whether I should tell my partner or not."

650

An insurance adjuster tells of a life policy that was taken out in the name of Abraham L. Brown in a small Southern town. For five years the insurance company received the premium payments when they were due, and then without warning they stopped. The company sent several notices. Finally there came a reply:

"Dear Sirs: Hope you all will excuse us. We can't pay no more insurance on Abe because he died last September. Yours truly, Mrs. A. L. Brown."

651

A man in a jewelry store was looking at $10 watches.

"That's exactly what I have to pay for them," the jeweler said.

"There's no profit in that," observed the customer.

"The profit, sir," the jeweler said, "is in repairing them."

652

The father of a little boy gave him a dollar for his birthday. The boy spent the afternoon going the rounds of the tradesmen and having them change the dollar, first into silver, then back to a bill, and so on. When the father heard of it, he inquired the reason.

"Well," said little Sandy, "sooner or later somebody is going to make a mistake, and it ain't going to be me."

653

A druggist is a merchant who maintains his poise, equanimity or what have you when a customer interrupts the compounding of a $2.00 prescription to buy a two-cent postage stamp. Sometimes, however, he gets in a little dig at this sort of trade.

One Sunday morning a man entered the store, put down a dime, and asked for two nickels. The druggist was obliging, and as he handed out the change, he said:

"I hope you enjoy the sermon."

654

The girl at the switchboard answered a call the other morning and heard a woman's voice say:

"Hello, is this the Fidelity Insurance Company?"

On being assured that it was, the woman continued:

"Well, I want to have my husband's fidelity insured."

655

When he was at the height of his fame, Charles Dana Gibson was invited by an automobile company to submit a drawing in a competition. In writing to the artist, the company specified that the drawing would win a cash prize if accepted, but if it was rejected it would become the property of the company. Gibson's eminently fair reply was:

"I am running a competition for automobiles. Kindly submit one of yours. If acceptable, it wins an award. If rejected, it becomes my property."

656

In these days you've got to go some to beat the other fellow, but when a certain war plant produced a piece of 120-gauge wire, which is virtually invisible, the boys felt that they had reached the ultimate in skill. They were so proud of it that they sent a section of it to a rival plant with the message, "This is just to show you what can be done."

No word came back for some weeks. Then a package arrived. Inside was a steel block on which were mounted two steel standards between which was the same piece of hairlike wire. A small microscope was delicately focused on a certain spot. When the engineers looked at it, they found their rivals had bored a little hole in the wire.

657

The telephone bell rang and the dumb cluck answered it.

"Couldn't say. Why don't you call the weather bureau?"

"Who was that?" asked his wife when he had hung up.

"Oh," said the husband, "it was some dope who wanted to know if the coast was clear."

658

The red-headed girl at the hotel cigar stand asked for a vacation. She said her beauty was beginning to fade.

"What makes you think that?" the boss asked her.

To which she replied:

"My men customers are beginning to count their change."

659

The merchant laid in a supply of cushions and then put a sign in his window that announced "underthings for Nudists."

660

An electrician returned home one night to find his small son's hand swathed in bandages.

"Hello, big boy!" he said. "Hurt your hand?"

"No, Pop," was his reply. "I just picked up a pretty little bee and one end wasn't insulated."

661

The National City Bank, operating in all corners of the earth, receives from its clients some very strange communications. A short time ago, a furrier in Australia wrote the following:

"Dear sirs:

Am sending draft for a thousand pounds, with which please credit my account. Last year I crossed a kangaroo with a raccoon, and now I'm raising fur coats with pockets."

662

A publicity man for a small middle western town sold himself so thoroughly on patronizing home industry that when he went to the hospital for an operation and they asked him whether he would take chloroform or ether, he said:

"I want a local anesthetic or nothing."

663

A clerk in a department store, receiving a very nominal salary, suddenly began to lead a very gay life. He dressed in the height of fashion, bought an expensive car, and gave every evidence of having great wealth. The personnel manager kept an eye on him, and finally called him into his office.

"How is it, young man, that you, who are receiving a salary of only $25 a week, can spend what must certainly amount to well over a $100 a week. Have you been left a fortune, or what's the answer?"

"It's very simple, sir," the clerk replied, unabashed; "there are more than 200 employees upstairs here, and every payday I raffle off my salary at $1 a ticket."

664

W. C. Fields, the uninhibited comedian, decided that a tract of land near his home would make a convenient and inexpensive graveyard for himself and other members of his community.

He approached the town undertaker with the idea that the latter should purchase and improve the land.

"You can manage the whole thing on $20,000," he said breezily.

"Well, I can only raise about $15,000. Will you put up the remaining $5,000? After all, you thought of the whole idea, and you have plenty of money."

"Ordinarily, I would be only too happy to oblige you. Unfortunately, I am now in the strange situation of having all my available funds completely tied up in ready cash," he said with great sadness.

665

It was during one of those periods of prosperity for the real estate business, and the landlord was making the most of it. To a prospective tenant he said:

"This is a very quiet and orderly house. Have you any children?"

The answer was "No."

"Have you," the landlord continued, "a piano, phonograph or radio, or do you play any musical instruments? Oh yes, and have you a cat, dog or parrot?"

Again the answer was "No" to everything, but the prospective tenant added:

"Maybe I ought to tell you that I have a fountain pen that scratches like the devil."

666

According to that sterling lexicographer Ambrose Bierce, an *auctioneer* is a "man who proclaims with a hammer that he has picked a pocket with his tongue."

667

During World War II the demand for mechanics was so great that the test for availability got to be very simple. The applicant was put into a room with a leg of lamb, a dog collar and a screwdriver. If he picked out the screwdriver, he was hired.

668

During the war-time meat shortage, a Bronx butcher despairingly put up this sign in his window: "Leg o' Nuttin'."

669

A taxi driver whose meter registered twenty cents, received just that amount from a prosperous-looking customer.

"That's correct, isn't it?" the customer asked of the cabby as he stared at the two dimes.

"It's correct," answered the cabby, "but it ain't right."

670

A dignified looking gentleman went into a high-class bakery and asked:

"Can you bake a very special cake for me?"

"Certainly," said the baker. "What do you wish?"

"I want a cake," was the answer, "in the shape of the letter S. It must be exactly eighteen inches tall."

The baker assured him that it could be provided, but he warned him that it would cost plenty of money. A special tin would have to be made, and it would be a special job all along the line. The whole work would require two weeks.

Time and price meant nothing to the customer, however, and the order was given. At the appointed time the gentleman appeared and the baker brought out the cake.

"Dear, dear," said the customer, "I forgot to tell you that I wanted a script S—like handwriting, you know. Don't worry; I'll pay the bill."

Another two weeks went by and the customer called. There, ready for him, was a beautiful specimen of the baker's art, a handsome Spencerian S done in cake.

The man was delighted. He went into raptures. Said the baker: "Now where shall I deliver it?"

"Oh, don't bother to deliver it," said the customer; "I'll eat it right here."

671

Special notice to cigarette manufacturers: The world will make a beaten path to your door if you produce better claptrap.

672

A cleaning woman was rightly proud of her polished floors.

"When I first came here to work the floors was in a bad way. But since I've been polishing them," she said, "half a dozen ladies at least has fell down."

673

There was a Negro applicant for the job of mail carrier in Washington, D.C., and a civil service examiner was questioning him.

"How far is it," he asked, "from the earth to the moon?"

The Negro scratched his head and thought. Finally he said:

"I certainly don't know, boss, but if you're goin' to put me on that route, I don't want the job."

674

They tell this story on Lucius Beebe, but it could just as well be told on Monty Woolley, or Adolph Menjou, or any other swell dresser you know. Let's say it was Beebe.

He ordered a pair of striped trousers from his tailor, who took six months to make them. Beebe was furious, and exclaimed:

"It took God only six days to create the world, but you take six months to make one pair of pants."

"Hokay, hokay, Mr. Beebe," the tailor replied, "but look at the world, and then look at these pants!"

675

A man of means was desirous of building a luxurious hunting lodge up in the North Woods of Wisconsin. He had his plans drawn up by a famous architect and sent them to a local carpenter with instructions to go ahead and build it according to specifications.

A few days later a post card came from the carpenter, saying: "The plans is all wrong. I can't do nothing till you get them straightened out."

The owner, being in a hurry to have the lodge completed, sent a letter by return mail assuring the man the plans were all right and to proceed as ordered.

By return mail came the following:

"I don't aim to saw a plank until I get them plans straightened out. Why if I was to build your house the way it's laid out here you'd have two bathrooms!"

676

A celebrated detective died and applied for admission to Heaven. At the gates he was stopped by an attendant who said:

"We're full up; you'll have to go on the waiting list."

The detective wouldn't have it, however, so the attendant finally said:

"If you can pick Adam out of the millions of people in there, I'll let you stay."

So the detective elbowed his way inside. In a quarter of an hour he was back, arm in arm with Adam. The guardian of the gates was amazed.

"How on earth did you find him?"

"Quite simple," the detective replied. "I just looked for a man without a navel."

677

A pleasant-faced little man went into a hardware store and said to the clerk:

"Will you be so good as to give me twenty-five cents' worth of rat poison?"

"Certainly," the clerk replied; "shall I wrap it up?"

"Oh, no, thank you," said the man; "I'll just eat it here."

678

They were searching for a statue that had disappeared, and then they looked under the sink. Eureka! But no, it wasn't the statue; it was the plumber.

679

Pharmacist: A white-coated man who sells ice-cream sodas, fountain pens, cigars, postage stamps and books in a drug store.

680

A smart newspaper headline writer called that lingerie model who got in dutch with the police "A model of the undieworld."

681

A small boy went into a country drugstore and said to the man behind the counter:

"Gimme a dime's worth of asafoetida."

The druggist weighed and packaged it. When he had finished, the boy said:

"Pop wants you to charge it."

"Okay, son; what's your name?"

"Loudenslager."

The druggist looked blank, then scratched his head and said:

"Look here, kid; take it for nothing. I ain't going to spell asafoetida and Loudenslager for a dime."

682

Little Willie Brown *was* to have a new governess.

"Willie, dear," said his mother, "come here and kiss Miss Jones."

"I don't dare," said Willie, holding back. Then he explained:

"I saw Papa kissing her yesterday, and she slapped his face."

683

The woman of the house came back to find the kitchen sink full of dirty dishes. The maid had apparently taken the afternoon off.

The woman looked about in dismay and saw stuck in the cupboard a note, which read, "So what!"

684

The cook was a good cook, as cooks go; and as cooks go, she went.

"Saki," H. H. Munro

685

The dowager was giving instructions to a new maid just before a dinner party. Said she:

"Now remember, Anna, don't wear any jewelry when you serve my guests."

Answered the maid:

"I have nothing valuable, madam, but thanks just the same for the warning."

686

After completing arrangements for hiring William, the new butler, a dowager said:

"By the way, William, I am in the habit of addressing my help by their surnames instead of their Christian names. What did you say your surname was?"

"Darling, Madam."

"Er, well," said the dowager, "that will be all for the present, William."

687

Barbara Hutton (or whatever her name is now) is said to have summoned her butler one afternoon and said:

"James, I am curious to know what my household expenses amount to, really truly. Now James, if you will please omit from the bills your commissions on food, beverages, washing, car expense, and other sundries, I shall be most happy to add the sum to your salary at the end of the week."

The butler gulped. Then he replied with the utmost decorum: "Madam, you couldn't afford it."

688

The lady of the house, hoping to keep the new maid for at least a week, said, "What beautiful scallops you have made on the pies, Lucinda! How do you do it?"

"Ah's pleased to goodness you lak dem, Mam. Ah just used mah false teeth to make de impresses."

SECTION 7

CHILDREN

689

"Revenge is sweet," said Ernest Coulter, founder of the Big Brother Movement; "especially so to the youthful soul. I have a tiny friend who is inclined to be rather naughty. The other day she was so very naughty that her mother found it necessary to shut her up in a big dark closet. For fifteen long minutes the door was closed and there wasn't a sound from behind it. At last the stern but anxious parent opened the door and peered into the darkness. She could see nothing.

"What are you doing in there?" she cried.

Slowly and with emphasis a small voice made reply:

"I'm thpitin' on your new hat, and thpitin' on your new dress, and I'm thpitin' in your new thatin thlippers, and—and—"

There was a breathless pause.

"And what are you doing now?" anxiously cried the mother.

"Waitin' for more thpit!" said the voice of vengeance.

690

A young father came home after a hard day at the office to find his two little daughters misbehaving. He gave them both a scolding and sent them to bed without their supper. The next morning he found a note pinned to his bedroom door:

"Be good to your children and they will be good to you.

(Signed) God."

691

Dorothy, three years old, having lived in southern California, had never seen snow before.

"What is it, Mother?" she shouted, pressing her button nose against the window pane.

"Why, that is snow, Dottie. Whatever did you think it was?" asked her mother.

"Snow!" said Dorothy incredulously. "Why, it looks like popped rain!"

692

Sammie's spirits naught could check,
And today at breakfast he
Broke his baby sister's neck,
So he shan't have jam for tea.

693

Little Will, with Father's gun,
Punctured Grandma just for fun.
Mother said, "You hateful lad,
'T was the last shell Father had."

694

Bernard Shaw found himself sitting next to a gushing matron at a dinner party.

"What a wonderful thing is youth," she burbled.

"Yes," Shaw agreed, "and what a pity to waste it on children."

695

A doting uncle from a distant city was testing his little niece's knowledge.

"Margie," he asked, "what are little girls made of?"

Immediately and very seriously came the answer:

"Sugar and spice and everything nice."

"Right; and what are little boys made of?"

"Snips and snails and puppy dogs' tails," was the quick reply. Then Margie added, "I told that one to Junior yesterday and he could scarcely believe it."

696

A little brother and sister were discussing their favorite colors. The little boy asked his sister, what was her favorite color. She said, "Pink and Blue."

"But you can't have two favorite colors," he protested.

"Blue, then," said she. "What is your favorite color, brother?"

"Plaid!" said he, manfully.

697

In this day and age, youth is nothing if not ambitious. Just the other day a small boy was asked by one of his elders what he wanted to be when he grew up. And the boy answered:

"Alive."

698

"Uncle Arthur," said little Betty Ann, "do you know that a baby fed on elephant's milk gained 20 pounds in a few weeks?"

"I don't believe it," exclaimed Uncle Arthur. "Whose baby was it?"

"The elephant's baby," laughed Betty Ann.

699

The conductor on the train looked down at Roy and asked his mother how old he was.

"He is just four, Conductor," she answered truthfully.

"All right, madam. He's a strapping fine boy," the conductor acknowledged.

Roy looked up at the conductor and thought perhaps further information should be given.

"And Mother," he said solemnly, "is just thirty-five."

700

If anyone complains that all the good names for country places have been pre-empted, you might remind him that Alexander

Woollcott called his Wit's End; Jerome Beatty dubbed his Writer's Cramp; Dorothy Parker named hers Rising Gorge; and Corey Ford hung up the sign Stony Broke. Besides which a well known heart specialist called his place Bedside Manor.

701

When Papa Dionne found that he had quintuplets, he could hardly believe his own census.

702

If thine enemy wrong thee, buy each of his children a drum.

Chinese Proverb

703

A worried old gentleman met a friend on the street. In answer to his friend's question, he said: "I've cause enough to be worried. My son just sent word that a child had been born, but he didn't say anything about the sex of the infant, so I don't know whether I'm a grandfather or a grandmother."

704

Janie had just received a scolding from her mother. Weeping violently, the child said:

"You don't love me any more."

"Certainly I love you," the mother protested.

"No you don't," the child said; "if you did, you'd talk to me as you do when we have company."

705

The cold weather and an empty stomach finally drove the mountain woman down into the valley to ask for relief. She said she had four children, all cold and hungry like herself.

"How old are your children?" she was asked.

"I jest am not fixin' to know the precise ages of them but I got one lap chile, one creeper, one porch chile, and one yard young 'un."

706

One sunny afternoon two little girls were playing together in New York's Central Park. After a while, one was heard to say:

"I wonder what time it is." And the other replied:

"Well, it can't be four o'clock yet, because my mother said I had to be home at four, and I'm not there."

707

"Mother!" screamed little Mary. "Come quick! I've hurt my toe."

"Which toe, darling?" her mother inquired, as she examined the foot Mary held up to her.

"My youngest one," sobbed Mary.

708

The quiz-minded child said to his parents: "I'm going to have a nickel. True or false?"

Walter Winchell

709

Familiarity breeds contempt—and children.

Mark Twain

710

Two kangaroo mothers were discussing their offspring. Said one of them:

"Junior is very irritating." And the other commented:

"I always understood that he was a very good child."

"In most ways he is," said the first; "but he *will* eat crackers in bed."

711

Maybe we shouldn't mention it to the young folks, but you know, they didn't invent any of this deviltry.

from The Nuggets

712

Childhood's worst disappointment is to crawl under a big tent to see a circus and discover that he is on the inside of a revival meeting.

713

Children begin by loving their parents; as they grow older they judge them; sometimes they forgive them.

Oscar Wilde

714

Alibi by Ring Lardner: "I can't come—it's the children's night out and I have to stay home with the nurse."

715

A New York lad went to Texas to live, and one day at school the teacher asked him to tell about the Alamo. He replied:

"That's pie with ice-cream on it."

716

An Italian youth, visiting Rome for the first time, was observed to resemble the Emperor so much that it was the subject of general conversation. Emperor Augustus summoned him to court, and asked him if his mother had ever been in Rome.

"No," was the innocent reply, "but my father has."

717

The following saying, attributed to the Chinese, would be equally applicable to grown folks: "Give your child a whipping every day. If you don't know why, your child does."

718

Charles was often called to account for his carelessness in leaving his clothes about on the floor and chairs.

"Who didn't hang up his clothes when he went to bed?" asked his mother severely.

From under the bedclothes came a muffled voice: "Adam."

719

Old Pop Dinkle had something when he said, "A pat on the back develops character if administered young enough, often enough, and low enough."

720

A certain man-about-town was for some reason chosen to be the godfather of an infant at a christening party. He became somewhat panicky just before the ceremony started, and asked one of his friends:

"What'll I do if they give me the baby to hold?"

"Don't worry about that," his friend reassured. "Grab it the same way you would a cocktail shaker."

721

Young Buck Smithers came home from college for the holidays dressed in the most extreme collegiate style. The effect did not please Old Man Smithers, who was a conservative in his tastes if not his expression.

"You look like a damned fool," he said to his son.

Buck saw no point in an argument, so he held his tongue. Later in the day a family friend dropped in and greeted the boy with:

"Buck, you're getting to look more and more like your father." And the boy answered:

"Yes, so Dad was telling me."

722

An addition to the Smith family was imminent. It seemed like the sensible thing to do to send 10-year-old Margaret to her grandmother's, but 12-year-old Tommy was kept home. Then one morning Papa Smith came downstairs and told Tommy that the angels had brought him a dear little baby brother.

"Here is a dollar," said Papa Smith; "you'd better send a telegram to your sister and tell her the good news."

So Tommy, very much excited, rushed to the Western Union office and sent off the following wire:

"You win; it's a boy."

723

A little girl looked up at her mother and said:

"Mother! How can I button my dress when the buttons are in the back and I'm in the front?"

724

One of Josh Billings's wise remarks was: "There iz two things in this world for which we are never fully prepared, and them iz—twins."

725

Little four-year-old Maribelle was alone in the nursery with the door closed when her small brother tapped on the door and asked to come in.

"But you can't come in, Bruvver; I'm in my nightie and nurse says little boys mus'n't see little girls in their nightie gowns."

Brother was very quiet while he reflected on the strangeness of women. Finally Maribelle called out:

"You can come in now, Bruvver—I tooked it off."

726

Johnny was especially fond of chocolate cake and had got away with two helpings.

"Johnny, if you eat any more cake you will burst," cautioned his mother.

"Well, pass the cake, Mom," he replied, "and then watch out for yourself."

727

Little Peter didn't like kindergarten, and refused to go any more. His mother reasoned with him, scolded him, and then insisted on his going.

"Okay, Mother," he said, "if you want me to grow up to be a damn bead-stringer, I'll go."

728

Little Willie came home one day greatly excited. He rushed into the house and said:

"Oh Mother, I just saw a man making a horse."

"Junior, that isn't possible," his mother said.

"Well, anyway," Willie replied, "I just saw him tacking on the feet."

729

They were two small boys. One of them was crying bitterly. The other wanted to know why. Said the first:

"It's because Duke, my nice old collie, is dead."

"Shucks!" the other countered. "My grandmother died last week, and you don't catch me crying."

"Maybe not," the grief-stricken lad replied, "but you didn't raise your grandmother from a pup."

730

During World War II a proud parent announced:

"We just got a new baby at our house; seven pounds."

And his absent-minded friend asked:

"How many ration points?"

731

He was the smallest and most timid boy in the Boy Scout troop and when the group went to summer camp most of the unpleasant tasks of camp housekeeping fell on his outwardly uncomplaining shoulders. Among his jobs was that of filling the boys' canteens from the water barrel before starting on hikes.

On this particular day the group broke its hike at midday and settled down to lunch and copious swigs of water. The smallest and most timid boy ate sparingly and drank none of his water—offering the contents of his canteen to his companions.

"What's the matter—aren't you thirsty today?" asked one of the other boys.

"Oh, I'm thirsty all right—but a mouse drowned in the water barrel this morning," he replied.

732

When I was a boy of 14, my father was so ignorant I could hardly stand to have the old man around. But when I got to be 21, I was astonished at how much the old man had learned in seven years.

Mark Twain

733

"Well, son, today you are twenty-one. You are of age, with all of a man's responsibilities. And I think, son, that you ought to dig in and help me a little."

"Yes, father, I agree with you," said the boy, swelling out his chest. "What can I do?"

"Well," the parent answered, "you might pay the last three installments on your baby perambulator."

734

Back in the middle of the 19th century the wife of one of the '49ers took her infant to the theater one evening. As might have been expected, it began to cry just as the orchestra started playing. A grizzled miner in the pit shouted:

"Stop those fiddles and let the baby cry. I haven't heard such a sound in ten years."

The audience made the rafters ring with their applause. The

orchestra stopped playing, and the baby continued its solo amid wild enthusiasm.

735

"When Lot's wife looked back," said the Sunday school teacher, "what happened to her?"

"She was transmuted into chloride of sodium," answered the little brother of one of the Quiz Kids.

736

A little girl celebrated her eighth birthday. Among her gifts was a wrist-watch and a bottle of perfume. She was very proud of them and chattered about her new possessions all day long, wearying her parents of the subject. Guests were expected for dinner and her Mother warned the child in advance, saying, "Now, darling, everybody has seen your gifts and everybody is very happy for you. But you mustn't talk about them all the time."

The little girl was very quiet and never mentioned her gifts at the table, but later, she burst forth, "If anyone hears anything or smells anything, it's me!"

737

Babies: Little rivets in the bonds of matrimony.

Arthur Gordon

738

John's mother was out of patience with him. It was late in the day, and nerves were frayed and on edge.

"One more word out of you and I'm going to give you a good spanking," she said to twelve-year-old John.

"It isn't the first time I've been spanked," whined John.

"So you've been spanked before," twitted his mother.

"Spanked before! I've been spanked as far back as I can remember, Mom."

739

The Snatz kid was weeping bitterly. Dear old Mr. Hoogenkamp from down the street asked him why.

"Ma drowneded one of my little kittens," wailed the child.

"Never mind, my little man, you have another," comforted the old gentleman.

"Yes," the kid blurted, "but she promised I could drown the kitten."

740

Willie, bedecked in bows and sashes,
Fell in the fire and was burned to ashes.
Presently the room grew chilly,
But no one cared to stir up Willie.

741

Willie fell down the elevator,
Where they found him six weeks later.
All the neighbors said, "Gee whiz,
What a spoiled child Willie is!"

742

Into the cistern little Willie
Pushed his little sister Lily.
Mother couldn't find her daughter;
Now we sterilize the water.

743

Little Willie hung his sister.
She was dead before we missed her.
Willie's always up to tricks.
Ain't he cute! He's only six.

744

The modern kid is pretty good at that. A mother who was expecting another child took a five-year-old on a crowded bus the other day, and they both had to stand up. After a minute or so, the five-year-old sang out:

"Won't some gentleman give my pregnant mother a seat?"

The $64 question is: Did somebody give her a seat?

745

A child awakened out of a deep sleep protested drowsily, "Oh, dear! I have lost my place in my dream."

746

During the Labor Day rush that is always most apparent in New York's Grand Central Station, a suburban mother lost her five-year-old girl. She searched frantically and finally located the kid with a group of nuns.

"Gracious," the mother exclaimed, "I do hope my daughter hasn't been causing you too much trouble."

"No indeed," said the Mother Superior, "but it's the first time we have ever been mistaken for penguins."

Section 8

CLIMATE AND PLACES

750

New Yorkers, it is said, never boast, but some of them do complain. One of them was telling a friend what a hot summer there had been in the metropolis.

The friend said, "Shucks, you don't know nothing. One day last week in New Orleans I saw a dog chasing a cat, and they were both walking."

751

Another 't ain't-so story: A western cowboy needed some hot water for shaving one morning, and put the kettle on to boil. The kettle boiled over before he realized it, so he put it outside the door to cool. Three minutes later it had frozen solid—so quickly, in fact, that the ice was still warm.

752

A visiting Britisher was riding with a cowpuncher through a western canyon. For some reason or other he got off his horse, when a sudden gust of wind blew him flat. He picked himself up and said to the cowboy:

"I say, old thing, but don't you rather overdo the ventilation out here?"

753

One of the soldiers stationed in Alaska with our troops had been a crackerjack salesman before he was inducted and seemed loath to lose his skill. He went from freezing barracks to freezing barracks trying to get orders for small air cooling units sold by his former employer.

"Are you crazy?" his buddies asked. "What do we need with an air cooling system with the temperature fifty below zero?"

"But you gotta have foresight," pleaded the salesman. "To-morrow it may leap up to zero."

754

In one of the counties of Arkansas the dogs are so skinny they have to lean against a tree to bark.

755

A visitor from England was being shown around Boston by a native of that city.

"And this," the Bostonian said, "is Bunker Hill Monument, where Warren fell, you know."

The visitor looked at the lofty shaft and commented:

"Nasty fall, eh what! Killed him, of course?"

756

He called himself a Southerner because he was born in southern New Hampshire.

757

Spain may have her matadors, but the United States has its Senators.

758

Wherever there is a tall, gaunt building and an artistic cynic in a city, the following story may be told with suitable variations.

William Morris, British poet and artist, spent a great deal of his time in the restaurant of the Eiffel Tower, where he ate all his meals and did much of his writing. A friend remarked:

"You must be very much impressed by the Tower."

"Impressed nothing!" exclaimed Morris. "I spend my time here because it's the only place in Paris where I can avoid seeing the blasted thing."

759

During the Civil War, General Philip H. Sheridan is reported to have said: "If I owned Texas and Hell, I would rent out Texas and live in Hell." And a Texan editor retorted: "Quite right; every man to his own country."

760

"I first saw the light of day in San Francisco," said the great man who was being interviewed.

"But," the reporter protested, "it is generally understood that you were born in Pittsburgh."

"True enough," the great man agreed, "but it was a year later that I first saw the light of day—in San Francisco."

761

In some of the arid regions of the West the people have gone so long without water that they can't get used to it. At one place a drop of water fell on a man, and his friends had to throw two buckets of sand in his face to bring him to.

762

A Texan of the exceedingly State-conscious variety was overheard taking his son to task. "Just now," he said, "I heard you asking a man what State he was from. Now, Son, remember this: if a man comes from Texas, he'll tell you; if he doesn't, there's no need for you to embarrass him."

763

This story of the size of Texas may be proved up with a map and a pair of dividers. A traveling man out of Kansas City reported to his home office that he had arrived in El Paso, and the sales manager wired back:

"Now that you're in Texas, just run over to Texarkana and collect that old account."

The salesman telegraphed back:

"Run over there yourself and collect it; you're nearer than I am."

764

The following is adapted to San Francisco and Los Angeles, Portland and Seattle, St. Paul and Minneapolis, and some other rival cities of the United States.

A man from Dallas, Texas, said:

"I'll have to admit that Fort Worth has just one thing that Dallas doesn't have."

The man from Fort Worth bit.

"What's that?" he asked.

"A real city just thirty-three miles away," was the reply.

765

Broadway is a main artery of New York life—the hardened artery.

Walter Winchell

SECTION 9

CLOTHING AND APPEARANCE

770

A man was holding forth on the shortcomings of the younger generation.

"Take clothes, for instance," he said. "Look at that youngster over there, the one with short hair, a cigarette, and breeches. What is it, a boy or a girl?"

"It's a girl," was the reply; "she's my daughter."

"I beg your pardon, sir," the man apologized. "I wouldn't have said that if I had known you were her father."

"I'm not," was the comeback; "I'm her mother."

771

Lorgnette: French name for a dirty look you can hold in your hand.

772

A maiden lady was on a personally conducted tour of Southern California and continually showed her interest by asking questions. One day she pointed to a tree and said:

"What is that?"

"That is a fig tree, madam," the guide answered.

"No it isn't," the lady replied sharply. "The leaves are much larger than that."

773

Evening gown: Low and behold.

774

Maybe they deserve all they get, including the girl who, when asked what size shoes she wore, said she took sixes, but sevens felt so good that she bought eights.

775

The flunkey entered.

"Sire," he said to his master, "Lady Godiva rides without."

Milord glanced out of the window, and remarked:

"Very tactfully put, my man."

776

Shirley Gladstone believed that clothes had a lot to do with social advancement, so she had her dresses made so that she is always seen in the best places.

778

Pity the poor moth; he spends the summer in a fur coat and the winter in a bathing suit.

779

Nudity: An inexpensive style but becoming to few.

Oliver Herford

780

When dressed for the evening, the girls now-a-days
Scarce an atom of dress on them leave;
Nor blame them; for what is an evening dress
But a dress that is suited for Eve?

781

Cadwalader Bean said that when he went to a nudist colony it reminded him of his first trip in an airplane. Pressed for an explanation he said:

"I'll never forget the first take-off."

782

The fashion wears out more apparel than the man.

Shakespeare

783

If the experts who control women's fashions are not careful, one of these days they are going to find themselves out of a job.

784

It is time to get your shoes re-soled if, when you step on a nickel, you can tell whether it's heads or tails.

785

Ph.D.: A signal between women signifying "Petticoat hanging down."

786

Take Ambrose Bierce's word for it, *armor* is the kind of clothing worn by a man whose tailor is a blacksmith.

787

The instructor was teaching a young thing how to drive a car.

"This," said he, "is the hand brake. It is used to put on quickly in case of an emergency."

"Oh, I see," the young dame exclaimed; "it's something like a kimono."

788

The poor benighted Hindu,
He does the best he kindu;
He sticks to caste
From first to last;
For pants he makes his skindu.

789

The new baseball dresses the girls are wearing have a diamond back, a grandstand view in front, and a whole lot of curves.

790

Irvin Cobb is reported to have met Fanny Hurst, the novelist, at a party one evening but failed to recognize her.

"Hello, Irvin," she said; "don't you recognize Fanny Hurst?"

"Well," he replied, "the Hurst eluded me, but I sure recognized the Fanny."

791

My sense of sight is very keen,
My sense of hearing weak,
One time I saw a mountain pass,
But could not hear its peak.

Oliver Herford

792

The body is but a pair of pincers set over a bellows and a stew-pan and the whole fixed upon stilts.

793

A spare little man remarked to a friend:

"You know, I weighed eleven pounds when I was born."

"Do tell!" remarked the friend dryly; "you haven't lost many pounds since then, have you?"

794

Why don't you get a haircut? You look like a chrysanthemum.

P. G. Wodehouse

795

Her face was calm as a custard.

Anne Parrish

796

Your eyes—they shine like the pants of a blue serge suit.

George S. Kaufman

797

Definition of *Human Being* by the poet Dryden: An unfeathered two-legged thing.

798

Isn't (or ain't if you prefer) Nature wonderful? Ages and eons ago the old Dame didn't know we were going to wear spectacles, but look at the way she placed our ears.

799

A little boy and girl lived next door to a nudist colony. One day they discovered a knothole in the fence about the colony. The little girl took the first peek.

"What are they?" the little boy asked. "Men or women?"

"How should I know?" she replied, "they haven't any clothes on."

Robert Carson

800

Clothes make the man, but with a woman they simply serve to show how she is made.

Section 10

EATING AND DRINKING

Eating

810

A skinny little chap strutted into the manager's office of an educational side-show on New York's 42nd Street.

"Who the dickens are you?" the manager asked.

"Egmont Essen," was the reply. "I am known as Egmont the Egg King."

"What's your act?"

"I eat a coupla dozen hens' eggs, the same number of ducks' eggs and a dozen goose eggs, raw, at a single sitting."

"Well, well," the manager said. "But I suppose you know that we give four shows every day."

"That's okay by me," Egmont answered.

"Besides that," the manager continued, "on Saturdays there are six shows, and sometimes on holidays we give a show every hour."

Then Egmont the Egg King showed his first trace of balkiness.

"Looka here," he exclaimed, "it don't matter none how rushing business is, you gotta give me time enough to eat my regular meals at the hotel."

811

There was a young man so benighted,
He never knew when he was slighted;
    And out at a party
    He'd eat just as hearty
As if he'd been really invited.

812

It was in the general vicinity of Boston, and a group of people were in the living room awaiting food. Presently the host appeared and announced:

"For those who don't like beans, supper's over."

813

One balmy day an inmate was looking out of the window of a retreat for mentally indisposed persons. He noticed a gardener with a wheelbarrow and said to him:

"What're you doing there?"

To which the gardener replied:

"I'm a-puttin' fertilizer on the strawberries."

"Well," the "case" observed; "they call me crazy, but I always put sugar and cream on mine."

814

Revised adage: What is one man's fish is another man's *poisson.*

815

There was a young lady of Munich,
Whose appetite simply was unich.
"There's nothing like food,"
She contentedly cooed
As she let out three tucks in her tunich.

816

A Southerner came to visit in New York and only believed the tales he had heard about the difficulty of securing restaurant service and the insolence of waiters after he had been curtly denied admittance to 11 restaurants during the dinner hour.

After much weary wandering he came upon a small eating place half hidden away on a side street and, wonder of wonders, he was ushered to one of the several empty tables. To his even greater surprise a waiter immediately popped up beside him and said "What does the gentleman desire?"

"Just a plate of beef stew and a few friendly words," he asked.

A few minutes later a steaming plate of stew was ceremoniously placed before him. "Well, I declare," said the Southerner happily, "that sure is just the food I ordered. But how about those few friendly words?"

The waiter bent low and whispered into his ear, "Don't eat that stew."

817

Add newly filed saws: A bird in the hand is bad table manners.

818

Dinner in an insane asylum is just a matter of serving soup to nuts.

819

The customer in a quick lunch ordered a Swiss cheese sandwich. Then he decided that he would rather have American cheese, so he asked if he could change the order. The counterman called back to the cook:

"Naturalize that Swiss!"

820

Restaurant: An eating place that does not sell drugs.

821

During World War II the OPA doubtless did some good, but there were exceptions. One day a man went into a restaurant. He had folding money with him, and he decided to have a real meal. Said he to the waitress:

"I'm going to have your $3.00 special dinner."

"On white or rye?" she asked.

822

There was a young soldier of Leeds,
Who swallowed a package of seeds.
In a month, silly ass,
He was covered with grass,
And he couldn't sit down for the weeds.

823

The man who drank sulphuric acid said he wasn't bothered by it particularly, but he said that for days every time he blew his nose, it left burnt holes in his handkerchief.

824

The young bride started out to make angel cake, but in the process of baking it fell, so she called it Lucifer cake.

825

Into one of the smart Park Avenue restaurants came a man of evident means but somewhat on the uncultured side. He was shown to a table. When he sat down he tied a napkin around his neck. The manager was scandalized and called a waiter, saying:

"Tell that man, as tactfully as possible, that that sort of thing simply isn't done."

The waiter was equal to the occasion. He stepped over to the table and said:

"Pardon, sir; shave or haircut?"

826

Adult: A person who has stopped growing at both ends and started growing in the middle.

827

Rhubarb: A kind of celery gone bloodshot.

828

Edible: Good to eat, and wholesome to digest, as a worm to a toad, a toad to a snake, a snake to a pig, a pig to a man, and a man to a worm.

Ambrose Bierce

829

Methuselah ate what he found on his plate,
And never, as people do now,
Did he note the amount of the calory count;
He ate it because it was chow.
He wasn't disturbed as at dinner he sat,
Devouring a roast or a pie,
To think it was lacking in granular fat
Or a couple of vitamins shy.
He cheerfully chewed every species of food,
Unmindful of troubles or fears
Lest his health might be hurt
By some fancy dessert;
And he lived over nine hundred years.

830

Fat people ought not to complain if others occasionally have a little fun at their expanse.

831

Willie Smart was asked to define *hors d'oeuvres* and came pretty close to it when he answered, "A sardine sandwich divided by twelve."

832

Dinnertime: As the Texas darky said: "dinner-time fur some folks; but just twelve o'clock fur me!"

Irvin Cobb

833

Charles Lamb had a somewhat ascetic countenance, and this, combined with the fact that he generally wore a white cravat, accounted for his frequently being taken for a minister. One day this led the host at a dinner to ask him to say grace. Lamb looked around at all the guests, and then with his usual stutter inquired:

"Is there no c-c-clerygyman present?"

The guests replied that there was none, so Lamb bowed his head and said:

"Then let us thank God."

834

When Oliver Wendell Holmes was asked by a woman friend what he thought of the institution of afternoon tea, the literary Doctor replied:

"It's giggle, gabble, gobble, git."

835

That stout early 19th century statesman John Randolph of Roanoke was at dinner in a tavern when he pointed to his cup and saucer and said to the waiter:

"Take that away; change it."

"What is it that you want, Mr. Randolph?" asked the waiter, and Randolph replied:

"If that stuff is tea, bring me coffee; if it's coffee, bring me tea."

836

To eat is human; to digest, divine.

Mark Twain

837

When Thackeray visited America he expressed a desire to taste some Massachusetts oysters. His publisher, James T. Fields, wishing to gratify his desire, took him to an opulent oyster bar. Six enormous bivalves were put before him, nested on ice and accompanied by a tempting sauce. He looked in amazement upon them, but not knowing how to eat them, asked his host in obvious perplexity, "How do you attack them?"

"This way," said Mr. Fields, and showed him.

Thackeray followed his example but made no comment. After a moment of profound silence, Mr. Fields ventured to ask how he liked it. Thackeray drew a long breath and said: "I feel as if I had swallowed a baby."

838

I sat next to the Duchess at tea;
It was worse than I thought it would be.
Her noises abdominal
Were simply phenomenal,
And everyone thought it was me.

839

Eat, drink, and be merry, for tomorrow ye diet.

William Gilmore Beymer

840

Among a party of ecclesiastics who attended a religious conference was Bishop Davidson of Winchester. As he was about to sit down at the dinner party tendered them after the conference one of his pious companions remarked: "This is the time to put a bridle on our appetites."

To which the Bishop replied: "No, this is the time to put a bit in our mouths."

841

After walking three miles to work, the new hand at the shipyard discovered he had left his lunch box at home.

"Faith and I've gone and done it this time," he grinned. "My grub is at home and I'm to work."

Then he laughed goodnaturedly, as he added:

"And it's a good thing I left it there, because I left my teeth at home, too."

842

Irrepressible little Audrey was sitting at dinner with the family. Her father asked her to pass the cream. So she passed the cream. Father poured some into his coffee. When he put the pitcher down, little Audrey noticed a drop of cream on the spout all ready to fall. It amused her no end, for she knew that the cream pitcher couldn't go *sniff, sniff.*

843

How can these women expect to reduce when their only exercise is pushing themselves away from the table three times a day?

844

It isn't so much what's on the table that matters, as what's on the chairs.

W. S. Gilbert

845

There's a lady in Kalamazoo
Who bites all her oysters in two.
She has a misgiving,
Should any be living,
They raise such a hullabaloo.

William Bellamy

846

The desire to be regarded as a tough guy is not confined to small boys. Two soldiers and a marine happened to go into a small-town restaurant at the same time. The first soldier thought he would make an impression on the waitress, so he ordered a steak "as thick as me two fists."

"Gimme a steak too," the second soldier said; and added, "Make it thick, raw and dripping with blood. If it ain't right, I'll send it back."

The trembling waitress approached the marine for his order. He took a long drag at his cigarette and said:

"Just drive the steer in here, sister, and I'll bite a chunk out of it."

847

A diner in a restaurant noticed that there were two prices for steak on the menu.

"What," he asked, "is the difference between a two-dollar steak and one for two and a quarter?" The waiter explained:

"With the two and a quarter steak we furnish a sharp knife."

848

"Just get an eyeful of that," said the waiter as he brought his customer a particularly nice portion of grapefruit.

849

A man who looked as if he had lost his last friend entered a restaurant one morning and sat down at a table. Said he to the waitress:

"Bring me two eggs fried hard, a slice of toast burned to a cinder, and a cup of very weak coffee."

"Will you repeat that order," said the mystified waitress.

He did, and in a few minutes she brought the order. As she set it in front of him, she asked:

"Anything else, sir?"

"Yes," he answered; "now sit down and nag me. I'm homesick."

850

A well known millionaire was host at a dinner party not long ago. He was not only hospitable, but wished everyone to know of his liberality. During the dinner, he spoke of the various foods being served, and gave their value in dollars and cents. In speaking of some hot-house grapes that were grown on his estate, he bored the guests with a careful calculation as to just how much a stem of them had cost him.

The guest of honor smiled and passed her empty plate, saying:

"I'll thank you to cut me off about $1.87 worth more, please."

851

Americans going to England begin by wondering why the English are such tea drinkers. When they try English coffee, they know.

852

Four men went to an expensive restaurant for luncheon. When they finally finished, the waiter brought the reckoning. Immediately Sandy MacGregor said:

"Waiter, give me that check!"

The following day an alarm was sent out by the police for a Scotchman who was wanted for murdering a ventriloquist.

854

The diner had waited interminably for his meal. When the waiter finally arrived with the food, the man asked:

"Have you ever been to the zoo?"

"No sir," the waiter replied; "why?" And the man answered:

"You sure would get a thrill the way the turtles race around."

855

Waiters are not supposed to say what is on their minds to unreasonable guests, but a headwaiter who was better bred than his customer achieved the general effect rather handsomely. Said he:

"My position does not permit me to argue with you; but, sir, if it ever came to a choice of weapons, I would choose grammar."

856

When a W.C.T.U. leader approached the late Dr. Charles W. Eliot for his assistance in an anti-tobacco crusade, the lady said:

"You know, Dr. Eliot, that man is the only animal that uses tobacco."

"Yes, I know," the doctor agreed; "but man is also the only animal that wears clothes."

857

Two cigarettes were conversing, when one of them was heard to say:

"I hope I won't get lit tonight and make an ash of myself."

858

Definition of Smoker: A person who claims that the more he fumes the less he frets.

859

Tobacco is a filthy weed;
  I like it.
It satisfies no normal need;
  I like it.
It makes you thin, it makes you lean,
It takes the hair right off your bean;
It's the worst darned stuff I've ever seen . . .
I like it.

Drinking

860

A farmer who seldom came to town, arrived one day with his pockets full of money from the sale of his crops. He walked over to the saloon and gaming house over the entrance to which was a large sign proclaiming, "BILLIARDS."

He swaggered up to the bar and ordered, "A glass of them there billiards."

The barkeeper took a good look at him and disappeared into the kitchen behind the bar. He came out with a large, foamy glass of dark and soapy dishwater, which he shoved across the counter to his customer. The farmer drank it down in one long draught. Banging the glass back on the counter he wiped his mouth on his sleeve and said, "Waal, efen I warn't an old and hardened billiard drinker, I'd 'a said that there was dishwater!"

861

Ambrose Bierce defines an *abstainer* as "a weak person who yields to the temptation of denying himself a pleasure," and adds that "a total abstainer is one who abstains from everything but abstention, and especially from inactivity in the affairs of others."

862

A Scotchman was on the tip-top floor of the Empire State Building when he dropped a nickel. The coin bounced and went over the edge down to the street a hundred floors below. The Scotchman began to cry. Thus we have the true origin of the Scotch high bawl.

863

One swallow may not make a summer, but it can break a New Year's resolution.

864

Fermentation: Something Moses forgot to forbid when he wrote the Ten Commandments.

865

A Bowery drunkard with keen business instincts got to seeing so many pink rabbits, white snakes, purple tigers, and such unusual fauna that he hired a shop and put up a sign reading:

"25 cents to see the zoo."

Two customers soon came in, but they saw nothing but four bare walls, so they swore out a complaint. A cop came in to make the arrest, whereupon the proprietor brought a jug out from under the counter. The cop took four snifters, and paid $750 for a half interest in the show.

866

Alcohol: A liquid good for preserving almost anything except secrets.

867

A New York business man who travels back and forth to his Staten Island home by ferry discovered a forgotten bottle of good old pre-war scotch in his desk and proceeded to taste the stuff with the result that he arrived at the ferry wharf an hour late and wabbling noticeably. But as he walked toward the end of the pier he saw a ferryboat about 15 feet out in the water.

Gathering all his reeling resources, with a fit of energy he leaped off the pier in a breathtaking jump that brought him right onto the deck of the ship.

He turned to the amazed passengers and hiccuped proudly, "I took a chance but I made it alright—for the wife and kiddies."

"You certainly jumped beautifully," agreed a passenger. "But why didn't you wait? The ferry was just coming in to the dock."

868

A drunk was on his wobbly way home late one night when he ran smack into a tree. He backed off and tried again; and bumped into the same tree. Once again he tried; but he couldn't seem to miss that tree. Then he burst out weeping, and exclaimed tragically:

"Lost—lost in an impen'trable forest!"

869

Believe it or not, a Scotchman got aboard the water wagon.

"Do you mean to tell me, Sandy," a friend asked, "that if you were standing in a lake of whiskey up to your knees, you wouldn't bend over just a bit?"

"No," said Sandy righteously.

"All right, Sandy, but if it was up to your chin—real Scotch whiskey—wouldn't you sip it?"

Sandy licked his chops and gulped. Then he replied:

"Well, I'm no saying I would, d'ye mind, but I might make a wee ripple with me hand."

870

God made Man
Frail as a Bubble,
God made Love,
Love made Trouble.
God made the Vine;
Was it a Sin
That Man made Wine
To drown Trouble in?

Oliver Herford

871

A souse who was in the habit of playing the slot machines one day reeled into an Automat. He got a lot of nickels at the change booth, went to the sandwich section, and put nickels into all the available slots. When he had collected about twenty sandwiches, the manager discovered him and said:

"Excuse me, sir, but I think you've got enough now; why don't you stop?"

"I should quit now?" exclaimed the drunk. "Why I'm just on a winning streak."

872

Youth must be served, but it shouldn't have to be carried out.

873

During hay-fever season the favorite barroom toast is, "Here's looking at-choo!"

874

Not the least of the war's tragedies occurred to the confirmed liquor-lover who was assigned by the U.S. Army to act as aide to an Arabian official, a strict Mohammedan who refused to permit any intoxicating beverages within 5 miles of his camp.

"I've never recovered," the American tells his pension board, "from the horror of those months of living on nothing but food and water."

875

In America we drink our cocktails out of glasses; in France they drink them out of doors.

876

Nobody needs to believe this if he doesn't want to, but at a big London dinner the Lord Mayor had done rather well by himself. Mr. Choate, the then Ambassador, saw His Lordship to the door. As he let go of him, he said:

"Now your Lordship, if I may presume to advise you, when you get to the walk you will see two hansoms. You should take the one to the right; the one to the left isn't there."

877

There was a young lady of Kent
Who said that she knew what it meant
When men asked her to dine
With cocktails and wine.
She knew what it meant, but she went.

878

One night in late October,
When I was far from sober,
Returning with my load of manly pride,
My feet began to stutter,
So I lay down in the gutter,

And a pig came near and lay down by my side.
A lady passing by was heard to say:
"You can tell a man who boozes
By the company he chooses;"
And the pig got up and slowly walked away.

879

Not drunk is he
Who from the floor
Can rise again
And still drink more;
But drunk is he
Who prostrate lies
Without the power
To drink or rise.

Thomas Love Peacock

880

Another of the quips attributed to the scintillating Dorothy Parker concerns a drunk who was annoying her at a New York restaurant. He took pains to assure her that he was a high class gentleman and a person of real genius. At first Miss Parker said nothing, but at length she observed:

"I see; you're a rhinestone in the rough."

881

Yesterday upon the stair
I saw a man who wasn't there.
He wasn't there again today;
Gee, I wish he'd go away!

882

When they took a census of all the American people who are in the habit of drinking, the results were staggering.

883

It was on a suburban train running out of New York (or Philadelphia, Chicago or other metropolis), and the conductor knew the passenger.

"Did you get home all right last night?" he asked.

"Sure; why?"

"Well," the conductor answered, "when you got up and gave the lady your seat, you two were the only people in the car."

884

Drink and the world drinks with you; swear off, and you drink alone.

885

Candy
Is dandy
But liquor
Is quicker.

Ogden Nash

886

The Irish physician, author and wit, Oliver St. John Gogarty, visited a friend of his who proved to be disappointingly shy in his supply of liquor both with meals and between. A few days afterward he met his host, who spoke disparagingly of a young army officer who also had been his guest.

"Gogarty," he exclaimed, "that fellow actually got drunk in my house. What do you think of that?"

"It shows marvelous industry," the author replied.

887

An Englishman traveling in the West for the first time met and became friendly with an American, and the two repaired to a barroom for a drink together. The American ordered a horse's neck, whereat the Englishman said:

"I'll have a horse's tail. There's no use killing two horses."

888

The following story has been vouched for by a man whose name we have forgotten.

A tough hombre breezed into a New Mexico drinking place and ordered a side-car cocktail. He drank it at a gulp and then had another. Then he began to eat the glass itself. He chewed and swallowed until he had finished all but the stem, which he tossed aside.

A runty little fellow watched him closely, fascinated. This irritated the tough one and he said, "What the blazes are you so interested about?"

"Well," said the runt, "you don't know how to eat those glasses. The stem is the best part."

889

The city hall in New York (or a hundred other towns you might mention) has a tower clock that is illuminated at night. Late one evening a drunk walked on rubber legs up to a mail box, dropped a nickel in the slot, looked at the clock, and exclaimed:

"Sufferin' cats! I'm eighteen pounds overweight!"

890

A couple of men were talking about what happened after they got to bed. Said the first one:

"I suffer something awful from insomnia."

"What do you do for it?" asked the second.

"I take a glass of whiskey at regular intervals."

"Does it make you sleep?"

"No, it doesn't, but it makes me perfectly contented to stay awake."

891

Two men returning from a club meeting were in a state of exhilaration and driving their car hell-bent-for-election toward home. "Shay, George," said one of them, "be sure to turn out for that bridge that's coming down the road toward us."

"What on earth do you mean?" said the other. "I thought you were driving."

892

Three gentlemen, each with at least that many drinks under his belt, were on a late train bound for the suburbs. They were all silent for a little while, when one of them said thickly:

"What time is it?"

"Thursday," another answered. Whereupon the third jumped to his feet, and exclaimed:

"My goodness, that's my station!"

893

"Casey is a fine judge of whiskey."

"Sure he is that; a fine judge and a merciless executioner."

894

A foul-looking individual rushed into a gin mill shooting a revolver and shouting:

"Get out of here, all you stinking so-and-so's."

The crowd fled, dodging a hail of bullets—all except an Englishman who stood at the bar quietly sipping a Scotch and soda.

"Well?" the gunman barked at him.

"Well," drawled the Britisher, "there certainly were a lot of them, weren't there!"

895

A man was brought before a judge on a charge of intoxication.

"What is your name?" asked the judge sternly.

"Sandy Angus MacDonald," was the answer.

The judge hesitated a moment, and then thundered:

"And who bought the whiskey for you?"

896

Two drunks were leaning against a bar. The stout one had his right hand closed and occasionally peeked into it.

"Whatcha got?" his friend asked.

"Guess what," was the reply.

"June bug?"

"Nope." The drunk took another peek.

"Bluebird?"

"Nope. Guess again."

"Hownell do I know; maybe it's an elephant."

At that, the drunk took a longer look, smiled, and asked:

"What color?"

897

Papa Hog went out for a stroll early one evening. Presently he came to where a barrel of beer had fallen off a truck, sprung a leak and made a big puddle. Papa Hog liked it so well that when he reached home he was staggering and squealing "Sweet Adeline" at the top of his voice. Mama Hog was shocked. She got the piglets to bed in a hurry, and exclaimed:

"Shame on you, William Hog, for making a human out of yourself in front of the children."

898

Three sheets in the wind and rolling slightly, a man entered a restaurant and sat down. The waiter appeared and asked for his order.

"Bring me a dish of prunes," said the groggy one.

"Stewed, sir?" the waiter asked; and the man answered:

"Thash none of your blankety-blank business."

899

A broad-minded father took his son to the village tavern for a glass of beer. Previous to this he had had several drinks, and in a mellow frame of mind he warned the young man against the evils of intemperance.

"My son," he said, "a gentleman never drinks too much. He realizes that it is a disgrace to be drunk."

"You're right, Dad; but how can I tell when I've had enough, or when I'm drunk?"

The parent pointed to the corner of the room and answered:

"Take, for instance, those two men sitting at that table. If you saw four men there, you would know you were drunk."

The boy took a good long look. Then he said in a puzzled tone:

"But Dad, there is only *one* man in that corner."

900

A policeman with both eyes open happened to notice a man who was walking along the curb with one foot in the gutter and the other on the sidewalk. He followed him for a time just to make sure. Then he went up to him and said:

"Come on, Bud, I'll help you home. You're just a bit pi-eyed."

The man looked around, saw the cop, and exclaimed:

"Thank Heaven; I thought I was a cripple."

901

A blustering Arizona cowpuncher breezed into a saloon and accosted a quiet looking man.

"Have a drink with me," he exclaimed.

"No thanks," the man replied.

"Well, I'd like to know why not!" The cowboy was inclined to be ugly.

"There are two reasons," answered the quiet man.

"Name them," the range rider roared. And the man did.

"First, I promised my grandmother on her deathbed that I would touch not, taste not the devilish stuff."

This rather softened the hardboiled cowboy, and he asked: "What is the other reason?"

"Well," said the mild one, "I just had a drink."

902

Two old friends met again after a long separation and repaired to a drinking place they had frequented in former days. But it wasn't the same, for it had been refurbished and modernized.

"I don't like it much, Bill," one of them said, "but most of all I miss the old spittoon."

"Eddie," came the answer, "you always did."

903

A rotund red-faced man in a barroom made the boast that he had drunk nineteen glasses of beer at one sitting. One of his audience said:

"While you were about it, you should have made it an even twenty."

"What!" the boaster bellowed. "Do you think I'd make a hog of myself?"

904

A three-hundred pound gentleman and a stringy little fellow had had several drinks at a Sixth Avenue bar when the big chap became confidential.

"D'ye know," he said, "when I was born I weighed only four and a quarter pounds."

"Wunnerful," said his companion; "and did you live?"

"Goonness yes," returned the fat man; "you should see me now."

905

A certain Admiral of the U.S. Navy came home for ten days recently, and it was natural that there was a reception given in his honor. It was all rather sudden, and sufficient help could not be had, so his ten-year-old daughter offered to help serve the cocktails. She wasn't too bad as an assistant hostess, either, but her mother was somewhat horrified when the kid went up to a Brigadier General's wife and said:

"Won't you allow me to get you your ninth Manhattan?"

906

A little lady had been invited out to a party, and when the drinks were passed around she refused a scotch and soda, saying:

"I never touched one in all my life."

"Well," the host urged, "why don't you try one now? Just see if you don't like the taste."

So, as she shyly consented, he poured her out a drink and she tasted it.

"Great Scott," she exclaimed; "you've given me Irish whiskey."

907

A man was brought up before a magistrate for being drunk. The magistrate was stern. Said he:

"Here you are before me, charged with being drunk. What have you to say for yourself?"

"Oh, your honor, it ain't true," said the culprit; "I've never been drunk in my life. I never intend to be drunk. It always makes me feel something terrible the next morning."

908

This yarn is distinctly to be classified as a "denatured story," but in whatever guise it appears, it is usually good for a chuckle.

A temperance speaker drew very good crowds, but he was continually annoyed by hecklers. Finally he hired an ex-prizefighter to sit in the gallery and keep order. He launched forth, contrasting the sweet content of home life with the dirt and squalor of a drunkard's abode.

"What," he asked dramatically, "do we look for when we return from our day's work?" He paused; no answer. "What," he continued, "do we wish to ease our burdens, to gladden our hearts, to bring smiles and joy to our eyes?"

The speaker paused for breath. And the plugugly in the gallery was heard to exclaim:

"The first dirty loafer that says beer goes out on his head."

909

Into a western bar swaggered a big hulking fellow with a black mustache and a mean disposition. He jostled a little man and didn't apologize. Suddenly the runt yanked out a six-gun and said evenly:

"When God created men He made some little and some big; but when Colonel Colt made his invention he made all men equal. Move over, you yellow-bellied so-and-so!"

The big fellow moved over.

910

A Scotchman was brought into court on a charge of drunkenness, and the magistrate asked him what he had to say for himself.

"I fell into bad company," he answered.

"Who were they?"

"Well, I came down from Albany last night with a bottle of whiskey and three teetotalers, so I had to drink every bit of it by myself."

911

There was a temperance lecturer who had a son named William who was also a temperance lecturer. William didn't have his Pa's punch, and he didn't reform the drunkards too well. One day an awful wreck called on the father and asked for his help. He said:

"I am appealing to you because it was your son William who reformed me."

The old man took a look at him and remarked wryly:

"Well, you sure do look like one of William's jobs."

912

A souse got on a Pennsylvania (or Southern Pacific, or Erie, or Santa Fe, or what have you) railroad train carrying a shoe-box very gingerly. The car was nearly filled, but he found a seat next to a rather colorless individual who showed considerable interest in the box. He could hardly keep his eyes off it, but he said nothing until the train started. Then:

"I beg your pardon, sir, but I am frankly curious about the contents of that box you handle so carefully."

"Imagine that," the drunk replied with evident surprise.

"Yes sir, I am," said the curious one. "Do you mind?"

"Not at all, not at all," was the answer. "And I'm going to tell you. It's a mongoose."

"Well, well," his new friend exclaimed. "May I see it?"

"No, you may not. You see, I'm taking it to the hospital where a friend of mine has the D.T.'s and sees snakes. Mongooses—mongeese—are hell on snakes, so this will solve his problem."

"But," objected the newfound friend, "those snakes are imaginary."

"Yes indeed, yes indeed," said the teed one, "but so is this mongoose."

913

A bachelor who prided himself on his good taste in all social matters took a young lady out to dinner. They began with cocktails, and, as the girl was slow in drinking hers, the man ordered a second one.

Conversationally, the dinner was off to a good start. The bachelor found himself talking better than he ever had talked before, so, in order to keep himself in form, he had another cocktail. Presently he began to wonder whether the girl noticed anything peculiar about his behavior, so he sought to reassure her. Said he:

"Although you may consider that I am under the affluence of inkahol, I'm not as think as you drunk I am."

914

Here's to champagne, the drink divine,
That makes us forget our troubles;
It's made of a dollar's worth of wine
And three dollars' worth of bubbles.

915

Here's to Hell! May we have as good a time there as we had getting there.

916

Here's to old Adam's crystal ale,
Clear, sparkling and divine,
Fair H_2O, long may you flow,
We drink your health (in wine).

Oliver Herford

917

May we kiss everybody we please; and please everybody we kiss.

918

To woman: The only loved autocrat who elects without voting; governs without law; and decides without appeal.

919

To our sweethearts and wives; may they never meet.

920

Here's to the ships of our navy
And the ladies of our land;
May the first be ever well rigged,
And the latter ever well manned.

921

Here's champagne to our real friends, and real pain to our sham friends. (At a barbers' convention dinner this was changed to: Here's shampoo to our real friends, and real pooh to our sham friends).

922

To Woman: The fairest work of the great Author; the edition is large, and no man should be without a copy.

923

Here's to tomorrow and what it holds in its hot little hand for all of us.

924

Here's to the modern mother; she can hold safety pins and a cigarette in her mouth at the same time.

925

Here's to the land we love—and the love we "land."

926

Back in Revolutionary days New York patriots would foregather at Fraunces Tavern where they drank thirteen toasts, one for each of the original States. One of the most pungent went as follows:

"Cobweb breeches, a porcupine saddle, and a hard-riding horse to all the enemies of freedom."

927

Let us have wine and women, mirth and laughter;
Sermons and soda water the day after.

Byron

928

To the idle rich; would to God they were related to us.

929

If all be true that I do think,
There are five reasons we should drink;
Good wine—a friend—or being dry—
Or lest we should be by and by—
Or any other reason why.

Henry Aldrich

930

Here's to God's first thought, Man!
And here's to God's second thought, Woman!
Second thoughts are always best—
So here's to Woman!

Section 11

EDUCATION

933

Maybe the old colored lady had something when she said: "Lawd, honey chile, when yo ain't got no education, yo jus' got to use yo brains."

934

In one of the ancient academies there was a three-year course. In the first year the students were called wise men; in the second they were called the philosophers—those who wished to be wise men; in the third year they were called disciples, learners.

935

A highbrow is a person educated beyond his intelligence.

Brander Matthews

936

The trouble with present-day education is that it covers the ground without cultivating anything in it.

Dr. E. N. Ferris

937

Woodrow Wilson deplored the promiscuous bestowal of honorary degrees:

"Our universities have learned of late," he said, "to distribute honorary degrees judiciously. But in the past—well, in the past I met an uncouth person at a dinner, and, being told by an acquaintance that he had three degrees, I asked why it was.

" 'Well,' said my friend, 'the third was given because he had two, the second because he had one, and the first because he had none.' "

938

William Howard Taft could be depended on to give a classic twist to his humor. Some of it may have been on the highbrow side, but it was funny just the same. In one of his talks to an educated group he said:

"Some men are graduated from college *cum laude,* some are graduated *summa cum laude,* and some are graduated *mirabile dictu.*"

939

The well-loved Yale professor William Lyon Phelps found this message written on a pre-Christmas examination paper:

"God only knows the answer to this question. Merry Christmas."

Dr. Phelps returned the paper to the student with this cheery notation:

"God gets an A; you get an F. Happy New Year."

940

Some for renown, on scraps of learning dote,
And think they grow immortal as they quote.

Edward Young

941

The question "Does education pay?" has some sort of official answer in the fact that the United States food rationing values included the following: Brains, three points; tongue six points.

942

A schoolboy found this question in his examination paper: "What was the import and export of coal for any one year?" His answer was: "1492—none—none."

943

If all the university students who slept in class were placed end to end, they would be much more comfortable.

944

A girl at college, Miss Breese,
Weighed down by B.A.'s and Litt.D.'s,
Collapsed from the strain.
Said the doctor, " 'Tis plain
You are killing yourself—by degrees."

945

Stephen Leacock tells a story on himself that concerns the pride he felt when he first received his Ph.D. degree. On a trip abroad he signed himself "Dr. Leacock" on the liner's passenger list. The ship was hardly away from the dock before a steward knocked at the door of his stateroom and asked him if he was Dr. Leacock. The Doctor answered that he was.

"Then," said the steward, "the captain's compliments, Doctor, and would you please come and take a look at the second stewardess's leg?"

Doctor Leacock responded immediately. "But," he says, "I didn't have any luck. Another fellow reached the spot first. He was a Doctor of Divinity."

946

A university education is always an advantage to anyone who is willing to learn something afterward.

947

Let our teaching be full of ideas. Hitherto it has been stuffed only with facts.

Anatole France

948

"A reasonable amount of fleas," said David Harum, "is good for a dog; they keep him from broodin' on bein' a dog." Maybe that is the function of politics in this great and glorious land of ours; and perhaps there is a slight parallel in the story of the school teacher who asked:

"Who is responsible for all the new bridges, Willie?"

"Roosevelt," came the answer.

"Now, Johnny, who made all the great new public buildings?"

"The WPA," said Johnny.

"Very well, Horace," continued the teacher; "who made our beautiful trees?"

"God did," Horace replied.

But Johnny jumped to his feet and said:

"Teacher, that's Republican propaganda; don't pay any attention to him."

949

A mellow old college professor was asked for advice by a newly appointed one. His counsel was as follows:

"Experience has taught me more than the theoretical study of pedagogy. You will doubtless find in your teaching that when you are holding forth there will be some lad in the class who will disagree with you. You will be tempted to nail him down and convert him right then and there. Don't do it. No doubt he is the only one who is listening."

950

The teacher of a high school class began her course with the question:

"Can you give me any well known date in Roman history?"

"I can," replied a dapper little maiden of sixteen; "Antony's date with Cleopatra."

951

Jimmie hated arithmetic but he liked his teacher. She was pretty and she had a sense of humor. She asked:

"If I laid four eggs over there, Jimmie, and four over here, how many eggs would I have?"

Jimmie scratched his head and answered: "I don't think you can do it, teacher."

952

It was nearing the close of the afternoon session and the teacher was having difficulty in holding the attention of the class.

"Johnny," she asked, "can you tell me what a hypocrite is?"

"I think so," answered Johnny. "It's a boy who comes to school these days with a smile on his face."

953

Miss Smith had been transferred from a school on the right side of the track to a school on the wrong side.

"If I say 'I have went' it is wrong, isn't it, Antonio?" she asked, patiently.

"I guess maybe it is, teacher," he agreed.

"Why is it wrong?" she asked.

"Because you ain't went yet," he said.

954

The wealthiest man in town was a man of little education, but being a respected citizen, admired for his genius in making money and his generosity in dispensing it for the advancement of the village, he was asked to distribute the prizes at school and make the usual speech of good counsel.

"Now, boys," he said, "always remember that education is a great thing. There's nothing like education. Take arithmetic. Through education we learn that twice two makes four, that twice six makes twelve, that seven sevens make—and then there's geography."

955

A well known New Jersey educator was taking an overnight trip in a Pullman. He was undressing behind the curtains of his berth, but one of his legs hung over the edge and his foot protruded into the aisle. Presently a stout woman came along and stepped on it.

"Ouch!" the man cried. "Get off my foot."

"Why don't you put your foot where it belongs?" she snapped. And with wrath in his voice, the educator replied:

"Don't tempt me, lady!"

956

The earnest college senior sought out his English professor and asked, "What would you advise me to read after graduating?"

"The 'Help Wanted' column, my boy," was the immediate rejoinder.

957

The arithmetic teacher felt like a heel when he had to mark this answer wrong:

The problem was as follows: If someone buys an article for $20.37, and later sells it for $2.97, does he make money or lose it?

The pupil certainly showed that he had given a lot of thought to the problem when he wrote on his paper:

"He makes on the cents, but loses on the dollars."

958

In a certain boarding house near Boston, there was a group of young engineering students who were in the habit of monopolizing the dinner-table conversation with scientific discussions in which technical terms were freely used. One evening there came a slight lull, and a hitherto inconspicuous fellow began:

"This morning I examined a new machine that is most astonishing in the way it works."

The students were all attention, and one of them immediately asked:

"How does it work?" So the speaker proceeded:

"Well, by means of a pedal attachment a fulcrumed lever converts a vertical reciprocating motion into a circular movement. The principal part of the machine is a huge disk that revolves in a vertical plane. Power is applied through the axis of the disk, and work is done on the periphery, so that the hardest steel may, by mere impact, be reduced to any shape."

"Wonderful!" the men chorused. "What is this marvelous machine?"

"A grindstone," was the answer.

959

A woman who taught in the mountain schools of Virginia tried to impress the virtue of honesty on her students. When examinations were held, she required them to give a pledge that they had neither given nor received help with their answers. One of the girls wrote on the top of her paper:

"I ain't received no help in this examination; and God knows I couldn't have gave any."

960

"If a farmer raises 2,500 bushels of wheat and sells it for $1 per bushel, what will he get?" asked the teacher.

"An automobile," answered a precocious child.

961

Crowns of glory had been the subject of the Sunday-school lesson and the teacher spoke of the heavenly rewards for good people.

"Tell me," she said at the close of the lesson, "who will get the biggest crown?"

A bright little girl said, "Him wot's got t' biggest 'ead."

962

"Who can tell me what the former ruler of Russia was called?" asked the substitute teacher.

"Tsar," came the answer.

"Yes; and what was his wife called?" she asked.

"Tsarina."

"What were the Tsar's children called?" she asked.

There was a pause, and then an eager voice piped up: "Tsardines!"

963

"What did you learn at school today, darling?" asked the doting mother.

"I learned two kids bettern' to call me mamma's little darling!"

964

The teacher informed the class that Sir Isaac Newton discovered the law of gravity.

"Sir Isaac Newton," she explained, "was sitting on the ground looking at a tree. An apple fell on his head and from that he discovered gravitation. Wasn't that wonderful?"

"Yes, but if he had been settin' in school lookin' at books, he wouldn't have discovered nothin'," said a small boy in the front row.

965

Mortie came home from his first day of school.

"Well, boy," said his father, "how did you like it?"

"Not too good. They asked me my name and I told them. Then they asked me your name, and I told them. Then they asked me where I was born. I didn't want to be a sissy and say in a maternity ward, so I just told them the Yankee Stadium."

966

The teacher had drilled her pupils day after day and at last they seemed to understand the fire drill and would obey her commands at once.

"What would you do if I told you the building was on fire?" she asked once again to make sure.

Like one voice came the children's response.

A few days later a well known lecturer visited the school. With a beaming smile the teacher said, "What would you do, children, if I were to tell you that Dr. Wellman is going to lecture here today?"

"We would rise promptly, put away our books, then quietly and without disorder file into the street," they answered in unison.

967

Bobbie watched his father lay the paper down and reach for his pipe and he knew from past experience that that was the psychological moment to ask him a question.

"Say, Pop," he ventured, "teacher said this morning that the law of gravity kept us on the earth. Is that right?"

"Yes, son, that is correct."

"Well, what I want to know is, how did we get along before that law was passed?"

968

Fred scowled at his father and said, "I got into trouble today, Dad, and it's all your fault."

"How's that?" asked his father.

"Remember I asked you how much $100,000 was?" said Freddie, still scowling.

"Yes, I remember. What of it?" demanded his father.

"Well, 'a helluva lot' ain't the right answer."

969

A formal banquet was to be given at Radcliffe College. In preparation for the event, the chairs had been given a new coat of varnish. The evening of the banquet was hot and humid, and as the speaker of the evening rose to deliver his remarks, he more or less stuck to the seat. However, he was equal to the occasion and said smilingly, "Ladies and gentlemen, I had expected to bring you a plain and unvarnished tale, but circumstances make it impossible to fulfill my intentions."

970

The teacher would ask the class to spell certain words and she would define them. Alice spelled *nonsense* correctly and looked to the teacher for the definition.

"Well," said the young and pretty teacher, "if an elephant hung over a cliff with his tail tied to a daisy,—that would be nonsense."

971

The English teacher in the Pawtucket High School tried the experiment of interesting her class in writing poetry, and she offered a reward for the best poem submitted. The contest lasted a week, and the verses were turned in. After reading through twenty-seven ghastly attempts by her pupils, the teacher had to award the prize to the following:

As I was laying on the green,
A stupid looking book I seen.
Addison's Essays was the edition,
So I left it lay in the same position.

972

Lady-in-waiting was defined by a college freshman recently as the feminine of *bachelor*.

973

"Abraham Lincoln," a schoolboy wrote in a composition, "was not cantankerous, while his wife was of the opposite sex."

974

"What's wrong with this sentence?" asked an English teacher of a class of small boys: "The horse and the cow was in the pasture."

A smart little fellow answered. His reply was:

"The lady should have come first."

975

A good many writers have very hazy ideas on the subject of punctuation. Some of them write their copy and then simply sprinkle it with a few commas and periods out of a salt-shaker, let the slips fall where they may. Others leave out all commas. This is a practice that is liable to lead to strange results. For example, what the writer had in his mind was the following sentence:

"The girl, said her mother, was a virgin."

But he left out the commas, and the sentence read:

"The girl said her mother was a virgin."

976

The head-mistress of a fashionable girls' school was interviewing a young lady who had just been entered in one of the classes. She told her the general rules, and finally said:

"There are just two words I want you to refrain from using. One is 'swell' and the other is 'lousy.' "

"All right," the girl answered brightly; "what are they?"

978

A professor of English in a large university was about to make a telling point in his lecture when the bell rang. The students began to get up, push their chairs back, and collect their books.

"Gentlemen, gentlemen," the professor remonstrated; "Wait a minute while I cast a few more pearls."

979

The boy at the foot of the class was asked by his teacher if there was anything he could do better than anybody else.

"Yes'm," said the boy, "I kin read me own handwriting."

980

A teacher asked one of her pupils to give an example of the opposite uses of *pro* and *con*, and the boy replied promptly, "Progress and Congress."

981

A high school student defined a morality play as one in which the characters are ghosts, goblins, virgins and other supernatural beings.

982

During the Allied invasion of Italy there was a quiz program on the radio, and the question was asked:

"What kind of people live in the Po Valley?"

A Southern boy got the question, and answered:

"Why, po' people, of co'se."

983

Little Harold's mother finally allowed her darling child to attend public school. She gave the teacher a long list of instructions.

"My little Harold is so sensitive," she explained. "Don't ever punish him. Just slap the boy next to him. That will frighten Harold."

984

A little Negro boy came to school one morning, his face wreathed in smiles. He told his teacher that he had a new baby brother.

"What is his name?" the teacher asked.

"Nicodemus," the boy replied.

Some days afterward the teacher asked how little Nicodemus was getting along.

The boy looked somewhat perplexed for a minute. Then he brightened:

"Shucks, teacher, we calls him Abraham now. We found we already had a Nicodemus."

985

Mr. Shapiro met his friend Mr. Waddell in a hotel lounge and showed him a roll of bills amounting to ten thousand dollars.

"Where'd you get it?" asked Mr. Waddell.

"A week ago I dreamed of number seven," Shapiro answered. "Then the next night I dreamed of number seven again. So I said to myself, 'Seven times seven is forty-six,' and got myself a lottery ticket number forty-six, and it won all this money."

"You big dope," said Waddell. "Seven times seven isn't forty-six; it's forty-nine." And Shapiro replied:

"Oh well, you should have the education."

986

A native clerk of India prided himself on his mastery of the English language. He sent the following telegram in announcement of his mother's death:

"Regret to announce that hand which rocked the cradle has kicked the bucket."

987

Little Jean was suffering from a cold, and her mother suggested that she remain home from (progressive) school.

"But I can't, Mother," Jean objected. "This is the day when we start to make a clay model of a cow, and I'm chairman of the udder committee."

988

A man of great wealth declared he never could understand the popular belief that because a man makes a lot of money he has a lot of brains. "For example," he said, "a man won a million dollars on Number 11. When asked how he had figured it out, he said: 'I had a dream. One night I saw in my dream a great big

7, and next I saw a 3, so I used my brains and figured that 7 and 3 is 11.' "

989

There is hardly a youngster in the land who will not appreciate this story of a schoolteacher who was given a ticket in Detroit for driving through a red light. When she appeared in the traffic court, she went to the judge and asked him for immediate attention to her case as she was due to be at her class. The judge looked at her sternly and said:

"So you are a schoolteacher. Well well, that's fine. Young lady, I am just about to realize a lifelong ambition. For years I have longed to have a schoolteacher before me in this court. Now" —and he pounded his fist on the desk—"you sit down at that table over there and write 'I went through a stop sign' five hundred times."

990

We were taught at school that a preposition is not a good word with which to end a sentence. A small boy, ill on the second floor, used this sentence that ends with five of them in a row:

"Mother, what did you bring that book I didn't want to be read to out of up for?"

991

A pretty young school teacher by the name of Mary Murphy was teaching her class to repeat together the 23rd Psalm. As the young voices intoned the words, she thought she detected a false note. She heard the children one by one, until at last she came to a little boy who was concluding the Psalm with these words, "Surely, good Miss Murphy shall follow me all the days of my life."

992

There was great commotion in Room 5. The principal, passing the door, stopped and asked what all the noise was about. A substitute teacher was in tears. "I was explaining the difference between *concrete* and *abstract*," she explained, "and I said that *abstract* is something you can't see, and *concrete* is something you can see. Then I asked Willie Jones to give me an illustration."

"What did he say?" the principal asked.

The teacher blushed and answered:

"He said, 'My pants are concrete. Yours are abstract.' "

993

A teacher of American history asked if anyone in her class could answer the question:

"What was the reason for the Puritans coming to this country?"

Queried later as to what she considered the best reply, she said that it came from one whom she had always considered her dullest pupil. He said:

"They came to worship in their own way and to make the other people do the same."

994

Arithmetic is one thing, but logic is something else again.

Teacher gave this problem to her class:

"If there were six flies on your desk, and you killed one, how many would remain?"

"One," shouted a boy; "the dead one."

995

Professor Smith said to his afternoon biology class:

"I am going to show you a very fine specimen of a dissected frog that I have brought in this parcel."

He then proceeded to undo the package and disclosed a sandwich, a hard boiled egg, and an orange.

"But surely," he mused, "I ate my lunch."

996

A facetious toastmaster introduced the speaker, a college president, as a man of great wisdom and mature judgment.

"Dr. Blank has shown rare discernment on several occasions. During that heavy rainstorm last Tuesday he was without an umbrella, so he went right inside a hotel and waited for the rain to abate.

"At another time he didn't try to correct the grammar of the police officer who bawled him out for a minor traffic violation.

"And," continued the toastmaster, "he always allows Mrs. Blank the last word in any controversial matter that may arise."

There was more in the same spoofing vein. But the college president caught the spirit of the build-up. After acknowledging the introduction, he turned to the toastmaster and exclaimed:

"Do you think I'm a dope?"

A very short pause, and then he shouted:

"DON'T ANSWER!"

997

Professor Fogle was giving his class a quiz.

"What," he asked, "is the most outstanding result of chemistry in the last thousand years?"

And one of his brighter students answered:

"Blondes."

998

The school psychologist told the teacher of the third grade that she didn't hold her pupils' interest.

"When they come in from recess, I'll prove to you that they are not paying the least attention to what is going on."

In a few minutes the kids straggled in and sat down. The psychologist asked for a number and a boy gave 36. This the critic wrote on the blackboard as 63. She then called for another number and a little girl said 81, which was chalked up as 18. Several other numbers were given and treated similarly by the psychologist. Finally there came a squeaky little voice saying:

"Eighty-eight. See what you can do with that."

999

Two country school teachers had an argument as to which was the correct form, "The hen is setting" or "The hen is sitting." They finally agreed to abide by what Farmer Brown decided; he knew his hens and he knew his eggs. So they went and placed the matter before him.

"Gals," he said, "that ain't what interests me. What I want to know when I hear a hen cackle is whether she's laying or lying."

Section 12

FIGHTING FORCES

1000

During a battle in Italy, a private suffered shell shock. He started running toward the rear. An officer stopped him, saying, "Here, what's the matter with you? Don't you know there's a battle going on up at the front?"

"Yes-s-s. I-I-I- know," stuttered the frightened soldier.

"Then what are you doing here?"

The boy did not answer, but hung his head.

"Why don't you answer?" yelled the officer. "Do you know who I am?"

The boy shook his head.

"I am your general," roared the officer.

"Gosh amighty! Am I that far back?" exclaimed the soldier and fainted away.

1001

During the heroic defense of the Battle of Cassino, one of the commanding officers lined up his men and asked for a volunteer for a mission of the gravest danger. Those willing to serve were told to step forward two paces from the line.

For a moment he was busy making notations. When he looked up, he was shocked to see the ranks unbroken.

"What," he said unbelievingly, "not a single man will volunteer?"

"You misunderstand, sir," said the aide at his side, "the whole line has stepped forward two paces."

1003

One night a sentry was standing guard at Fort Dix. He heard a sound and saw someone approach.

"Halt! Who goes there?"

"Friend—with a bottle," came the answer.

"Pass, friend; halt, bottle," said the sentry.

1004

The captain ordered the sergeant to drill his men for a coming military funeral, so he began at once to put the men through their paces. When they were drawn up, he opened their ranks to allow the passing of the supposed cortege and gave the order:

"Rest on your arms reversed."

He illustrated by walking down the open space formed by the two ranks, saying:

"Now I'm the corpse; attention!"

When he reached the end of the squad, he looked critically at them and then said:

"Youse guys has got your hands right and your heads right, but you ain't got the look of regret you oughta have."

1005

In one of the Army camps a second lieutenant asked of a Negro mule-driver if a mule ever kicked him.

"No suh," he answered, "not yet, but frequently he kicks the place where I recently was."

1006

Two soldiers were gossiping in a USO clubroom. One of them said:

"In this morning's paper I saw an item about a sergeant who was struck by lightning while he was swearing."

"That's nothing at all," the other replied. "If he'd been struck while he wasn't swearing, that would have been news."

1007

Sailors, Bob Hope observed, are the only fellows who roll when they walk. Soldiers do it from a kneeling position.

1008

His girl's mother brought out the family photograph album and was showing the young soldier the relatives' pictures, many of whom were military men.

"And here," she finally said, "is my great great grandfather. He fought in the War of 1812. Soldiers run in our family."

1009

Two non-coms were returning to camp in a jeep one night after a somewhat rosy day in the city. After they had been on the road a while, the driver said:

"We must be getting closer to camp."

"Why?" asked the other.

"Because," the first replied, "we seem to be hittin' more people."

1010

The modest soldier was telling how he won the D.S.C.

"It was this way," he explained. "The Captain said he wanted somebody to step out of the line to volunteer for a dangerous mission."

"And you stepped forward from the line," one of the women exclaimed admiringly.

"No," said the soldier, "the rest of the line stepped back."

1011

A newspaper man was interviewing a soldier whose term of enlistment was nearly over. Among the questions he asked was:

"When you're discharged, what is the first thing you'll do?"

"I'm a-going to poke the second lieutenant in the nose," he answered.

"The heck you are," objected a nearby buddy. "You're going to get in line and wait your turn."

1012

It is told of a man who worked with the French Underground that he advised always giving a Nazi officer an impressive Heil Hitler before kicking him in the midriff. When the Nazi raises his arm for the return salute, the going is easy.

1013

Sam Evans took great pride in the global war map, covering one wall of his office. Blue pins represented the Allies, red pins indicated the Axis, all enemy lines. One white pin stood out on the map.

"What's that white pin for, Sam?" asked a friend.

"That," he explained, "is Mrs. Roosevelt."

1014

The girl was sounding out the soldier as to his bravery.

"Would you come to me in distress?" she asked. And he answered:

"Babe, it wouldn't make any difference to me what you were wearing."

1015

An American Legion post had their annual dinner in the banquet hall of a St. Louis hotel. A nervous and clumsy waiter in serving the soup spilled a plate of it down the neck of a visiting Chaplain. During this supreme test of fortitude the Chaplain gritted his teeth, sputtered and squirmed. Then he burst forth:

"Come on now; one of you sinful comrades say something appropriate!"

1016

A farmer in the region of a training camp for paratroops was walking through a field and saw one of the troopers dangling from a tall tree.

"I was trying to make a record," the soldier explained.

"Well, you sure did, stranger," the farmer observed. "You'll be the first man around these parts that ever clumb down a tree without climbing up it first."

1017

After all, a German censor can't know everything, and so he passed the following letter from a Yankee doughboy in a Nazi prison camp:

Dear Jack:

Everything is very comfortable here, and there is plenty to eat. The officers in charge of the camp are gentlemen in every sense of the word. The discipline is not severe, we do not have too much work to do, and there are frequent entertainments. Your affectionate brother, Bill. P.S. Please tell this to Sweeney.

1018

An objector, whether conscientious or not, was inclined to argue with the draft board officer.

"No one can make me fight," he said.

"Possibly not," replied the officer, "but they can take you to where the fighting is going on, after which you can use your own judgment."

1019

"Have you any special qualifications?" asked the recruiting officer of the man who appeared for enlistment.

"Yes sir, I am a descendant of John Quincy Adams, Daniel Boone, and John Van Astorbilt."

"Quite so, quite so," replied the recruiting officer, "but it's fighting we want you for, not breeding."

1020

An enthusiastic young selectee was being given an intelligence test.

"What," asked the examiner, "does R.F.D. stand for?"

The light of recognition shone in the lad's eyes, and he answered proudly:

"Relano Fanklin Doosevelt."

1021

Ginsburg had been in the Army a week and was writing his first letter home. He was critical of the camp, his fellow rookies, and the officers; but most of all the food displeased him.

"The rations are not fit to eat; they are garbage; I would not feed them to the pigs. *And such small portions!*"

1022

Little Maxie Cohen was flattered when some larger boys on his block taught him the Nazi salute. When he went home and began parading around the house with his right arm extended and exclaiming, "Hi-ya Hitler!" his parents felt different. They were so worried that Mr. Cohen sent for Dr. Minsky.

The doctor was worried too. He tried to reason with the boy, but it didn't work. Then the doctor was silent for some minutes. Finally Cohen could stand it no longer.

"Doctor," he exclaimed, "do you t'ink we'll hev to amputate?"

1023

A soldier was returning to camp late one night after a strenuous 24-hour leave. When he was asked for his bus fare, he looked through all his pockets without finding any money.

"All right, guy; all right, put me off and I'll walk back. I had fifty dollars when I left camp and now I'm broke."

"Come, come," the bus man said; "how could you have spent fifty dollars in twenty-four hours?"

"Well, lemme see," the man said thickly. "I bought four quarts of liquor for twenty dollars. Had to treat the crowd. Then I lost five bucks in a crap game. Lessee now—oh, I took a blonde out to dinner for five dollars. Then we danced."

"What did you do with the remaining money?"

"Oh, I just spent that for damfoolishness."

1024

Back in 1933 when matters had been more or less straightened out for the time being, a German officer got chummy with a member of the British Embassy and said that the British were gentlemen but the French were not. He was asked to explain, and told the following story:

"In 1920," he said, "a commission under a French and a British officer visited the barracks in my charge. They said they had reason to suspect that I had rifles stored behind a brick wall, in defiance of the terms of the Peace Treaty. I gave my word as a German officer that I had no rifles concealed in the barracks. The British officer, gentleman that he was, accepted my word and left. The French officer, however, was not a gentleman. My word of honor was not sufficient. He tore down the brick wall, and he took away my rifles."

1025

The Confederate forces were falling back on Richmond when an old Negro, asked by his hopeful mistress for news, said:

"Well, Miss Lula, due to de lay of de land where dey's fightin', dem Yankees is retreatin' forward, while we is advancin' backwards."

1026

Her father believed in being patriotic but not in overdoing it. She was entertaining a Marine tonight, last night it was the air force. He had thrown both shoes on the floor and still the Marine was with his daughter.

"Doesn't that young man know how to say goodnight?" called her father in exasperation.

"I'll say he does!" came back the answer in the cuddly-coo voice of his youngest.

1027

In reviewing a new novel, a book critic wrote:

"Every soldier should wear a copy of this over his heart when going into battle. A bullet would never go past the first chapter."

1028

"Your American language," a British officer commented to a Yank, "seems just a bit on the subtle side."

"How come?"

"For one thing," he explained, "it is most difficult for me to get the distinction between the phrases 'a fat chance' and 'a slim chance.' "

1029

A dear old lady was visiting convalescent Navy men in a hospital. In talking with one of them, she asked:

"Where were you wounded?"

"In the Dardanelles," was the reply.

"Oh my poor boy," she exclaimed; "and were they broken?"

1030

A story comes back from Guadalcanal about a cannibal who asked an American Army officer who ate the tremendous quantities of human flesh made available by the war. He was told, of course, that white people do not eat their slain foes.

"What barbarians you are," the cannibal exclaimed in horror, "to kill without any real purpose."

1031

It was a rookie's first experience at sentry duty. When he saw a figure approaching, he snapped:

"Who goes there?"

"Captain Moses," was the reply.

"Glad to meet you, Moses," said the sentry; "advance and give the ten commandments."

1032

A regiment of Negro soldiers were billeted somewhere in England, and some of them taught the English lads the great American game of poker. The cards were dealt and a Britisher picked up his hand. He examined it carefully and said:

"I really don't know your poker game, but I'll wager a pound."

Then one of the colored boys looked at his hand and discovered that he had four aces.

"Well," he said, "I don't know much about you-all's money, but I'm a-gonna see your pound and raise you a ton."

1033

The lieutenant had just returned after a fifteen-day furlough. The captain asked him:

"Did you enjoy your leave?"

"Yes sir," was the reply, "but there's nothing to take the place of the feeling of a good desk under your feet again."

1034

An Army sergeant was quizzing a group of privates.

"Smith, what's the first thing you do when cleaning a rifle?"

"I look at the number," said the private.

"What's that got to do with it?"

"That," Smith answered, "is to make sure I'm cleaning my own gun."

1035

When the Hollywood star went to make a blood donation at the Red Cross station, he said:

"For Heaven's sake don't take it all. Remember that my agent has to get ten per cent."

1036

The soldier boy was home on a furlough, and his proud daddy asked him:

"Done much shooting lately, son?"

"Well, Dad, I won seventy-five bucks last payday," the lad replied.

1037

During Army maneuvers in the Dust Bowl a soldier took shelter from a storm by stopping in the cook's tent. He noticed that there was no lid on the soup kettle, so he called the cook's attention to it.

"If you'd put a cover on that kettle, we wouldn't get so much dust and dirt in our soup."

"Look here, wise guy," the cook answered; "your business is to serve your country."

"All right, all right," said the soldier; "my business is to serve my country, but it ain't my business to eat it."

1038

A couple of Australian kids of about ten and twelve paddled a canvas canoe up to the side of an anchored troopship. A gold-braided officer was leaning over the rail, and they asked his permission to come aboard. The answer was NO, but the lads persisted. Finally the officer got mad and said:

"Get to perdition out of here."

"Are you the captain of this ship?" the older boy asked.

"No," was the reply, "but I'm the fourth officer."

"In that case," said the Australian boy, "you'd better learn to be more respectful to your superior officers. I'm the *captain* of this one."

1039

The three daughters of Colonel Berry were visiting the camp when a sentry on duty halted them.

"I have orders to send everyone around to the main gate," he explained.

"Oh," said one of the girls, "but we are the Berrys."

"Can't help it if you're the cat's pajamas," the sentry retorted; "you'll have to go around to the main gate."

1040

Military precedence has been known to extend to wives of the officers concerned. Thus the wife of a first lieutenant feels privileged to snoot the wife of a second lieutenant, and so on upward.

One afternoon at a bridge party, a woman exclaimed:

"Well, at last Frederick has attained his majority."

A second dame added:

"Horace has just received his captaincy."

The third, rather meekly, said:

"Bill made his lieutenancy."

There was a pause. Then a girl who had that something that women despise, and men love, busted out:

"Well, thank God, Butch still has his privacy!"

1041

In writing to her boy in the service, a patriotic mother gave this advice:

"Now that you are in camp, try to be punctual in the mornings so you won't keep breakfast waiting."

1042

Two colored boys were discussing the draft.

"Is you ready to go?" one asked.

"No," said the other, "I ain't ready, but I'se willin' to go, unready."

1043

A marine on furlough was relating his experiences on Guadalcanal.

"We had fired our last round of ammunition. Our food and whiskey had run out, and we were nearly crazy with thirst."

"But," one of his listeners asked, "wasn't there any water?"

"Sure there was," said the marine, "but it was no time to be thinking of cleanliness."

1044

A horse in the remount division developed such an ugly temper that the soldiers were leery of approaching him.

One day a new recruit appeared, a gangling youth from rural Vermont, and he "allowed that he could handle the hoss."

So the horse was turned loose. He ripped and snorted around the corral two or three times, and then stood still for a moment.

The new recruit, with a halter in his hand, walked toward the fiery beast. Looking him straight in the eye, he said:

"So bossy, so bossy."

A change came over the horse. As he stood quietly, the soldier slipped the halter over his head without any difficulty whatever.

The horse was cowed.

1045

A Civil War colonel was something of a martinet, or, as it would now be termed, a dictator. One day an evangelist came into camp and said to him:

"I am a servant of the Lord trying to save the souls of the soldiers. Just recently I left the camp of the 18th New Jersey, where I had the good fortune to lead ten men into the paths of righteousness."

The colonel paused for a moment and then exploded:

"Adjutant, detail twenty men for baptism. No d— New Jersey regiment is going to get ahead of mine in anything."

1046

An Army sergeant had charge of a bunch of recruits on the rifle range. They were almost uniformly poor shots. At a hundred yards not one of them hit the target. When they were moved up to fifty yards there was no improvement. Then the range was decreased to twenty-five yards and still there were no hits.

The sergeant became enraged, and with withering scorn he ordered:

"Fix bayonets and charge!"

1047

Entering an English club, an austere and unapproachable major-general sat down heavily in a leather chair and glared about him. A young second lieutenant, wishing to make an impression, said to him:

"Good morning, General."

"Harrumph," the older officer replied.

"Splendid weather, General," the younger man continued. There was a similar acknowledgment. Then the lieutenant went further.

"General," he said, "please pardon me for being personal, but I read in the Times that you buried your wife yesterday, and I wanted to extend my deepest sympathy."

"Oh yes, oh yes," the general answered. "Buried my wife . . . had to of course—dead y'know."

1048

This was brought back from London by an American member of a military commission, who overheard the conversation.

Two charwomen were chatting in the hall of an office building. Said one:

"She wanted me to 'ave a finger in the pie, but I smelt a rat an' nipped it in the bud."

"Lor', Mrs. 'Arris," said the other, " 'ow you do mix your semaphores."

1049

Two young lieutenants were back from the Pacific area. They were introduced to a pretty girl who said to them: "Did you really kill Jap soldiers?"

"Yes."

"With which hand did you do it?" she asked.

"With the right hand, of course," said the young officers, grinning.

The pretty girl seized their right hands and kissed them, one after the other.

A comrade at arms looking on said: "Jeepers, why didn't you tell her that you bit 'em to death?"

1050

During the First World War an American officer was up at headquarters, when a pleasant-looking British subaltern came toward him.

"Who are you?" asked the American officer.

"The Prince of Wales," the young man said good-naturedly, continuing on his way.

"Oh, yeah," was the retort. "And I'm the King of England."

A few weeks later at a Red Cross hut, the two men met again. The American was greatly disturbed to find that the young man was actually the Prince of Wales. He was still more embarrassed when the Prince smiled, and waved to him from across the room, calling out blithely, "Hello, there, Dad."

1051

A young lieutenant, short of stature and fresh from the Officers Candidate School, was assigned to a new detachment. He barely met the army regulations for height and seemed very inefficient as he appeared before the company. There were some half-audible comments made about his size and rank. Then from the rear, a voice was heard to exclaim: "And a little child shall lead them!" There was a roar of laughter.

The next day the lieutenant posted a notice on the bulletin board: "Company A will take a 25-mile hike today with full packs. And a little child shall lead them . . . on a big horse."

1052

The general was an impulsive man, but he was careful of the welfare of his men. One day in Africa he encountered two soldiers coming from the kitchen with a large soup kettle.

"Let me taste that," he ordered.

"But Gen—. . . ."

"No *buts!* Give me that spoon." Taking a taste, the General sputtered, "You don't call that soup, do you?"

"No, sir," replied the soldier, "I was trying to tell you, sir, it's dishwater."

1053

A private in the Air Corps was persuaded to attend chapel one Sunday morning, and heard the chaplain preach a powerful sermon on the Ten Commandments—all of them. He was greatly impressed and considerably sobered. Finally, however, he decided to look on the bright side of things.

"At any rate," he was heard to observe, "I have never coveted my major's wife."

1054

A somewhat bulbous old gentleman was talking with a young lieutenant junior grade and revealed the fact that he too had once been in the Navy.

"May I ask, sir, what was your official capacity?" said the lieutenant.

"To the best of my recollection," the old boy replied, "it was three quarts a day."

1055

Who says that soldiers don't worry? One of the boys in the Amphibian Corps has been worrying for months for fear the war would be over before he could get a furlough.

1056

Two WACS met in the lobby of Shepheard's Hotel, Cairo. They exchanged greetings, experiences and warnings. Said the blonde:

"Do you know what becomes of bad little Egyptian girls?"

"No indeedy," the brunette replied.

The blonde knew all the answers, including this one:

"They become mummies."

1057

Private Wentworth received his pay check and 24 hours' leave at the same time. When he returned to camp he had only a black eye to show for his absence.

"It was Princess Matilda what done it, sir," he explained to the officer of the day. "She has a place down at Troy. Wonderful looking girl, too; golden hair, blue eyes, gorgeous figure—"

"What kind of a place does she run at Troy?" asked the O.D.

"Oh, I thought I told you, Sir. She's a mind reader."

1058

He was on furlough from overseas, and a dimple and an armful of girl looked good to him.

"Listen, beautiful," he said, "would you like to make a bet? I'll bet a quarter I can kiss you without even touching you."

The dimple laughed and said, "I'll take you up."

"Get ready and let's go," he directed, kissing her several times.

"But you touched me when you kissed me," she pouted prettily.

"All right, so what—here's your quarter."

1059

A soldier got into one of the ordinary coaches on a suburban train and lighted a cigarette. When the conductor came along, he pointed to a NO SMOKING card and said:

"See that sign?"

"Yeh, pal, I see it," the jeep replied. "But there's a lot of dopey signs around here. Lookit that one—WEAR DAMSELFORM BRASSIERES. Why should I pay attention to any of 'em!"

1060

Women's girdles will probably go out of style long before this conundrum is outmoded:

"Why is a Jap like a girdle?" asked (here you name someone you want to introduce into your talk).

"Search me," replied (here you name someone else).

"Because," comes the payoff, "it creeps up on you, and it takes a Yank to bring it down."

1061

It was a long story that Poppa told five-year-old Johnny about his experiences in World War II. Finally he summed up:

"So there, my boy, is the story of your dad in the global war."

"But, Poppa," the boy asked, "why did they have to have all the other soldiers?"

1062

A Marine walked over to Zasu Pitts in the Stage Door Canteen, and said, "Hiya, Beautiful!"

Zasu smiled and said, fluttering her hands, "I know why you're calling me Beautiful. It's because I spent six hours in a beauty parlor."

"You're wrong, Cutie," the Marine answered. "It's because I've been spending six months in the Solomon Islands."

Johnny Morgan

1063

A leatherneck, member of the Marine band, was returning to camp late one night after a furlough in the city. It had been a gay and festive occasion, and it wasn't any wonder that the gyrene couldn't find his ticket. Finally the conductor became impatient.

"Look again, man," he said, "you simply couldn't have lost your ticket."

"Couldn't have lost it, hell," the Marine exclaimed; "why I lost my bass drum."

1064

A sergeant in a Negro regiment was discussing their chances of coming out of battle with a whole skin. Said he:

"You see it's this way, Amos. Every bullet and piece of shell has on it the name of the man it's a-goin' to hit. If it's your bullet, your time's up."

"Yes, Rossiter, you're absolutely right," said the other, "but what worries me is those bullets that have written on 'em 'To whom it may concern.' "

1065

American mechanical precision is sure wonderful. Nobody has ever complained of one of our parachutes not opening.

1066

A parachutist was cornered by a maiden lady who was out after thrills. Said she:

"You must have had some perfectly terrific experiences."

"Yes," said he, "some of 'em have been awful. Would you believe it, once I came down where there was a sign that said, 'Keep Off the Grass.' "

1067

An Army Colonel had occasion to visit a retired soldier who had inherited a nice piece of change from a rich uncle. The Colonel was curious about an apparently useless man-servant. "What does that man do?" he asked.

"Oh, him?" said the soldier. "I pays him a salary to wake me up at six o'clock every morning. I says, 'Whatdye want?' and he says, 'The Colonel orders you to report immediately.' So then I says, 'Tell the Colonel to go to blazes,' and I goes back to sleep."

1068

A soldier at a U.S.O. dance met a girl and fell for her charm. At the end of the evening he said:

"Gimme your phone number, Marge, and I'll call you up sometime."

"It's in the phone book," she said.

"Good," the jeep came back. "By the way, what's your last name?"

"That," the girl answered, "is also in the phone book."

1069

There was an enlistment drive in Los Angeles in December, 1941, and one of the drawing cards at a big rally was Bing Crosby. There was great enthusiasm when he sang "Anchors Aweigh," and ten men signed up for the Navy. Then when he sang "The Caissons Go Rolling Along," twenty men enlisted for the Army. But when he sang "There's a Gold Mine in the Sky," forty Scotchmen joined the Air Corps.

1070

Dating from World War I, there is an inscription on a marker over the grave of an Army mule that reads:

"In memory of Maggie, who in her time kicked two colonels,

four majors, ten captains, twenty-four lieutenants, forty-two sergeants, 432 other ranks and one Mills bomb."

1071

An American soldier took an English lassie to the first baseball game she had ever seen. After it was over, he asked her how she liked it.

"Perfectly ripping," she said. "But what I liked best was the way the pitcher hit the bat every time."

1072

McLandburgh Wilson wrote this quatrain about Theodore Roosevelt and entitled it "A Man of Peace":

Our hero is a man of peace,
Preparedness he implores;
His sword within its scabbard sleeps,
But mercy, how it snores!

1073

One of the best but half forgotten stories about Lincoln has a new pertinence today when so many arm chair strategists and statesmen are in evidence.

During the siege of Washington, Lincoln decided to visit the front lines, see how operations were progressing and perhaps cheer up the soldiers.

He became so interested in following the progress of a bitter skirmish further down the line that he stood up to his full length in an exposed trench—a magnificent target wearing his traditional tall silk hat. When enemy bullets immediately began to whine around the President, the youthful lieutenant assigned to him unceremoniously shouted "Get down, you fool" and dragged Lincoln to the ground.

When he realized what he had done the Lieutenant felt sure

that disciplinary action of some sort would fall upon his shoulders.

But Lincoln only smiled and said "I'm happy to see that you know how to talk to a civilian."

1074

A light-hearted young man was idly brandishing an automatic pistol.

"I don't like the way you're pointing that gun," his companion expostulated.

"Well," was the careless reply, "I don't aim to please."

1075

General McClellan's "waiting campaign" is remembered by students of Civil War history. When President Lincoln had become thoroughly disgusted with the policy, he wrote this short letter to the General:

"My dear McClellan: If you don't want to use the Army I should like to borrow it for a while. Yours respectfully, A. Lincoln."

1076

When that grand gagster of the radio and screen, Bob Hope, was on an entertainment tour of Great Britain during World War II, he saw a British soldier standing beside a winch from which a cable ran straight up into the foggy sky. Curious but friendly, Hope asked the Tommy if there was a barrage balloon at the other end of the cable. And the soldier answered:

"If there ain't, Chief, then I'm doin' the bloomin' rope trick."

1077

The artist Whistler during the Boer War heard of a dispatch from General Buller in the Transvaal, in which the British general said that he had retired without losing a man, or a flag, or a cannon. To which the artist added: "Or a minute."

1078

During the Civil War President Lincoln sent out an order that detailed reports from the front must be dispatched to the White House. It irritated General McClellan, and he presently sent the following telegram:

"We have just captured six cows. What shall we do with them?"

Immediately President Lincoln answered:

"As to the six cows captured—milk them. A. Lincoln."

1079

History not only repeats itself; it parallels itself. William Pitt received a document from a body of London volunteers who offered to enlist as a company. Various exceptions were stated, however. Presently Pitt came to a clause setting forth as one condition of their enlistment that they would never be required to leave England. Pitt seized a pen and wrote in the margin, "except in the case of actual invasion."

1080

The French statesman Talleyrand heard an army officer speaking contemptuously of a class of people whom he called *pékins*. He asked the military man to tell him who these contemptible persons were. The officer replied:

"We soldiers call everybody a *pékin* who is not military."

"Ah, I see," Talleyrand said; "it is just like what we do when we call anybody military who is not civil."

1081

Two American doughboys in England had to stand up in a well-filled tram car. At length an English lady and her daughter showed signs of getting off. Suddenly the mother nudged her daughter, and said:

"Mind this, Helen. When we get off the tram, do what I do. Back out of the car. I'll tell you why later."

The daughter obeyed, and both women backed out of the car. On reaching the pavement, the young woman asked the reason.

"Well," said the mother, "of course you noticed those two Yankee soldiers. I knew they were up to no good, because I heard one of them say, 'When those two dames get off, we'll pinch their seats.' "

1082

Thrusting my nose firmly between his teeth, I threw him heavily to the ground on top of me.

Mark Twain

1083

During the Civil War, a number of Confederate prisoners were held at a Western military post under not too difficult conditions. Most of them appeared to appreciate the situation, but one fellow wasn't reconciled, and took every opportunity to express his views. He rubbed it in continually about the Battle of Chickamauga that resulted so disastrously for the Federal forces.

Finally it got under the skin of the Union men, and they complained to General Grant, who brought the prisoner before him.

"Look here," Grant said; "you are being very insulting to the men here with reference to the Battle of Chickamauga. Now you've either got to take the oath of allegiance to the United States, or you'll be sent to a Northern prison. Make up your mind."

The prisoner took some time to come to a decision. Finally he said:

"I reckon, General, I'll take the oath."

The oath was duly administered. Then the subdued soldier asked if he might speak.

"Yes," said Grant; "what is it?"

"I was just a-thinkin', General, that they certainly did give us hell at Chickamauga."

1084

GI's of whatever age or country have always regarded it as their sacred right to indulge in what is now known as "griping."

Back in ancient times, a group of Macedonian soldiers were having a gripe outside of King Philip's tent. It continued for some time, when the King stuck his head out and said:

"I think you men ought to go a little farther away to talk. The King might hear you."

1085

The rookie didn't mean no harm. He was from Mississippi, where men are men, and very much inclined to be pleasant about it. He happened also to be a new recruit in camp.

Well, he met up with a second lieutenant, and feeling that the occasion demanded courtesy, he said:

"Mawnin'."

The shavetail was outraged. He stopped the rookie, gave him instructions as to military courtesy, and then sailed into him on the important subject of saluting. The rookie looked at him aghast for a minute. Then he said:

"Holy mackerel! If I'd a knowed you was gonna carry on like that, I woodna spoke to you a-tall."

Section 13

JOURNALISM

1101

A man's death was mistakenly noted in the obituary column of a local paper, and he rushed to the editor in high dudgeon.

"I'm awfully sorry," said the editor. "And the worst of it is, it's too late to do much about it. The best thing I can do for you is to put you in the Birth Column tomorrow morning, and give you a fresh start."

1102

"And," the press agent went on enthusiastically, "our show at the Summer Garden has a chorus of fifty."

"Well," said the newspaper critic, "from where I sat, they certainly looked it."

1103

The newspaper editor fears libel suits as the devil fears holy water. One of them had occasion to warn a cub reporter against making statements that might prove libelous. Said he:

"Be absolutely sure of being able to prove anything you write. If you're not sure, use the words *alleged, claimed, reputed, rumored,* et cetera."

It wasn't long after that when the following item appeared in the society news:

"It is rumored that a bridge luncheon was given by a group of reputed ladies. It is said that Mrs. William Jones was hostess, and it is alleged that all the guests were local people. Mrs. Jones claims to be the wife of William Alan Jones."

1104

One of the curses of modern civilization is the dignity of printer's ink. Write it with a pencil on a piece of scratch paper, and it isn't important. Set it up in type and print it in any rag that appears regularly, and it acquires authority.

A newspaper editor in the Middle West said to his landlady one morning:

"I think we'll have an excellent potato crop this year."

She didn't believe it, and she said so with vigor.

When the editor reached his desk, he wrote a filler that read:

"An excellent potato crop is expected this fall."

After a long hard day, he came back to his boarding house and was met by his landlady. She beamed on him, and said apologetically:

"I've decided that you're right. I too think that the potato crop this fall will hit a new high."

1105

The cub reporter was being lectured by the city editor, who cited the ancient gag, "When a dog bites a man, it's old stuff, but if a man bites a dog, that's news."

The lad was much impressed. A few hours later he returned to the city room, sat down at his typewriter and began to bang furiously. Wondering what all the enthusiasm was about, the editor strolled over and looked at his story. It was headed: "Hydrant Sprays Dog."

1106

Late one night a newspaper man stopped in a restaurant and ordered a cup of coffee, specifying that it was to be without cream.

In a minute or so the apologetic waitress hurried back without the coffee.

"Sorry, sir," she explained. "We got no cream. Do you mind taking it without milk?"

1107

A script writer was arguing about a scene.

"What's so difficult about it, the way I want it?" the movie magnate yelled. "Give me four writers and I could write it myself."

1108

Vital statistics in country weeklies are usually hot news, so you can imagine the pressure when this item appeared in the Bingham *Bugle:*

"Owing to lack of room and shortage of paper, several births and deaths have to be postponed until next week."

1109

The editor of a little weekly newspaper in a Nevada town was hard up one week for matter with which to fill his columns, so he had his compositor set up the Ten Commandments, and ran them without making any editorial comment. Three days after the paper was published he received a letter saying:

"Cancel my subscription. You're getting too darned personal."

1110

An earnest young aspirant to poetic laurels had an interview with the editor of a well known magazine and asked for a lot of advice. His final question was:

"Do you think that I ought to put more fire into my poetry?"

"Not at all," the editor replied; "you should do just the opposite."

1111

An English cub reporter had been bawled out by his editor for turning in stories that were much too long. He was told to make them short and to the point, and he took the advice to heart. His next story read as follows:

"A shocking incident occurred last night. Sir Basil James, who was a guest at Lady Smithers' ball, complained of feeling ill, took his hat, his coat, his departure, no notice of his friends, a taxi, a pistol from his pocket and, finally, his life. Nice chap. Regrets and all that."

1112

A western paper ran an item stating that "The departing Mr. Smithers was a member of the defective bureau of the police force." The chief of police made a strong protest, whereupon the paper published an apology as follows:

"Our announcement should have read 'The detective branch of the police farce.' "

1113

In their fight to get circulation, newspapers will do most anything. In one of our large cities a morning paper advertised a free accident insurancc policy to all subscribers for six months. It was a whoop-her-up campaign for several weeks, but the top was reached when the journal ran an item on the front page as follows:

J. Wellington Snook subscribed to the *Sun* yesterday morning, and with it received his free accident policy. When he was on his way home in the evening, he was struck by a bus, suffering a fractured jaw, a broken arm and internal injuries. Because he had our accident policy, he will be allowed five hundred dollars. Just think—you may be the lucky one tomorrow.

1114

The printing press is either the greatest blessing or the greatest curse of modern times, one sometimes forgets which.

J. M. Barrie

1115

There's never anything new in the newspapers. All the same old things are happening—only to different people.

1116

A midwestern newspaper once chartered a locomotive to rush a cub reporter to a nearby town to scoop all rival journals with the first news of a fire that was sweeping through the business section. In an hour or so the editor received a telegram from the green reporter reading: "Have arrived at fire. What shall I do?"

The editor replied: "Find the place the fire is hottest, and jump in."

1117

The editor of a small-town newspaper had treasured for many years a set of old-fashioned wooden scarehead type of some 60-point size. His assistants on more than one occasion had urged him to use it, but he had refused.

One day he was called out of town. A cyclone struck the town; tore off the church steeple, unrooted several houses, sucked a couple of wells dry, and scattered a few barns around. Never before had the town suffered such a calamity. His assistants decided that now was their chance to get down the 60-point type and set up a startling front page headline with it.

When the editor returned and saw what they had done, he shouted: "What do you mean by taking down that type for a cyclone? All these years I've been saving it for the Second Coming of Christ!"

SECTION 14

LAW AND LAWYERS

1125

A Negro was before the judge for deserting his wife and received a thoroughgoing reprimand. The man took it patiently and then replied:

"Jedge, if you knowed that woman like I do, you wouldn't call me no deserter. I'm a refugee."

1126

Two fighting Irishmen were brought before a judge, who said:

"Why don't you two settle this case out of court?"

"Sure, that's what we were doin'," one of them answered, "and the police came and interfered."

1127

A Negro had just been sentenced for stealing chickens. He muttered something and the judge said:

"What's that! It sounded like profanity."

"I didn't say nuthin'," said the man uneasily.

"Yes you did," said the judge. "Now repeat it out loud."

"Well, your honor," the Negro drawled, "all I said was 'God am the judge—God am the judge."

1128

When he was practicing law at Springfield, Illinois, Abraham Lincoln replied to an out-of-town inquiry as to the credit of one of his townsmen. He wrote:

"First of all, he has a wife and a baby; together they ought to be worth $500,000 to any man. Secondly, he has an office in which there is a table worth $1.50, and three chairs worth, say, $1.00. Last of all, there is in one corner a large rathole, which will bear looking into. Respectfully, A. Lincoln."

1129

There was an awful stew in the courtroom. The prosecuting attorney said to the judge:

"Your bull pup has just chewed up the court Bible."

"Okay," the judge replied; "the witness can kiss the pup; there's no time to get a new Bible."

1130

The court was impatient. It was the fifth day, and the twelfth juryman was still unconvinced.

"Well, gentlemen," said the court officer, entering the jury room, "shall I, as usual, order twelve dinners?"

"Make it," said the foreman, "eleven dinners and one bale of hay."

1131

Down on the Mexican border, back in the old gun-totin' days of yore there was a judge whose duty it became to sentence a Latin-American to the gallows. He made rather a neat job of it, as the following seems to prove:

"Pedro Gonzalez, you have been tried by twelve good men and true; not your peers, but as high above you as Heaven is above Hell; and they have said that you are guilty.

"In a few weeks, Spring will spread a carpet of green grass and beautiful flowers on every hill and dale. Then will come hot Summer with its shimmering waves on the horizon; then Fall with her yellow harvest moon and hills growing golden under the sinking sun. And finally Winter, with its howling winds and all the land clad in snow.

"But you, Pedro Gonzalez, will not be here to see all this, for it is the order of the court that you be taken to the nearest tree and hanged by the neck until you are dead, dead, dead, you saddle-colored so-and-so!"

1132

A little old lady went into a lawyer's office one day and began: "I have a grandson who is working here."

"Yes," replied the boss, "but he's away today attending your funeral."

1133

A Pennsylvania judge was likewise a cashier in his home town bank. A stranger presented a check one day at his window and asked to have it cashed. His identification was not satisfactory to the cashier.

"Why, Judge," said the man reproachfully, "I've known you to sentence a man to be hanged on no better evidence than this!"

"Maybe so," replied the judge. "But when it comes to letting go of cold cash, we have to be mighty careful."

1134

A famous judge, reprimanding a criminal, called him among other things a scoundrel. The prisoner retorted: "Sir, I am not as big a scoundrel as your honor—" the culprit stopped and looked the angry judge in the eye, but hurriedly added—"takes me to be."

1135

In a certain prairie town some years ago there was a case to be tried that involved testimony of an exceptionally racy order. When the judge entered the courtroom, he noticed that it was crowded with women. He looked them over, and then said:

"Guess the folks here don't know the kind of case we're going to try. Therefore I feel I ought to ask all the respectable women to withdraw."

Not one of them made a move.

"All right," the judge continued; "now that all the respectable women have gone, I order the bailiff to put the others out."

1136

A suburban widow was discussing her troubles with her very best friend. "Don't talk to me about lawyers," she said; "I've had so much trouble over John's property that sometimes I wish he hadn't died."

1137

The plaintiff was confused by the attorney for the defense.

"Are you sure," the lawyer asked, "that the prisoner is the man who stole your car?"

"Well," came the reply, "I was quite sure until you cross-examined me. Now I'm not sure that I ever had a car at all."

1138

Paul Kruger, President of the Transvaal, once decided a dispute between two brothers about an inheritance of land in South Africa.

"Let one brother divide the land, and let the other have first choice."

1139

Man is an able creature, but he has made 32,647,389 laws and hasn't yet improved on the Ten Commandments.

1140

I sometimes wish that people would put a little more emphasis upon the observance of the law than they do upon its enforcement.

Calvin Coolidge

1141

A psychiatrist was asked by a lawyer if he could prove that his client was crazy. The answer was:

"Absolutely; and what's more, if you are ever in trouble and need my services, I will do the same thing for you."

1142

Lawyer: A man who gets two other men to strip for a fight and then takes away their clothes.

1143

America's well-loved fabulist, George Ade, made an after-dinner speech. There was a lawyer as toastmaster, and when he rose to comment he informally kept his hands in his pockets.

"Doesn't it strike you as a little unusual," he said, "that a professional humorist should be funny?"

"Doesn't it strike this company as unusual," Ade returned as the laughter died down, "that a lawyer should have his hands in his own pockets?"

1144

Joseph H. Choate was at one time defending a client in Westchester County, New York City's silk-stocking suburban area. He was doing so with his usual suave skill, and the opposing lawyer was not happy about it; in fact, when the opponent rose to address the jury, he began by saying:

"Gentlemen, I sincerely hope that your decision will not be influenced by Mr. Choate's Chesterfieldian urbanity."

When Choate addressed the jury, he smiled and said:

"Gentlemen, I am sure you will not be influenced, either, by the Westchesterfieldian suburbanity of my opponent."

1145

It was Abraham Lincoln's habit to discourage unnecessary lawsuits, though it cost him a pretty penny. One day a man stormed into his office and demanded that he bring suit for $2.50 against a debtor. Lincoln gravely demanded ten dollars as a retainer. Half of this he gave to the poor defendant, who immediately confessed judgment and paid the $2.50. Thus the suit was terminated to the entire satisfaction of everyone concerned.

1146

The following can be told (and has been) on almost any law firm:

A New York attorney had to go to Carson City, Nevada, to handle a very important case. It dragged somewhat, but finally the lawyer was able to telegraph his partner:

"Justice has triumphed."

Immediately the New York partner wired back:

"Appeal at once."

1147

Roy Bean, who, back in the so-called halcyon days, was known as "the law west of the Pecos," was equally well known in Texas as a bartender and judge. As the former, he had an aversion to giving change. One day a lawyer came in and ordered a glass of beer, for which he put down a twenty-dollar gold piece. When Bean was slow about giving him his change, the lawyer began to swear. But the Judge was equal to the situation, saying:

"I fine you $20; $6.66⅔ for public profanity; $6.66⅔ for abusive language; and $6.66⅔ for being a public nuisance. The beer is on me."

1148

Another favorite Texas story concerns Judge Bean. The defunct body of a stranger was found, and in his pockets were a six-shooter and forty dollars. The Judge fined the corpse forty dollars for carrying a concealed weapon.

1149

A motorist who was arrested for speeding lost his temper and called the traffic officer an ass. In addition to fining him, the judge reproved him for the name-calling.

"Then I mustn't call the policeman an ass?" he inquired.

"Certainly not," the judge answered.

"But," the man continued, "you wouldn't mind if I called an ass a policeman, would you?"

"Not at all," grinned the judge, "if it gives you any satisfaction."

Whereupon the motorist turned to the cop who had arrested him, and said:

"Good-bye, policeman."

1150

Whether justice has been served better or worse since women have been sitting on juries is a moot point, but the gentler sex has lent additional interest.

A certain judge, after a three-hours charge to the jury, finally said:

"Is there any other question before the jury retires?" And a woman juror piped up:

"Please, your honor, tell us what is a plaintiff and what is a defendant."

1151

A colored woman name Sally White had her husband before the judge for wife-beating. She showed a broken nose, bleeding mouth and a closed eye, and on that basis demanded that Rastus be punished.

"Rastus," said the judge, "you have heard what your wife says. Now what have you got to say for yourself?"

"What I says, Judge," Rastus replied, "is not to pay no attention to that woman. She's punch drunk."

1152

Having just been graduated from law school, a man wrote to the postmasters of several towns inquiring as to the possibilities for an honest young Republican lawyer. The reply he received from an Arkansas town said:

"If you are a Republican, the game laws will protect you, and if you're an honest lawyer, you won't have any competition."

1153

Having told her story, the lady witness in a civil suit was followed by a witness of the opposite sex. His story was the exact opposite in almost every detail.

"Do you mean to call this lady a liar?" a lawyer snapped.

"Not at all," said the man. "I merely wish to make it plain what a liar I am if the lady is telling the truth."

1154

Two small boys were discussing each other's parents. Said one:

"A little bird told me what kind of a lawyer your father is."

"What did he say?" the other asked.

"Cheep, cheep," was the reply.

But the No. 2 lad was quick on the trigger, as he said:

"Well, it was a duck that told me what kind of a doctor your father is."

1155

Under cross-examination, the witness was asked if his watch stopped when it fell to the pavement.

"Oh, yes," the witness replied, "it couldn't have gone through."

1156

A colored woman was on trial before a magistrate in a southern town charged with inhuman treatment of her offspring.

Evidence was clear that the woman had severely beaten the youngster, aged some nine years, who was in court to exhibit his battered condition.

Before imposing sentence, his honor asked the woman whether she had anything to say.

"Kin I ask yo' honah a question?" inquired the prisoner.

The judge nodded affirmatively.

"Well, then, yo' honah, I'd like to ask yo' whether yo' was ever the parent of a puffectly wuthless cullud chile?"

1157

A hobo, arrested for vagrancy, was asked by the magistrate why he was in that condition, and replied thus:

"Good God! I ain't had no chance to get a damn job."

The bailiff sprang to his feet and exclaimed:

"Here, you. What kind of language is that to use in a courtroom! For one thing, you used a double negative, and besides that, you ought to know that 'ain't' is incorrect."

1158

A very young lawyer addressed the jury for several hours, and every one of the twelve good men and true was in a highly belligerent frame of mind. When he finally finished, a veteran attorney stood up, looked pleasantly at the judge, and said:

"Your Honor, I will follow the example of my young opponent who has just finished, and submit the case without argument."

1159

The foregoing story has an ancient parallel, dug up by Ben Richards, the sage of Chappaqua, in an epigram by the Greek poet Nicarchus.

Two deaf men brought their quarrel to a deaf judge. "Your Honor," said one of them, "this man owes me five months' rent."

"It's a lie," said the other. "I always ground my meal at night."

The deaf judge looked at them sternly. "After all," he decided, "she is your mother. You should both support her."

1160

A woman witness was asked by a judge if she had ever appeared as a witness before.

"Yes, your honor," she said.

"In what suit?" he asked.

"My blue serge," she replied.

1161

A man who had been convicted of stealing was brought before Judge Blank, who, as you all know, is well known for his tender-heartedness.

"Have you ever been sentenced to imprisonment?" asked the judge, not unkindly.

"Never!" exclaimed the prisoner, suddenly bursting into tears.

"Well, well, don't cry, my man," said Judge Blank consolingly; "you're going to be now."

1162

A Negro woman entered a law office and was asked what she wanted.

"Mister lawyer," she answered, "I wants a divorce from my man."

"Now what's that scoundrel been doing now?" asked the lawyer.

"Dat old fool's gone and got religion, he has, and I ain't tasted chicken for nigh on to three months."

1163

A technicality prevented Rastus Johnson from getting a divorce. His attorney discovered that his marriage wasn't legal on account of the girl's father not having a license to carry a gun.

1164

A county sheriff in Vermont was suspected of being very lenient with his prisoners. Early one evening a fellow townsman passed the lockup and saw five or six prisoners coming out of the jail. In the doorway stood the sheriff, watching them depart. The townsman hid behind a tree and heard the sheriff say to the prisoners, "Now you fellers be back here by 9.30, or, by Heaven, you'll be locked out."

1165

A California newspaper reported the following:

"Mrs. Blank was granted a divorce when she told the judge that since their marriage her husband had spoken to her but three times. She was awarded the custody of their three children."

1166

At an important dinner party a lawyer was seated next to a lady whose name he did not catch. During the second course he noticed at the host's right another lawyer who had won a case from him.

"See that man?" he said to his fair dinner partner. "I hate him worse than anybody else on earth."

"That," the lady replied, "is my husband."

"Yes, I know," the lawyer lied glibly—"that's why I hate him."

1167

Pat O'Grady had been brought before the bar of justice charged with wife desertion and nonsupport. Pat admitted his guilt, said his wife talked too much, he couldn't stand it.

"That's no excuse for desertion, Pat," the judge said. "Don't you know that the Constitution guarantees every woman the right to talk all she wants to?"

"But Ellen never stops talkin'. She keeps it up steady, mornin', noon, and night, day in, and day out, 'til I get so fed up I can't stand it, Jedge."

"What does she talk about, Pat?" asked the judge.

Pat shook his head sadly.

"She don't say, Judge."

1168

Mr. C., a distinguished lawyer of Boston, was on his way to Denver to transact some important business. During the afternoon he noticed, in the opposite section of the Pullman, a sweet-faced, tired-appearing woman traveling with four small children. Being fond of children and feeling sorry for the mother, he soon made friends with the little ones.

Early the next morning he heard their eager questions and the patient "Yes, dear," of the mother as she tried to dress them, and looking out he saw a small white foot protruding beyond the opposite curtain. Reaching across the aisle, he took hold of the large toe and began to recite; "This little pig went to market, this little pig stayed at home; this little pig had roast beef, this little pig had none; this little pig cried wee wee all the way home."

The foot was suddenly withdrawn and a cold, quiet voice said: "That is quite sufficient, thank you."

Mr. C. hastily withdrew to the smoker, where he remained until the train arrived in Denver.

1169

A woman in a highly nervous state visited her lawyer and told him that she wanted to get a divorce.

"On what ground?" asked the lawyer.

"He hit me," the woman exclaimed, "and closed one of my eyes. Isn't that enough?"

"Absolutely," the lawyer assured her; "it's an open and shut case."

1170

A certain judge in a Western city passed sentence on a culprit in a long-winded discourse that lasted half an hour. Shortly before he reached the end of his discourse, the prisoner, visibly bored, interrupted, saying:

"Look here, Judge, is this a sentence or a filibuster?"

1171

A poor woman begged King Philip of Macedon to grant her justice, which Philip refused.

The woman said she would appeal the case.

The King, astonished, asked to whom she would appeal.

The woman replied, "From Philip drunk to Philip sober."

Section 15

LOVE

1200

The captain and the junior lieutenant on one of the smaller warships were both in love with the same girl. Consequently they were not fond of each other and they took underhanded means of showing it. They alternated on making the day's entries in the ship's log, and one day the lieutenant was annoyed to find in the captain's handwriting the entry: "July 5; lieutenant jg drunk." For a moment he was practically nonplused. Then he smiled, grabbed a pen, and wrote: "July 6; captain sober."

1201

A woman is as old as she looks, and a man is old when he stops looking.

1202

After two days in the hospital, I took a turn for the nurse.

W. C. Fields

1203

A college sophomore was discussing a girl he had just met at a party. "At dancing," he said, "she's not so hot, but at intermissioning—WOW!"

1204

Once upon a time a little miss of sixteen summers was walking through the woods. She came to a foot-bridge that was very narrow and was suspended across a brook swollen by the spring rains. She hesitated, fear clutching at her heart.

"Don't be afraid, little one," called a deep voice. "The bridge will hold you. Walk across."

The young girl looked in the direction of the voice but saw no one.

"Who's there?" she cried in alarm.

"It is I, the Prince. Come across the bridge and join me," answered a pleasant, reassuring voice.

She ran across the bridge, looking about, expecting to see the handsome Prince, but she saw only an ugly frog sitting on a log.

The frog said, "I am the Prince. A wicked fairy changed me into a frog because I would not marry her daughter. I cannot become myself again until some kind person picks me up and carries me to her home. Will you, pretty child?"

"Certainly, I will carry you to my home, dear Prince," she said sweetly. She stooped and picked up the ugly frog and put him under her coat to protect him from the wind and rain.

When she reached her home she put him to bed, telling him she would care for him until the wicked spell was broken and he became the Prince again.

The next morning she woke up and there beside her lay a handsome young man—the Prince himself.

But her mother would never believe her story.

1205

The following conversation between two Negro women took place just prior to the Yuletide season:

"Mandy, are you goin' to hang up any mistletoe when Christmas comes?"

"No indeed I ain't. I got too much pride to advertise for the ordinary courtesies that a lady has a right to expeck."

1206

An argument was on the point of being started. In fact, it had started. The boy loved her but he realized her shortcomings.

"The first time you contradict me," he said, "I am going to kiss you." Whereat she quickly replied:

"You are *not*."

1207

There are few of the great philosophers who have made a greater contribution to the science of happiness than the hard-working Negro woman who had a thoroughly lazy but likable husband. When she was asked why she put up with him, she answered:

"Well, it's this way; I makes the livin', and he makes the livin' worth while."

1208

Darling: The popular form of address used in speaking to a person of the opposite sex whose name you cannot at the moment recall.

Oliver Herford

1209

Flirtation: Attention without intention.

1210

They were discussing modern music and dancing, and the young woman said:

"I don't like dancing to swing and jive. Why it's nothing but hugging set to music."

"Humph," said the young man, "what is there about that you object to?"

"The music," the girl replied.

1211

A young man in the country had been sparking a girl for several months, and was battling with the problem of how to ask her for her hand in marriage. Finally he consulted the hired man on his father's farm. He said:

"I haven't the slightest idea of the right way to ask Alice to marry me."

"Son," the man replied; "there ain't no wrong way!"

1212

A woman in the Zoological Park in New York (or Chicago, Philadelphia, St. Louis, or elsewhere) seemed to have a mania for asking questions of one of the keepers. The keeper answered politely for a while, but finally he tired, and when the inquisitive woman asked whether the hippopotamus was a male or female he replied:

"What earthly difference does it make, ma'am—unless you are another hippopotamus?"

1213

A diffident young man brought a young lady a bouquet of orchids. She was that pleased she threw her arms around him and kissed him heartily. He reached for his coat and hat and started to leave.

"Oh, Billy, I'm sorry if I have offended you," the girl exclaimed.

"Offended hell," the young man replied; "I'm going out for more orchids."

1216

The front door at last closed, and Mary Ann came upstairs. She was met by her mother, who exclaimed:

"Mary Ann, your hair is all mussed up." Then she added with a gleam in her eye, "Did that young fellow kiss you against your will?"

"Well, he thought he did, Mummy," the girl replied.

1217

"James," exclaimed J. Horace Van Fayer to his chauffeur, "how on earth did this blonde hair get on the back seat of the car?"

"I can explain that, sir," said the chauffeur.

"To heck with an explanation," Mr. Van Fayer burst forth. "Can you give me an introduction?"

1218

A little later in life the girls stop looking for their ideal man and start looking around for a husband.

1219

Charlie Snerd couldn't think of much to talk about when he called on Helene Lamour, but he stayed, and he stayed, and he stayed. Finally he burst forth with:

"Do you know I can imitate any bird you can mention?"

"No, Charlie," was the reply; "but I'd love to see you imitate a homing pigeon."

1220

After a very earnest courtship, Jack Smith proposed to the heiress to the Rich millions, was accepted, and then went to her father for his permission. The old man was inclined to be skeptical.

"Would you love my daughter just as well if she had no money?" he asked.

"I would indeed," said Jack.

"In that case," said her papa, "get out of here quick. I don't want any idiots in the family."

1221

"Is your girl friend beautiful?" asked Robbie McTavish of Sandy McGregor.

"That she is," replied McGregor. "When I take her home in a taxi I can hardly keep my eyes on the meter."

1222

Men don't make passes at gals who wear glasses.

Ogden Nash

1223

Gals who wear slacks should not turn their backs.

H. I. Phillips

1224

A careful swain used to begin his love letters: "My own precious girl and gentlemen of the jury."

1225

One can find women who have never had one love affair, but it is rare indeed to find any who have had only one.

La Rochefoucauld

1226

When a woman really loves a man, he can make her do anything she wants to do.

Anon

1227

The man got his girl via a ladder from the second-story window, helped her into the taxicab, and they were off. Said he to the driver breathlessly:

"Grand Central Station, New York. How much is the fare?"

"You don't have to pay a cent," the driver replied. "The lady's father took care of that."

1228

Love: A season's pass on the shuttle between heaven and hell.

Don Dickerman

1229

I used to love my garden,
But now my love is dead,
For I found a bachelor button
In black-eyed Susan's bed.

1230

The turtle lives 'twixt plated decks
Which practically conceal its sex.
I think it clever of the turtle
In such a fix to be so fertile.

Ogden Nash

1231

"I saw you take his kiss." " 'Tis true."
"O, modesty!" " 'Twas strictly kept:
He thought me asleep: at least, I knew
He thought I thought he thought I slept."

Coventry Patmore

1233

I'm Smith of Stoke, and sixty-odd,
  I've lived without a dame
From youth-time on; and would to God
  My dad had done the same.

Thomas Hardy

1234

There was a young man from the West
Who loved a young lady with zest.
So hard did he press her
To make her say, "Yes, sir,"
He broke three cigars in his vest.

1235

The reason girls kiss each other, while men do not, is that girls have nothing better to kiss, and men have.

1236

There once was a maiden of Siam,
Who said to her lover, young Priam,
"If you kiss me, of course
You will have to use force;
God knows you are stronger than I am."

1237

"May I print a kiss on your lips?" he asked,
And she nodded her sweet permission.
So they went to press, and I rather guess
They printed a large edition.

1238

A bottle of perfume that Willie sent
Was highly displeasing to Millicent;
Her thanks were so cold,
They quarreled, I'm told,
Through that silly scent Willie sent Millicent.

1239

I'm past my days of wooing,
As years are now accruing.
How time flies by!
I wish that I
Had done some more wrongdoing.

Ned Allen

1240

A young blade in the Ozarks had been courting a girl of the region for some time. The girl's father, after a long time, finally said to the lad:

"Looka here! You been seein' Elviry for pretty close to a full year. I wanta know what your intentions are—honorable or dishonorable."

The young man looked a bit sheepish, shifted from one foot to the other, and said:

"Do you mean I got a choice?"

1241

THE FLEA

And here's the happy bounding flea—
You cannot tell the he from she.
The sexes look alike, you see;
But he can tell, and so can she.

From "Not for Children," by Roland Young. Doubleday, Doran. 1930

1242

At the tender age of 90 the Duchess of Queensbury was asked, "When does a woman stop hoping for romance?" She answered, "Goodness, I don't know yet!"

1243

Zeke Daniel says: "Kissing a girl is a good deal like opening a bottle of olives. It's a mite difficult to get the first one, but the rest come easy."

1244

An ancient Greek philosopher and humorist once said to a despairing lover, "Don't tear your hair out—baldness is no cure for sorrow."

1245

Many a girl who fails to give a man any encouragement is the kind who prefers a man who needs no encouragement.

1246

In the musical comedy "One Touch of Venus," Mary Martin, the lovely and provocative star has this line:

"Love isn't the dying moan of a distant violin; it's the triumphant twang of a bedspring."

1247

They say that high heels were invented by a girl who never got kissed anywhere but on the forehead.

1248

If a fellow can drive a car safely while he is kissing a girl, he is not giving the kiss the attention it deserves.

1249

Platonic Love: The gun you didn't know was loaded.

1250

Love: The tenth word in every telegram.

1251

He slipped the ring upon her third finger and waited for her exclamation of delight.

She looked at it critically.

"Do you think the diamond is too small, maybe?" he asked, crestfallen.

"Oh, no! It's not that it's too small, it just looks as though it were paid for, that's all."

1252

Hug: Energy gone to waist.

1253

Women, said Oscar Wilde, were made to be loved; not to be understood.

1254

Kiss: The anatomical juxtaposition of two orbicular oris muscles in a state of contraction.

Dr. Henry Gibbons

1255

She was that kind of a girl. The young man showed a very definite interest—a tremendously definite interest. Said he:

"Darling, I love you: I worship you: I adore you: I have always wanted you. Kiss me, sweet!"

And the girl answered:

"Why?"

1256

Men always want to be a woman's first love. Women have a more subtle instinct; what they like is to be a man's last romance.

Oscar Wilde

1257

Love, said a male cynic, is the delusion that one woman differs from another.

1258

A bad man of the West, bad because he was drunk and carried a six-gun in each hand, menaced his way into a railroad coach and shouted:

"I'm going to rob every man on this here train, and I'm going to kiss all the women."

Whereat a determined looking Texan got up and said:

"Look here, pardner, you can rob us men, but I'm blowed if you're going to kiss the women."

At this point a spinster rose and shouted:

"You leave that man alone; *he's* a-robbin' this train."

1259

"Well, so long," said one young man to another; "I've got to pick up a girl at Broadway and Forty-second Street."

"Who is she?" was the query. And the other answered:

"How do I know who's going to be at Broadway and Forty-second Street?"

1260

Two motorists were reminiscing about their experiences. One of them asked the other:

"Have you ever been arrested for going too fast?"

"No," was the reply, "but I've been slapped."

1261

"It's all over between us," said the earnest young man to his friend. "I showed the girl one of my boyhood pictures with my father holding me on his knee, and she said: 'My goodness, it's Edgar and Charlie to the life.' "

1262

The young lady had been most carefully brought up, so she knew her way around. She was out walking with a young man in the country, and apparently in a happy frame of mind. The man said:

"Come on over and let's sit beneath that apple tree."

"Not me," she said decisively.

"Why not?" the young man asked; "don't you trust me?"

"Sure I trust you," she said; "and I trust myself; but I can't quite trust the two of us together."

1263

Young Matilda was being kissed by Harry when the girl's small brother happened along. Harry was somewhat upset about it, and when the boy walked away whistling, the ardent lover said:

"How much should I give the kid to keep him quiet?"

And the absent-minded girl replied:

"He usually gets a quarter."

1264

A young man was paying ardent court to a beautiful girl. Finally, after proposing to her, he exclaimed:

"If you turn me down, I shall die."

She turned him down.

Sixty-three years afterward he died.

1265

A State of Maine villager had a pretty and popular daughter who received a good deal of attention from the boys. The father, however, was thoroughly lacking in hospitality when the lads would call to see the girl.

Abner Smith dropped in one evening and the old man opened the door but made no move to get the girl. The two sat down.

"It looks like rain," the young fellow observed.

" 'Taint a-goin' to rain," was the short response.

Not another word was said for a quarter of an hour. At length the host's curiosity got the better of him, and he growled:

"Who are ye anyway?"

"Abner Smith."

"Ye don't mean you're old Eliphalet Smith's son!"

"Yes sir, I am."

"Goodness gracious damn," the girl's father exclaimed. "In that case I guess it may rain."

1266

Ever tactful, the charming lady who was the guest of an Irish group made the remark:

"I really believe that I was meant for an Irish woman."

A courtly old fellow in the group immediately replied:

"Madam, the world would be with me in saying that you were meant for an Irishman."

Section 16

MARRIAGE AND MARRIED LIFE

1280

A suburban wife was complaining to her husband that they never had any money.

"Why is it?" she asked.

"It's the neighbors, darling," he replied. "They're always doing something we can't afford."

1281

A mountaineer woman went into a southern town to obtain ration books for the family, which included twelve children. The clerk said to her:

"If you will take these books over to that table, the man will stamp them and give you some literature." And the woman answered:

"Don't want any literature, thanks; I likes a big family."

1282

Two girls at a matinée couldn't get seats together, but were placed across the aisle from each other. One of them, who was anxious to have the man seated next to her exchange places with her friend, said, "Are you alone?" The man was disturbed and burying his face in his program, whispered, "Sh, wife."

1283

"Mother, are you the nearest relative I've got?" asked little Ruth.

"Yes, dear, and your father is the closest," sighed her mother.

1284

The young bachelor asked the old benedict what was the best month to be married in.

"Octembrary," was the quick reply.

"Why, there's no such month," said the bachelor.

"Just so," rejoined the benedict.

1285

A new family moved into the neighborhood and Mrs. Fenwick was very much interested in them.

"They seem to be such a devoted couple," she reported to her husband. "He kisses her every time he goes out, and waves to her from the sidewalk. Why don't you do that?"

"Good lord, Grace," replied her husband in astonishment. "I don't even know the woman yet."

1286

The man who has no secrets from his wife either has no secrets or no wife.

Gilbert Wells

1287

Prospective bridegrooms always have a lot to learn, no matter how worldly-wise they are. One of them was nervous, and said to his married pal:

"Give me the lowdown, Phil. Who is the boss in your house?"

"Well," was the reply, "Edith directs the children, the maid, the dog, the cat and the canary. But I can say anything I darn please to the goldfish."

1288

Frederick was to be married and was eager to learn the modus operandi.

"How much do I have to shell out for a marriage license, Jim? You've been through the mill and know the ropes."

"All you pay is two dollars down, Fred, and then your entire salary each week for the rest of your life."

1289

The blushing bride timidly approached the butcher.

"I would like a shoulder of smoked ham," she said.

"I'm sorry, Ma'am," the butcher answered, "but we haven't any just now. How about a nice fresh leg of spare rib instead?"

1290

There are two periods in a man's life when he doesn't understand a woman. Before marriage and after marriage.

1291

A man went to his doctor and asked him to look at his ankle.

After a careful examination, the doctor asked: "How long have you been walking around with this ankle like this?"

"About two weeks," replied the patient.

"Why, man alive, your ankle is broken in two places! I don't understand how you ever got about. Why didn't you come to me when you met with the accident?"

"Well, Doc, you see every time I say something is wrong with me, my wife vows I'll have to stop smoking."

1292

Women do find the weirdest things to worry about. If it isn't one thing, it's six others. I know a man and his wife who have been ideally happy for years. They have plenty of money; they have had no great griefs; they don't fight.

One morning at the breakfast table wifie had an awful sour puss and was snappish.

"Whatsa matter, Little bitta Heaven?" he asked.

Then she blew off the lid.

"If ever again I dream that you kissed another woman, so help me, I'll divorce you!"

1293

Sacred to the memory of Anthony Drake,
Who died for peace and quietness sake.
His wife was constantly scoldin' and scoffin',
So he sought repose in a twelve-dollar coffin.

1294

Little Barbara and her mother were discussing one thing and another, when the child said:

"Mother, if I get married, will I have a husband like Daddy?"

"Yes, darling," Mother replied.

"Well, if I don't get married, will I be an old maid like Aunt Martha?"

Mother agreed that she would, and Barbara came back:

"It certainly is a tough world for us women, isn't it!"

1295

One of the guests at a Negro wedding approached a man who was considerably dolled up.

"Pardon suh," he said, "but is you de groom?"

"No suh, I ain't," the man replied with a sorrowing look; "I was eliminated in the semi-finals."

1296

Mr. Botts was getting a curtain lecture after the musical evening to which his wife had dragged him. "You were impossible," said Mrs. B. "How?" grunted her sleepy spouse.

"Do you remember," continued the wife, "that Mrs. DeLancey exclaimed, 'What a large repertoire that soprano has,' and that you made a crude remark?"

"No, darling, what was it?"

"You agreed with her and said, 'What's more, the dress she has on makes it look even more conspicuous.' "

1297

The man who claims that he always has the last word in an argument with his wife may be telling the truth; but it's dollars to doughnuts that what he says is, "Yes, Darling."

1298

A celebrated writer, still in love with his wife, always celebrated the anniversary of their engagement. On one occasion he was away from home and he sent a telegram saying, "Many thanks." And she wired back to him, "The pleasure is mine."

1299

Papa, Mama and little Billy Kangaroo were leaping through an Australian field. Junior kept popping out of Mama's pouch and jumping back again, which delayed the progress of the tour. Pop started to scold Billy, but Ma came to his rescue.

"Don't be hard on the little fellow," she said. "It's actually my fault; I've got the hiccoughs."

1300

A stringy-looking farm woman entered the village drug store one afternoon with two prescriptions. She handed them to the druggist, who promptly started back to fill them.

"Be careful to keep them separate," the woman called after him. "One's for Pa and the other's for our hawg. He's a blue ribbon winner and State Fair starts next week. We can't take no chances."

1301

"How about it? Do you give the little lady a personal allowance?" asked Ruggles.

"We tried out that plan, but it didn't work," answered Jones.

"How come?"

"She always spent it before I could borrow it back."

1302

Maybe it marked the end of the honeymoon when the young husband said:

"But darling, this meat isn't cooked; neither is the pie."

"I know and I can't understand it," the bride pouted. "I followed directions, but the recipe was for four people, and as there are just two of us, I measured half of everything and cooked it half the time it said."

1303

One of the editors of the Army newspaper in France slipped in a gag when he was preparing the French lesson for American soldiers. He decided to tell the GI's how to say, "My wife doesn't understand me." Of course he didn't think of possible repercussions in case one of the wives at home should get hold of a copy.

But the situation was saved when a linotyper, who knew human nature as well as the French tongue, made the sentence read:

"My wife understands me too well."

1304

"I think you might talk to me while I knit," sighed his wife.

"Why don't you knit to me while I read?" suggested her better-half.

1305

"Does your husband prefer home cooking?" asked the newlywed.

"Oh, yes. We always plan to dine at a café that makes a specialty of it," answered her friend.

1306

They had been married a week and were having their first quarrel.

"I wish I were dead and buried," she sobbed.

"I wish I were, too," he cried in agony.

"Then I *don't* wish I were," she sniffled.

1307

"Do you let your husband carry a latchkey?" asked a strong-minded woman of another.

"Certainly," was the quick answer. "He likes to show it to his friends to let them see how independent he is; but between you and me, the key he carries doesn't fit the door."

1308

Mary believed in keeping up with the times but she still clung to the notion that John should ask her father for her hand in marriage.

"Was father furious when you asked for my hand, John?" she asked, clinging to him.

"Was he furious? I thought he would shake my arm off."

1309

Intrepid Fred had at last screwed up courage to ask Ethel's father for his consent.

"Sir," he said, "I want your daughter for my wife."

"And I, sir," her father replied, "am not willing to trade."

1310

The eloping bride received this wire from her parents.

"Do not come home and all will be forgiven."

1311

Every man who is high up loves to think that he has done it all himself; and the wife smiles, and lets it go at that.

J. M. Barrie

1312

Smith said his marriage was on a strictly 50-50 basis. When she bought a $50 dress, he bought a 50-cent shirt.

1314

When a man and his wife have a joint checking account, it's a perfectly simple arrangement. He makes the deposits and she draws the checks.

1315

"Keep next Friday free, Genevieve," said a young lady recently. "We're going to give Mary a shower."

"Count on me," burbled Genevieve, "I'll bring the soap."

1316

Then there was the man who said, before marriage, that nothing would be good enough for his wife. After the marriage he held to the same opinion.

1317

A man yearns for a woman before he married. Afterward, the y is silent.

1318

"Darling," said Alpheus, "I cannot live without you."

The girl was taut with emotion herself. Said she:

"If I should refuse to marry you, would you kill yourself?"

"That," Alpheus replied, "has been my usual custom."

1319

A young man went to the girl's father for his permission. In a shaky voice he said:

"Sir, I wish to marry your daughter."

The father looked at him sternly and asked:

"Young fellow, do you drink?"

And the lad answered nervously:

"Thanks a lot, but let's get this other matter out of the way first."

1320

A sturdy and determined woman lost her thumb in a bus accident, and sued the company for $50,000. In questioning her, the attorney for the defense asked:

"What makes you believe that your thumb was worth as much as $50,000?"

"Because," she answered, "it was the thumb I kept my husband under."

1321

Here is an ad that appeared in the classified section of a San Francisco newspaper:

> FOR SALE—By a young couple, twin beds, one slightly used.

1322

Evidently the bridal couple who occupied Lower 9 on the Pullman sleeper between Omaha and Chicago thought that the curtains kept their voices from being heard. But it didn't.

The other passengers listened in on their conversation, which went something like this:

"Kiss me, sweetheart."

A moment of silence and then a loud SMACK. A cough from the upper berth across the aisle and a snort from the end of the car.

"Kiss me again, darling."

A gasp and then another smack. A growl from behind another curtain. Yet again came the girl's voice:

"Kiss me, honey."

"Not now," said the man; "you must go to sleep."

"Oh, but you must," the girl insisted. "Kiss me and then I'll go to sleep."

That was too much for the man opposite, and he roared:

"For Pete's sake kiss her and we'll *all* go to sleep!"

1323

At a spiritualistic seance the medium called up the departed husband of a widow who was present. The widow asked him eagerly:

"Are you happy now, Bill?"

"Yes, Matilda," he replied; "extremely so."

"Happier than when you were with me, Bill?"

"I am," came the answer; "how could it be otherwise?"

"Tell me, Bill," the widow continued, "what is Heaven like?"

"Heaven," the spook exclaimed, "who said I was in Heaven?"

1324

The old tightwad protested at his wife's extravagance.

"Last week she wanted a dollar, this week she wants seventy-five cents, today she wants two dollars."

"Landsakes, what does she do with it all?" a sympathetic neighbor asked.

"I dunno," the henpecked husband replied ."I ain't given her any yet."

1325

When a friend called at the home of a girl who was planning to be married, there was no one at home except the Negro maid.

"No'm," said the maid, "she ain't here. She's down at the Y.M.C.A. taking the course."

"What do you mean, the course?"

"My Lawd," was the reply; "I done thought you-all knew. It's the course in domestic silence."

1326

One afternoon a young woman stepped up to a telegraph counter, and in a trembling voice asked for a supply of blanks. She wrote a message on one blank, which she immediately tore in halves; then a second message was written out that was treated in the same manner; finally a third was accomplished. This she handed to the operator with a feverish request that it be "rushed."

When the message had gone on the wire and the sender had departed, the operator read the other two. The first ran: "All at an end. Have no wish to see you again." "Do not write or try to see me," was the tenor of the second message. The third was to this effect: "Come at once. Take next train. Answer."

1327

"Horace, you shouldn't have kissed me like that when we went through the dark tunnel. Not with all those people on the train."

"I didn't kiss you," he said, looking at her with amazement. "If I knew who did I'd teach him a lesson."

"Horace," sighed the girl friend, "you couldn't teach that guy nothing."

1328

The couple sat on the rustic seat beneath the great elm through which the moonlight was filtering.

"Gloria," faltered Ralph awkwardly, "you believe that girls and boys should be perfectly frank with each other before getting married, don't you?"

"Yes, Ralph," she answered shyly.

"And that neither should keep any secrets from the other?"

"Yes, Ralph."

"Because you know one might find out later and it would cause all—all—"

"All sorts of trouble," she finished for him.

"Yes, Gloria, some men might not care, but I think it best to ask if—"

"Yes, Ralph," she answered, gazing confidently into his searching eyes.

"Gloria, perhaps I ought not to demand this, but I don't feel as though I could get along with a woman—who—who—"

"Be frank, Ralph, and I'll answer you honestly."

"Gloria," Ralph burst out nervously, "do you squeeze a toothpaste tube from the top?"

1329

Little Willie was a very sincere reader of Popular Science Monthly, and his father encouraged his interest in the subject.

"William," said Dad one day, "I want to see how much of a scientist you are. Tell me this: when the kettle boils, why does the steam come out of the spout?"

"That's easy," Willie replied. "It's so that Mother can open your letters before you get them."

1330

At breakfast Mr. Pettigrew was on the defensive.

"Well," he said to his wife, "you can't say I made any noise coming home last night."

"No," agreed Mrs. Pettigrew, "but the three men who were carrying you did."

1331

Mr. and Mrs. Pipp had been married a week, and they were having Thanksgiving dinner alone at home.

"There's my first turkey, darling," said Mrs. Pipp as she placed the bird on the table.

"Marvelous, sweetheart," exclaimed her spouse. "How beautifully you have stuffed it!"

"Stuffed it? Why, this one wasn't hollow."

1333

A definition of happiness, as given by Oliver Wendell Holmes, is "Four feet on a fireplace fender."

1334

When will women realize that the most seductive perfume is not "Passionate Peonies" or "Three Weeks in Paris," but the aroma that comes from a broiling beefsteak.

1335

Two married men were discussing their domestic arrangements in some detail. At length the older one asked:

"Does your wife do all her own washing?"

"Absolutely," said the other: "that is, all except her back."

1336

A freshman took his father to the first football game of the season.

"Gee, Dad," he yelled as they took their seats, "you'll see more excitement for your two dollars than you ever saw before."

"I'm not so sure about that," said the old man; "two dollars was all I paid for my marriage license."

1337

Here is another version of the "that was no lady, that was my wife" story. A man went to a church fair and a girl at the flower booth said to him:

"Won't you buy a bouquet to give to the lady you love?"

He looked uncomfortable and stammered:

"That wouldn't be right; I'm a married man."

1338

When Senator Arthur H. Vandenberg was told of the birth of his first grandchild, someone asked him how he felt about being a grandfather.

"I don't mind being a grandfather," he said, "but I'm a little dubious about being married to a grandmother."

1339

"Bill," said his wife, "you're plumb mean. You just sit there reading your newspaper and not paying any more attention to me than as if I weren't here. You just don't love me any more."

"Darling girl, that's nonsense," the husband replied. "I love you more than ever; more than life itself. I kiss the ground you walk on. I worship you. Your slightest wish is my command. Now for Gossakes shut up and let me read the baseball scores."

1340

The Joneses had company in for dinner, and Mr. Jones was trying to be entertaining by telling a comic story. When he had finished and the guests had politely laughed, little Willie Jones said:

"Now, Daddy, tell the other one."

1341

A sympathetic woman was listening to the woes of her married friend, who said chokingly:

"Jack has run away with another woman. I s-simply c-can't c-control myself!"

Then came the consoling words:

"There, there, dearie, don't try. You'll feel better after a good laugh."

1342

Two cronies were talking at the club, and one asked the other:

"Did you and your wife ever have any difference of opinion?"

"Yes indeed," was the answer, "but I was smart enough not to let her know it."

1343

Poets at their best may be very very good, but at their worst they can be very very trying. Their wives must have a Hades of a time.

At the poetry society recently they discussed a poet whose wife acts as his secretary and stenographer. Said one of the members:

"When he is lying awake in bed, if he thinks of something he will ask his wife to get up and put it down for him. He simply says, 'Get up, I've thought of a good word.' "

One of the younger women members spoke up at that point.

"Well," said she, "it's a good thing for him I'm not his wife. I'd answer, 'Get up yourself; I've thought of a bad word.' "

1344

Jackson was in great pain from a toothache when he reached the office. He got a lot of sympathy and some advice from his fellow workers, one of whom said:

"Last week I had a toothache, but it didn't last long. My wife simply kissed it away."

"That's fine," Jackson moaned; "is your wife home now?"

1345

Conversation overheard in the powder room:

"Two months ago I refused to marry Jack Aspinwall, and he has been drinking heavily ever since."

"Well, if you ask me, dear, I think that's carrying a celebration much too far."

1346

A certain author was trying to finish a book to meet a publisher's deadline, and one evening at home he told his wife he should have to have absolute quiet while he worked. His wife agreed, but having had no one to talk to all day, she couldn't help an occasional remark. Immersed in his work, the author made no reply. Finally his wife lost her temper.

"Well!" she exclaimed. "You might at least say 'Shut up.' "

1347

A pants manufacturer on New York's Seventh Avenue became a millionaire without having learned to read or write. He got along okay, however, by signing his checks with two crosses. One day his banker called him up and said:

"What's wrong; you've signed your check with three crosses?"

"Oh, that's all right," the pants maker retorted; "my wife has social ambitions and thinks I should have a middle name."

1348

Below stairs the help were discussing the family's affairs. Said the butler:

"The mistress has a new husband."

And the cook queried:

"Do you think he'll stay?"

1349

A Boston woman went into a store to buy her husband a comb. She said:

"I wish to obtain a man's comb."

"Do you want a narrow man's comb?" the clerk asked.

"No," she said precisely, "I wish a comb for a stout man with rubber teeth."

1350

"Why do I love Richard?" the girl repeated. "Why, father, he's wonderful. He has that certain something."

To which her father replied:

"He'd be a lot more wonderful if he had something certain."

1351

German: A man who lives by the sweat of his frau.

1352

"I made these biscuits all by myself," the new bride proudly informed her husband.

"Marvelous!" he exclaimed. "Who helped you lift them out of the oven?"

1353

"If I tell you anything," Mrs. Smith complained to her husband, "it goes in one ear and out the other."

"No doubt," Mr. Smith agreed; "but if I tell you anything, it goes in both ears and out of your mouth."

1354

The chances are that most girls are as anxious to get married as the boys are. Sometimes they give themselves away. A young man sneaked up behind the young woman of his choice a day or two ago and put his hands over her eyes. Said he:

"Unless you can guess who it is in three guesses, I'm going to kiss you."

The girl did her best. She replied quickly:

"Jack Frost, Davy Jones, Santa Claus."

1355

Among the most embarrassing questions was that of Baby Stork, who asked:

"Mama, where did I come from?"

1356

Smith and Jones met on the way to the 8.15 train. Said Smith:

"Whaddye say we get our wives together tonight and have a big evening?"

"Swell idea," Jones replied. "Where'll we leave 'em?"

1357

It didn't seem promising to the diners when the after-dinner speaker began:

"According to statistics, the average American family consists of 4.1 persons." But he continued: "I'll give you three guesses as to who the one-tenth person is."

1359

"Darling," said a tired husband, "what became of that unpaid bill from R. H. Saxe & Company?"

"Oh," his efficient spouse replied, "I sent it back marked 'insufficient funds.' "

1360

"My wife has the worst memory I ever heard of."

"Forgets everything, does she?" sympathized the friend.

"No; remembers everything."

1361

A recent society bride had six bridesmaids in primrose yellow, carrying old fashioned nosegays of violets, and two pages, in rich purple velvet, with gold lace. A pale bridegroom completed the color scheme.

1362

Mother (reading from a book of fairy tales)—

"Once upon a time—"

Little girl—"Mother, do fairy tales always begin like that?"

"No, darling; sometimes they begin, 'Awfully sorry, my darling, to have been detained at the office again tonight,' " explained the mother, jumping up to answer the telephone.

1364

"Ah well," said a middle-aged man to an acquaintance, "the old gentleman's dead."

"Too bad! Who was he?"

"My 90-year-old grandfather."

"Goodness! At 90, what was it that finally got him?"

The bringer of bad tidings sighed as he answered:

"Liquor and women."

1365

Casey had to spend thirty days in jail for wife beating. Finally his sentence came to an end, which happened on his birthday. As he came up the front steps to greet his wife, she said:

"Sure, Pat, and I wish yez many happy returns of the day."

And that's why Casey is spending another thirty days in jail.

1366

At a bridge party it developed that one of the girls was the second wife of her husband. The first wife had died soon after the marriage.

A rather thoughtless young woman, as she cut the cards, said:

"Of course it's perfectly all right, but somehow I wouldn't want to be a man's second wife."

"But somehow," quietly observed the woman who was, "I'd a lot rather be Jack's second wife than his first."

1367

"Hiram," said the wife of a Vermont farmer, "you'll have to pare your toenails again; you're wearing out my sheets."

1368

At any rate, Eve couldn't throw up to Adam the better men she might have married.

1369

"How long did your wife take to learn to drive a car?"

"Well, let's see; she started eleven years ago come next October."

1370

"Woman," exclaimed a disgruntled husband, "whereas you can see a blonde hair on my coat halfway down the block, you can't see a pair of garage doors six feet away."

1371

Farmer Jones made his clothes last a long time. In fact, he had worn his present suit for ten years. One day when he went to town to sell some potatoes he took a few snifters and got nicely oiled. In this condition he decided to surprise his wife by getting some new clothes. He bought a complete outfit, put the package in the back of his wagon, had a few more drinks and started home.

When he came to a river, he thought he would grasp the opportunity to bathe and change into his new clothes, thereby giving his wife an additional surprise. He peeled off his old garments, threw them down stream, and proceeded to wash himself. When he went to get his new clothes, they weren't there. Somebody had stolen them.

There was only one thing for Farmer Jones to do. Naked as he was, he climbed to the seat of the wagon and made for home.

"Well," he mumbled, "I guess I'll surprise Caroline anyway."

1372

The man with a chip on his shoulder was filling out a questionnaire. Presently he came to the question:

"Who was your mother before she was married?" To which he replied:

"I consider this insulting. I didn't have any mother before she was married."

1373

Bates was waiting for a trolley car when a man came up to him and said, "Can you tell me the time?" Bates didn't pay any attention to him. The man asked the same question again. Bates kept on ignoring him. The stranger finally walked away in disgust. A bystander remarked to Bates:

"What's the idea? Why didn't you tell that man what time it was?"

"I'll tell you," said Bates. "Here I am minding my own business and this fellow comes along and wants to know what time it is. Suppose I tell him. Then we get into conversation, and he says, 'How about a drink?' We have a drink. Then we have another and still another. Pretty soon I say, 'How about going home with me for something to eat?' We go to my house and we rustle up some ham and eggs in the kitchen. Then my daughter comes in, and my daughter's a very pretty girl. So she falls for the fellow, and he falls for her. Sooner or later they get married, and if a guy can't afford a watch, then I don't want him in my family."

1374

Nothing is hopeless if one has the proper attitude. Listen to this:

Two rabbits were pursued by two foxes and took refuge in the hollow stump of a tree. Of course the foxes laid siege.

Time marched on, but the foxes stood by waiting for their prey to emerge.

"What on earth'll we do?" asked the lady rabbit. And her gentleman answered:

"It looks like we'll just have to stay here until we outnumber them."

1375

Joseph Jones is always telling a hard luck story, and this is his latest heart-stabber: "My best friend ran away with my wife, and oh dear me, how I miss him!"

1376

The neatness of the New England housekeeper is a matter of common remark, and husbands in that part of the country are supposed to appreciate their advantages. A bit of dialogue reported by a New York paper shows, however, that there may be another side to the matter.

"Martha, have you wiped the sink dry yet?" asked the farmer, as he made the final preparations for the night.

"Yes, Josiah," she replied. "Why do you ask?"

"Wall, I did want a drink, but I guess I can git along till morning."

1377

As a man and his wife were crossing the street, an automobile slithered around the corner and knocked the woman for a loop.

The car stopped, and the man, very much excited, shouted at the driver:

"You've got to pay me a hundred dollars for injuries to my wife."

"A hundred dollars!" exclaimed the man at the wheel. "Why, your wife isn't even hurt. She's getting up."

"All right, so she's getting up. But you give me the money just the same, and if she isn't hurt, you can have another try at her."

1378

After a good deal of discussion, a farmer and his wife made up their minds to buy the tract of land adjoining theirs. The price was $5,000, and they carried their money to the bank in a milk can.

They turned out the contents on a desk and, while a vice-president looked on, counted the bills and silver. They were somewhat taken back when, after two countings, they found they had only $4900. Then the woman had an idea.

"Hank, you old fool," she said, "you brought the wrong can."

1379

An ambitious woman who sought to rise on the social ladder made her husband's life miserable trying to get him to rent a more expensive apartment.

He came home one evening in a wonderfully good humor.

"Good news, Dearest," he shouted. "We don't have to move. The landlord has just raised the rent."

1380

A Negro woman in a Southern city was never officially married, but she was the proud mother of four children and was a strong supporter of the church. When at last she was on her deathbed, the members of her church wanted to show her some recognition of her long service. And so a committee met, and before the woman died they conferred on her the Honorary Degree of Mrs.

1381

This story is a warning to parents not to stick their necks out. Mother told Tommy that liars do not go to Heaven.

"Did Papa ever tell a lie?" he asked her.

"Well, I suppose he did," she answered.

"Did you and Grandpa and Uncle Tad?" Tommy continued.

Mother had to admit that they all probably had once or twice.

"Gosh," Tommy exclaimed, "it must be awful lonesome in Heaven with nobody there except God and George Washington."

1382

"Mother, where were you born?" asked Bobby.

"In Massachusetts, my dear."

"Where was Dad born?"

"In Connecticut, Bobby."

"Where was sister born?"

"In New York."

"Where was I born?"

"In California, my son."

"Gee, how'd we all get together?"

1383

Papa Doolittle was in a hurry to leave for the office, so the grace that he said before breakfast was greatly curtailed.

"That was a short prayer," said 5-year-old Winnie.

"That," observed Mrs. Doolittle, "was a blessing."

1384

A motorist was arrested and brought before the magistrate who said:

"The traffic officer says you got nasty with him."

"Honest, your Honor, I didn't mean it," protested the car driver. "The fellow talked to me like my wife does, and I forgot myself and said, 'Yes, dear.' "

1385

The golfing judge said to the prisoner, "I'm not fining you for hitting your wife with a club; it's for using the wrong club."

1387

Whilst Adam slept, Eve from his side arose:
Strange his first sleep should be his last repose.

Anon. "The Consequences"

1388

A motor-car salesman was high-pressuring the customer. He rose to the heights when he said:

"Yes, sir, this car is absolutely the very last word."

"Well," the customer said, "if it's the last word, my wife will love it. Wrap it up and send it home."

1389

The Life of the Party told this one at a wedding breakfast recently. Mr. Jones strolled into the Blank Club one day and saw the usually dapper young Smith sitting dejectedly in a chair nursing a black eye.

"How come you have that lovely shiner?" Jones asked.

"I got it for kissing the bride after a wedding ceremony," said Smith.

"What's wrong about that? Isn't it the usual custom?" Jones inquired.

Smith stirred uneasily and replied:

"Quite! The point is that this was three years after the ceremony."

1390

The following verses are based on what the entomologists tell us about the female praying mantis—that, after the nuptial rapture, she eats her mate.

PRAYER FOR A HUSBAND

What does the praying mantis say
   To God when she gets on her knees to pray?
I've listened, and so I will spill the beans
   As to just what her prayerful attitude means:

"O Lord, I hereby supplicate,
  Do Thou send me another mate
Before the setting of the sun,
  And, Lord, let him be a digestible one."

Ned Allen

1391

Those who are curious as to the ritual observed in the old-fashioned Mormon marriage may be sure that the following is wholly acurate, for the man who told it swore to it on a stack of wheatcakes:

Said the preacher to the groom, "Do you take these women to be your lawfully wedded wives?"

And the groom answered, "I do."

Then the preacher turned to the brides and asked, "And do you take this man to be your lawfully wedded husband?"

Several voices responded in a weak tremolo, "We do."

"Hey," said the preacher, "some of you girls there in the back will have to speak louder if you want to be included in this.'"

1392

Not a great while after they were married, Bill Jones and his wife moved into a new apartment. Bill took a day off, and the two worked hard to get their furniture to rights. When he went to the office the next day, the new home was far from being settled. In the middle of the morning Bill received an agonized telephone call from his wife.

"Billy dear, you'll have to come home immediately. I'm in awful trouble. I must have got the wires crossed or something, because the radio is all covered with frost and the refrigerator is playing the Poet and Peasant Overture."

1393

George Ade had always been a sincere bachelor. One afternoon he was sitting with the seven-year-old daughter of a friend. She was quietly reading a tale by Hans Christian Andersen when she stopped and said:

"Mr. Ade, does m-i-r-a-g-e spell marriage?"

"Yes, my dear," said Ade.

1394

Mothers-in-law are not so bad after all; in fact, most of them are fair to meddling.

1395

If, as an authority has said, a bride wears white as a symbol of happiness and purity and joy, just why the heck does the groom wear black?

1396

Common sense, if applied, would prevent a great many divorces; but, on the other hand, it would prevent a great many marriages.

1397

My darling wife was always glum,
So I drowned her in a cask of rum,
And thus made sure that she would stay
In better spirits night and day.

1398

Bachelor: A man who thinks that the only thoroughly justified marriage was the one that produced him.

Harlan Miller

1399

This story is told about Abe Lincoln's father Thomas.

Mrs. Sally Lincoln said: "Thomas, we have lived together many years now and you have never told me whom you like best, your first wife or me." Thomas chuckled and replied, "Sarah, you remind me of old John Hardin down in Kentucky who had a fine looking pair of horses. A neighbor asked him which horse he liked best and John says, 'I can't tell; one of them kicks and the other bites and I don't know which is wust.' "

1400

Ambrose Bierce calls *bigamy* "a mistake in taste for which the wisdom of the future will adjudge a punishment called trigamy."

1401

Alimony: A situation that arises when two people make a mistake and one of them continues to pay for it.

1402

Doctor Samuel Johnson, who was good at definitions, called a second marriage, "the triumph of hope over experience."

1403

The name of Joseph H. Choate, American lawyer and diplomat, is revered as much for his urbane humor as for his legal astuteness.

On one occasion he was the guest of honor at a dinner of the Pilgrim Society, and was asked to respond to the toast, "The Pilgrim Fathers."

He paid a stirring tribute to the hardihood and fortitude of the Pilgrim fathers in enduring the rigors of the New England winters, the privations of the life they led, the dangers of marauding Indians, and so on. Then he stopped.

"But let us give a thought," he added impressively, "to the Pilgrim mothers. For they not only had to endure everything that the Pilgrim fathers endured, but, mark this, they had to endure the Pilgrim fathers."

1405

A lot of people say definitely that they will never marry, but the building of schoolhouses goes on just the same.

1406

The most tactful husband on earth is the one who always remembers his wife's birthday but never can remember which one it is.

1407

Shortly after former Prime Minister Menzies of Australia was sworn into office, the representatives of the press interviewed him. One reporter from the radical press said brusquely, "I presume, Mr. Prime Minister, that you will consult the powerful interests that control you when you begin choosing your cabinet?"

To which the Prime Minister replied, curtly, "Young man, keep my wife's name out of this."

1408

The man said his wife had a lot of liniment talk for him because she was always rubbing it in.

1409

When the late John Barrymore's yacht *Infanta* was launched, his wife of the moment was selected to christen it. The actor handed her a large bottle of champagne and told her to break it over the bow.

"I'm afraid I can't do it," she said; "it's too heavy."

"Oh yes you can," said John; "just make believe the yacht is me."

In telling about it later, Barrymore chuckled as he said:

"She did fine; she damn near wrecked the boat."

1410

At the silver wedding anniversary of a Washington diplomat one of the guests was a Frenchman who had recently come to this country and did not understand the significance of the occasion. One of the other guests tried to explain.

"You see, the couple have lived together for twenty-five years without separation."

"I see," said the Frenchman with enthusiasm. "And now he marries her."

1411

The man who boasts that he runs things in his house refers, very likely, to the lawn mower, vacuum sweeper, washing machine, baby carriage, the errands and occasionally the motor-car.

1412

Mrs. Billings was inclined to be talkative after she and her husband had gone to bed. Then came a few minutes' silence, during which time Mr. B. dozed. Suddenly the missus exclaimed:

"John, I'm sure I heard a mouse squeak." And John replied sleepily:

"Well, I suppose I'll have to get up and oil it."

1413

Mrs. Smith said that she could always tell when her husband was lying. If his lips were moving, he was.

1414

Maybe So, Maybe Not Department: A word to the wife is sufficient.

1415

Then there was the Scotchman who invited only married people to his wedding, figuring that the presents would all be clear profit.

1416

Divorced are Mr.
And Mrs. Howell;
He wiped the car
With her best guest towel.

1417

"How did you meet your wife?" asked one man of another.

"Oh," was the reply, "we got in a revolving door and started going around together."

1418

One of the more serious type of fathers was having a heart-to-heart talk with his son. Among other things he said:

"My boy, until I met your mother, I never kissed a girl. Will you be able to say the same thing to your son?" And the boy answered:

"Yes, Dad, but not with such a straight face."

1419

Mr. Jones's only comment when he saw the painting of Mona Lisa was: "Exactly the way my wife looks when she thinks I am lying."

1420

A bride and groom were starting off on a Caribbean cruise. The groom was very solicitous for his new wife's comfort, so he went to the ship's captain and said:

"My wife is very susceptible to seasickness. Can you tell her what to do in case of an attack?"

"That's hardly necessary," the captain replied politely; "she'll do it."

1421

A mother handed her younger son a suit of clothes saying:

"Take these, Johnny; your brother cannot wear them any longer."

"All right," said Johnny, who had become weary of wearing hand-me-downs; "but will I have to marry his widow when he dies?"

1422

Three girls were discussing the recent marriage of one of their highstepping friends. One of them said:

"It's reported that before she accepted him she came clean with a full confession of every one of her indiscretions."

"What touching confidence!" another exclaimed.

"What needless trouble!" still another added.

"What a *memory!*" the first concluded.

1423

Mr. and Mrs. Smith had separated. The Missis heard that her husband was going to advertise the fact in the newspaper and she was ready for him. That is why the following two notices happened to appear in the same column:

My wife Mary having left my bed and board, I will not be responsible for any of her debts. Henry Smith.

Directly following was the come-back:

Very hard bed, very little board, awfully bored. Mary Smith.

1424

A young fellow who had recently been married had not yet learned all the ropes of matrimony. He consulted a married friend:

"I simply don't know what to call my mother-in-law. Since my own mother is living, it doesn't seem right to call my wife's mother 'Mother.' "

"That's simple," his friend said; "I had the same problem. The first year I addressed her as 'Say,' and after that I called her Granny."

1425

Bobby was very proud of his father on account of his bravery. One day they were having a conference about one thing and another, and the boy asked:

"Dad, are you afraid of bugs?"

"No indeed, my son."

"Are you afraid of snakes?"

"Of course not."

"Aren't you even afraid of thunder and lightning?"

"Certainly not."

"Gee, Dad, aren't you afraid of anything in the whole world except Mama?"

1426

They were on their honeymoon trip, and the train went through a very dark tunnel. When it emerged the young man said:

"Darling, if I'd known that tunnel was so long, I would have given you a kiss."

"Goodness!" the girl answered. "Wasn't that you?"

1427

King George V and the Princess Victoria were in the habit of having an informal chat over the telephone at the same hour each morning. They spoke informally, and often joked about this and that. One morning the phone rang at the usual time, and the Princess picked up the receiver and said, "Hello, you old fool."

"I beg your pardon," interrupted the operator, "but His Majesty is not yet on the line."

1428

A woman was listening to her maid's matrimonial troubles, and said: "What was the difficulty; December wedded to May?"

"No'm," the maid replied; "it was Labor Day wedded to the Day of Rest."

1429

A Scot telegraphed a proposal of marriage to a girl who lived in the back country. He waited all day around the office for his reply. Finally at night came an affirmative reply. The clerk who delivered the message said to him:

"If I were you I would think twice before marrying a girl who kept me waiting so long for an answer."

"That's all right," the Scotchman replied; "the girl for me is the girl who waits until the night rates go on."

1430

Little Lucy's favorite uncle was to be married on the following Tuesday, and she was asking a great many questions about the wedding. Finally she said:

"Mother, is it true that the last three days they give them anything they want to eat?"

1431

Mr. J. Wintringham Jones was away from home for a few days. A courteous hotel clerk handed him a copy of his local paper, and Mr. Jones began to read it. What was his amazement to find on the obituary page a notice of his own death.

He rushed for the telephone and made a long-distance call to his wife.

"Darling," he said excitedly, "have you seen the notice of my death in the newspaper?"

"Yes, sweetheart," came the answer; "where are you calling from?"

1432

Two women were married to musicians. The one, a bride of a year, was pushing a baby carriage in which were three fine babies —triplets, all girls. The other woman had been in the bonds of matrimony only a couple of weeks.

"What beautiful children!" exclaimed the newlywed.

"Yes," replied the proud mother; "let me tell you the funniest coincidence. At our wedding supper the boys who played with my husband in the orchestra serenaded him, and they played 'Three Little Maids' from *The Mikado*. Isn't that funny?"

At this the other bride turned pale. "Mercy!" she gasped. "At our wedding supper Tom's friends serenaded him too, and they sang the Sextet from *Lucia.*"

1433

As the girls sat down for their weekly game of bridge, one of them said:

"I was feeling big hearted this morning, and I gave a bum five dollars."

"What did your husband say about *that?*" her partner asked.

"He said 'Thanks.' "

1434

Kid Gregory had spent his whole life on a remote cattle ranch where there were no women. When he was about twenty he decided to go to the nearest town to see the sights. It was all very new to him, including the pretty waitress in the hotel dining room. He fell for her like a ton of bricks, paid her ardent court, won her hand, and took her back to the ranch.

In a week he reappeared in town. He was alone. One of the men who knew him said:

"How are you and your wife making out, Kid?"

"Had some hard luck, Pardner," the Kid replied. "Three days ago she went to the well to get some water, slipped on a rock and broke her leg. So I had to shoot her."

1435

Of course the man didn't know too much about it, for he was a crusty old bachelor. A young person said to him:

"Do you believe it's unlucky to postpone a wedding?"

"No," he replied definitely; "not if you keep on doing it."

1436

Don't get married unless you want to start raising a family, and don't start raising a family unless you want to get married.

R. A. Lyman

1437

Take it from Socrates: By all means marry. If you get a good wife, you will become very happy; if you get a bad one, you will become a philosopher—and that is good for every man.

1438

The trouble with marriage is that, while every woman is at heart a mother, every man is at heart a bachelor.

E. V. Lucas

1439

The man who enters his wife's dressing-room is either a philosopher or a fool.

Balzac

1440

Then there was the young woman who rushed into police headquarters one day and demanded of an officer:

"Where do I go to apologize for shooting my husband?"

1441

Jones made a date to meet his wife at the corner of 36th Street and Madison Avenue, New York, at six o'clock. They were going to a nearby restaurant for dinner. He arrived on time. Then it began to rain, and he waited in a doorway for her to show up. After an hour, during which there was no letup in the rain, he got disgusted and went home. After a while his wife arrived at their apartment and found her husband fit to be lassoed.

"Where in Tophet were you?" he exploded.

"Oh," she said: "I was going to tell you. There wasn't any subway station at 36th Street, so I got off twice at 18th Street."

1442

Here is the ideally mated pair: the wife drives from the back seat and the husband cooks from the dining-room table.

1443

Men marry because they are tired; women because they are curious: both are disappointed.

Oscar Wilde

1444

Bobby was curled up in a chair, munching an apple, making a pretext of studying his history lesson.

"Who was it, Pop, that said we haven't started to fight yet?"

"A bride and groom who are still on their honeymoon, I guess, Bobby," mumbled his father.

1445

A bride of two years was lunching at the home of a newlywed.

"How do you like the potato salad?" asked the little bride.

"It's delicious, dearie. Did you buy it yourself?"

1446

She insisted upon taking every dress she owned with her for the week-end visit. Her husband, staggering under the load of luggage as they entered the station, remarked, "I wish that we'd brought the piano."

"Don't be funny," came the icy reply.

"I'm not trying to be funny," he explained. "I left the tickets on it."

1447

A bachelor is a man who thinks before he acts, and then doesn't act.

1448

Two Irishmen were speaking of their families. One was boasting of his seven sons, saying that they had never caused him a moment's trouble:

"Yes, indade," he said, "they are just about the finest boys in the world. An' would ye believe it, I niver laid violent hands on any one of them except in self-defense."

1449

In all thy humors, whether grave or mellow,
Thou'rt such a touchy, testy, pleasant fellow,
Hast so much wit and mirth and spleen about thee,
There is no living with thee, nor without thee.

Addison

1450

The days just prior to marriage are like a snappy introduction to a tedious book.

Wilson Mizner

1451

The legend that "matrimony" is a lottery has almost ruined the lottery business.

1452

A strong-minded woman took her meek little husband to a mountain resort. For several days he "Yes, my dear-ed" her. Then one morning, out of a clear sky, she said:

"This mountain air disagrees with me."

"Why, darling," he protested mildly; "I don't see how it would dare."

1453

The spinster laughed at anyone who suggested that it was too bad she did not have a husband.

"I have a dog that growls, a parrot that swears, a fireplace that smokes, and a cat that stays out all night. Why should I want a husband?"

1454

"Is it true, Miss Simpkins, that you are going to be married soon?" asked a well meaning friend.

"Well, no, it isn't. But I am very grateful for the rumor."

1455

A house is no home unless it contains food and fire for the mind as well as for the body.

Margaret Fuller

1456

A Negro explained how the weekly lodge meeting happened to be postponed. Said he:

"Well, suh, the Grand, Invincible, All-Powerful, Unconquerable, Most Supreme Potentate got the stuffin' knocked out of him by his wife."

1457

"Will you marry me, darling?" he begged.

The sweet young thing looked meltingly into his eyes and said, "First, I want to ask you a question."

"I'm yours to command," he answered.

"Do you drink anything?" shewhispered, cuddling her hand in his.

"Anything," he answered fervently.

1458

The way the quarrel began was this: Claude proposed again to Heloise. It seems rather stupid for her to object to his pertinacity, but one can't really blame the girl for being peeved, because only the night before, she had accepted him.

1459

A friend of ours explained why he called his wife his better half.

"You see," he said, "if she asks me for money, I'd better have some."

1460

"But my dear," protested the harassed husband, "you've been talking for half an hour, and I haven't said a word."

"No," snapped the wife, "you haven't said anything, but you've been listening in a most annoying manner, and I'm not going to stand for it."

1461

"Iisn't it time the baby said 'Daddy'?" asked the proud father.

"Maybe," explained the young mother, "but I've decided not to tell him who you are until he gets stronger."

1462

Two women were discussing their husbands' mechanical ability. One of them said:

"My husband can take a watch apart in the dark and then reassemble it without turning on the light. And what is more, it will run."

Said the other:

"My husband is pretty good too. He took our cuckoo clock apart and then put it together again so that now the cuckoo backs out of its nest and asks for the time."

1463

A man and his wife, both pompous looking and rather stuffy, entered the room. An acquaintance of the gentleman greeted him, and Mr. Pompous said:

"Allow me to present my wife." Whereat the newcomer said:

"No thanks; I have one already."

1464

A certain young couple had just returned from their honeymoon trip and spent their first night in the new home.

At 7.30 hubby rose and went downstairs to start the coffee. To his amazement, he found a horse in the kitchen.

"Darling, darling," he bellowed up the stairs, "there's a horse in the kitchen."

And from above there came a sleepy voice that said:

"Well, sweetheart, I always warned you I was untidy."

1465

An old fellow drove into Portland and looked up the Bureau of Missing Persons. He reported that his wife had been missing for 15 years. The Bureau clerk was shocked.

"You're just reporting it now? You want her back after all that time?" he asked.

The man nodded and explained: "I just got lonesome."

1466

A colored parson had just married a young couple, and the bridegroom asked him the price of the service.

"You can pay me whatever it is worth to you, my good man," he answered.

The young man looked long and silently at his bride. Then, he slowly rolled his eyes up to heaven, and said, "Lawd, suh, you has done ruined me for life; you has, for sure."

1467

A New England farmer, resting after his day's work, looked at his tired wife and said, "When I think of what you've meant to me for all these years, sometimes it's more than I can stand not to tell you."

1468

As they were being driven home from the dinner party, Mrs. Peck was telling her husband of his many shortcomings. She reminded him of the haircut he had promised to get, pointed out a spot on his shirt-front, told him he had drunk too many cocktails, and so on.

Mr. Peck listened in dejected silence.

"Finally," Mrs. Peck said, "you paid entirely too much attention to that silly young blonde."

The chauffeur pulled up in front of the Peck mansion and opened the door of the car. Mr. Peck got out first and turned to help his wife. She made a misstep. As Mr. Peck saved her from falling, he said sweetly:

"Be careful, Sweetheart, or you'll break your goddam neck."

1469

In consulting an undertaker for the interment of her late husband, the widow was asked:

"Do you wish to have the body cremated or buried?"

"Well, it's this way," the woman replied; "he was the laziest man that ever drew the breath of life, so I've decided to have him cremated and the ashes put in an hour glass."

1470

Children at school learn of the effect that the moon has on the tide. A little later in life they find out that it has fully as great an effect on the untied.

1471

Loyalty sometimes proves embarrassing. The story is told of a husband who was unusually late in coming home. His wife in alarm wired to five of his special friends, "Jack not home. Is he spending night with you?"

Her husband arrived home shortly afterwards, and was followed by five telegrams all saying, "Yes."

1472

The following letter appeared in an "Advice to the Lovesick" column of a metropolitan newspaper:

"Every time I sit in my husband's lap, he starts dictating letters. Should I get a divorce?"

1473

After the barber's wife had waited a solid hour for her husband in front of a movie house, the man appeared. It's a bit of an understatement to say that the woman was not entirely calm.

"Where have you been, Lug?" she inquired coldly.

"Well, I'll tell you, Honey," he answered. "I was shaving, and I talked myself into a shampoo and a massage."

1474

A couple of ham actors out of a job were overheard at the corner of 44th Street and Broadway in a discussion of their wives. It went this way:

"What kind of a girl did you marry?"

"An angel—nothing less."

"Gracious, but you're a lucky guy. Mine's still living."

1475

Before the days of sulfa drugs the widely advertised patent medicines seemed to be ample cure for almost everything. At any rate, the testimonials proved something. Here is a specimen:

"A month ago I was so tired and run down that I was unable to spank the baby. After taking four bottles of your marvelous vegetable compound I can now thrash my husband in addition to all my other housework. God bless you!"

1476

During the time in World War II when the telegraph companies would not accept congratulatory telegrams, there was a certain Mr. Smart who received news from two young couples. He tried to wire congratulations. No soap. Then he started his think-tank bubbling. The first couple had become the parents of a bouncing boy, so he wired:

"Glad to hear that you have declared a dividend."

The other couple had just been married, so Smart got by with: "Merger should be very productive."

1477

The woman was fully six feet tall and weighed around two hundred pounds. The man was under five feet and thin to the point of emaciation. The woman haled him before the justice of the peace and demanded that he marry her or go to jail.

"Did you promise to marry this woman?" the justice asked.

"I did," was the surly reply.

The justice turned to the woman and said: "Are you determined to marry this man?"

"I am!" she assured him, beyond question.

"Join hands," the justice said. When they had done so, he raised his own right hand and spoke solemnly:

"I pronounce you twain woman and husband."

1478

Two friends collided on the street corner.

"What are you doing with that rice?" asked one.

"I bought it by mistake," explained the other.

"Most people go shopping on purpose."

"Yes, but this was funny. I saw a man coming down the street with a shotgun, so I followed him."

"A shotgun? And then?"

"I thought there was going to be a wedding."

"And you stopped and got the rice?"

"Yes, but the joke was on me. It turned out to be just a bank robbery."

1479

The astounded husband greeted his wife, who had just presented him with twins:

"But—but honey, won't you ever get over the habit of exaggerating?"

1480

It was Leap Year, and the man really should have been careful. He was describing the church he attended. He said it was beautiful in every way, and then he added:

"But you should see the altar."

To which the girl quickly answered:

"Lead me to it."

1481

Once upon a time there was a girl who was so frugal that she went without her honeymoon so's her husband could save his money for her alimony.

1482

"I've decided on a name for the baby," said the expectant mother. "I shall call her Minerva."

The young husband didn't care very much for her selection, but being a tactful fellow, was far too wise to object verbally.

"Fine," he agreed. "That's a beautiful name. The first girl I ever loved was called Minerva, and the name revives happy memories."

There was a brief pause, then: "We'll call her Lucy Jane, after my mother," said the young wife firmly.

1483

"Dad, a man's wife is his better half, isn't she?" asked son George.

"They say so."

"Then if a man marries twice, there isn't anything left of him, is there?"

"Correct, my boy."

1484

"Pop," said Tommy, "we learned at school today that the animals have a new fur every winter."

"Hush, boy," said his parent, "your mother is in the next room."

1485

A man well known for his cynicism met a friend of his in a cocktail lounge one day with a woman old enough to be his mother.

Nodding, he started to pass by, but the man stopped him and said:

"Let me introduce you to my wife."

After the introduction was acknowledged, the cynic whispered in his friend's ear:

"Great Scott, man, how could you have married such an old bird? She has a glass eye, chemical blonde hair, and false teeth."

"Speak up, old fellow," the husband replied; "she's deaf too."

1486

"How did you cure your husband of staying so late at the club?"

"When he came in late I called out, 'Is that you, Bert, darling?' My husband's name is Percy."

1487

"Are they a well mated couple?"

"Perfectly; he snores and she's deaf."

1488

"Aren't statistics wonderful?" observed the man of the house. "They say the average woman has a vocabulary of only 500 words."

"What utter nonsense," the wife commented.

"Does seem like a small stock," agreed the man. "But think of the turnover!"

1489

"Darling, I've set my heart on a Rolls Royce," she purred.

"No kidding! Well, that's the only part of your anatomy that'll ever set on one," he assured her.

1490

The bride was all hot and bothered.

"I wish you would get out of the kitchen, Richard, when I'm cooking," she cried. "See what you have done—knocked the cook-book on the floor and lost my page. Now I haven't the faintest idea what I was cooking."

1491

"You mean to tell me you were not at your own daughter's wedding? Where in heaven's name were you?"

"I was looking for a job for the groom."

1492

"My wife doesn't understand me; does yours, Bill?"

"I don't know, John. I've never heard her even mention your name."

1493

"What's the matter, Harvey?" asked his wife.

"Matter enough! My razor is as dull as a hoe. It won't cut at all."

"Nonsense! Your beard can't be tougher than our linoleum."

Section 17

MEDICINE, ILLNESS AND HEALTH

1500

The family doctor had brought the boy into the world and had followed his career with great interest. The boy grew up, went to medical school, and was graduated. When he was ready to hang out his shingle he announced to the old physician that he was going to be a specialist—a nose specialist. He explained that the ear and mouth were too large a subject to be covered by one man.

The aged general practitioner seemed to be awed by the young man's learning. He nodded his head. Then he asked:

"Which nostril are you specializing in?"

1501

Mrs. Jones consulted the doctor about her husband's talking in his sleep. The doctor said:

"I can give him something to stop that."

"Oh no, Doctor," Mrs. Jones objected; "what I want is something to make him talk distinctly."

1502

Two psychiatrists met on the street, and one said to the other: "You're fine; how am I?"

1503

The doctor advised having little Mary's tonsils out. Her mother promised her that if she would be a brave little girl and go to the hospital and have Doctor Haven remove them, she should have the finest kitten to be found.

As Mary was coming out from the effects of the anesthetic, the nurse heard her mumbling, and stooping, heard her say:

"It's a bum way to get a cat."

1504

The doctor told his patient that he was coughing more easily.

"And why not?" the patient exclaimed. "Haven't I been practicing all night?"

1505

A woman and her small son were looking into a dentist's showcase.

The boy pointed and said:

"If I had to wear false teeth, Mom, I'd take that pair."

"Johnny, hush your mouth," his mother replied; "how often have I told you not to pick your teeth in public?"

1506

"How is your husband today?" the doctor asked Mrs. Smith. "Did you give him the sleeping powder?"

"Oh yes," she answered. "You told me to give him as much as I could get on a nickel, but I couldn't find one so I used five pennies instead. He's been sleeping like a log ever since."

1507

The patient was on the road to recovery and seemed grateful to the doctor. He said:

"Doc, I know I'm going to get better, but after all our years of close personal friendship I couldn't think of offering you money. I'll tell you what I'll do; I'll remember you in my will."

"That's mighty handsome of you, old pal," said the doctor as he started to leave. Then he hesitated and said, "By the way, let me see that prescription again. There's a little correction I want to make."

1508

After an operation for appendicitis, young Flossy Jones had not been long out of the ether when she asked a question:

"Oh Doctor Smith, will my scar show?"

"No, Miss Jones," the doctor reassured; "not if you're careful."

1509

In a London medical college one of the faculty wrote the following notice on the blackboard in his classroom:

"Professor Jenkins proudly announces to his students that he has just been appointed honorary physician to His Majesty, King George VI."

He modestly left the classroom after that, but when he returned later he found a line written below his notice:

"God save the King."

1510

For those who have wondered how medical fees are established, the following may give a ray of enlightenment.

A well known specialist lectured confidentially to a class of medical students on the subject of professional charges.

"The highest fees," he said, "are charged by the specialist. For instance, I charge twenty-five dollars for a call at a home, ten dollars for consultation at my office, and five dollars for advice over the telephone."

Then one of the boys in the back of the room piped up:

"Say, Doc, how much do you charge for passing a man on the street?"

1511

Then there was the doctor who had such a large and lucrative practice that when a patient had nothing the matter with him, he told him so.

1512

An old doctor had a son who was just hanging out his shingle.

"Can you tell me," the son asked his father, "some rules for success?"

"Yes," the father replied; "always write your prescriptions so they can't read 'em, and your bills so they can."

1513

The old medico was advising the young doctor just embarked on his professional career. He began:

"It isn't too easy for the young physician to get a good start."

"I know that," the young man replied, "but I'm raising a set of whiskers."

"That's a good beginning," said the veteran. "It will help a lot; and I'll lend you some of my magazines for 1899 to put on the table in your waiting room."

1514

A doctor was at one time serving as interne in one of the Philadelphia hospitals as well as holding his own with a coterie of rather gay friends. On a certain morning the physician awoke to find that he had sadly overslept. Sleepily donning his clothes, he hastened to the hospital and soon a stalwart young Irishman claimed his attention.

"Well, my man, what seems to be the trouble this morning?" inquired the doctor, concealing a yawn and taking the patient by the hand to examine his pulse.

"Faith, sor, it's all in me breathin', doctor. I can't get me breath at all, at all."

"Your pulse is normal, Pat, but let me examine the lung action a moment," replied the doctor, kneeling beside the bed and laying his head on the Irishman's chest. "Now let me hear you talk," he continued, closing his eyes and listening for sounds of pulmonary congestion.

A moment of silence.

"What will I be sayin', doctor," finally asked the patient.

"Oh, say anything. Count one, two, three and up," murmured the physician drowsily.

"Wan, two, three, fure, five, six."

When the doctor opened his eyes, Pat was continuing weakly, "Tin hundred an' sixty-nine, tin hundred an' sivinty, tin hundred an' sivinity-wan."

1515

There was a new nurse in the Army hospital, and the doctor was questioning her about a handsome young soldier patient.

"Have you kept a chart on this man's progress?" he asked.

"No," she replied, with just the hint of a blush, "but you can read my diary if you want to."

1516

An eminent psychiatrist finally got to the bottom of his subject's tendency toward deception. It seems that her father used to try to sing her to sleep when she was a baby. The father couldn't sing, and the baby began pretending she was asleep.

1517

One day a woman entered a doctor's office and said:

"Doctor, I want a little wart removed."

The doctor, who knew who she was and had seen her husband, hardly looked up as he replied:

"Madam, you're in the wrong office; the divorce lawyer is next door."

1518

The man determined to consult a doctor.

"I've been misbehaving, Doc, and my conscience is troubling me," he complained.

"I see, and since I'm a psychiatrist, you want something to

strengthen your will power?" agreed the doctor, studying his patient.

"No, something to weaken my conscience, I would suggest," said the man.

1519

By any standard whatever, Pat Casey was as homely as they came. One day a friend introduced him to a plastic surgeon, and in the course of conversation, the doctor convinced Pat that he would be helped in many ways if his face could be improved.

"And, Mr. Casey," he said, "with plastic surgery I could make you the handsomest man in this country."

This sounded like good sense to Pat, so he decided to go through with it. Just before the operation the surgeon asked him:

"Would you like to have me change your face entirely?"

"I would not," Pat replied; "I want people to know who it is that's so handsome."

1520

Lay this one to your favorite doctor. He was invited to a party, and when the refreshments were passed, his hostess asked:

"Do you like lobster salad, Doctor?"

"Not particularly," he replied, "but I'm grateful to it."

1521

"Doc," exclaimed a patient to his physician, "I've got a toothache and an earache at the same time, and I'll bet a million dollars there can be no greater misery on earth."

"Not so fast," the doctor replied; "how about rheumatism and St. Vitus dance?"

1522

Homely remedies have at times been extremely effective, and it sort of burns the doctors up. They want to use penicillin or sulfanilimide. One of them, however, had to listen in on a story about an English sailor who broke his leg by falling from a mast. The teller of the story said that he dressed it with nothing but tar and oakum and that within three days he was able to walk just as well as before the accident.

When he heard this, the doctor sneered. "Absolutely impossible," he exclaimed.

Whereupon the narrator cleared his throat and said:

"Oh, I forgot to mention that it was a wooden leg."

1523

The cleaning woman was tidying up the doctor's office.

"I spect you get paid a lot of money for tending that mighty rich Jameson feller," she observed, giving the table an extra polish.

"Why, yes," replied the doctor, looking up at her. "I get amply paid. Why do you ask?"

"I don't know, but I hope you won't forget that it was my Freddy what threw the stone that hit him."

1524

A patient called his dentist for an appointment.

"I'm very sorry," said the dentist, "But I can't take care of you today. I have eighteen cavities to fill."

Then the young Doc hung up the phone, picked up his golf bag and hat, and left his office.

1525

A worried-looking man consulted a doctor about his habit of talking to himself. Being the old-time, comfortable family-doctor type, the physician said:

"Lots of people do that. There's absolutely nothing to worry about."

"But," protested the patient, "I'm such an infernal bore."

1526

Medicine, the only profession that labors incessantly to destroy the reason for its existence.

Lord Bryce

1527

Dr. Jones slipped in the well.
He died without a moan.
He should have tended to the sick
And let the well alone.

1528

If you desire to paralyze
Your enemy, don't "damn his eyes";
From futile blasphemy desist;
Send him to Blank the oculist.

Walter Leaf, from "Nicarchus"

1529

Grandma had diabetes. Her family had to watch her very carefully to see that she didn't eat the things that disagreed with her. But she liked them just the same, and she ate them. Consequently once in a while she would have to go to bed. One time when she jumped over the traces she had to be sent to the hospital. The hospital was crowded, so Grandma had to be put in the maternity ward. After a day or so, her granddaughter, age seven, went to visit her. In asking for "Grannie" at the desk, she said, "I want to see my grandma, Mrs. Bristol. She's in the maternity ward. She's been cheating again."

1530

Over the doctor's telephone came a call from a man who said that his small son had swallowed his fountain pen. The doctor said:

"I'll come at once. What are you doing in the meantime?"

"I'm using a pencil," the man answered.

1531

A fat man didn't feel right, so he went to his doctor, who lectured him on the value of exercise.

"Exercise," the doctor said, "will kill all germs."

"Okay, Doc," the man replied, "but how can I get the germs to exercise?"

1532

Getting things free is a favorite thought with nearly everybody, including the two small boys who were overheard discussing the subject. Said one of them:

"My father is a doctor, so I can be sick for nothing."

The other kid was not to be outdone, and he replied:

"My dad's a minister, so I can be good for nothing."

1533

A perfectly healthy woman called often to ask the doctor about her heart. One day he said to her, "You need not worry. Your heart will last as long as you live." And she left the doctor's office in high spirits.

1534

If a man still has his appendix and his tonsils, the chances are that he is a doctor.

1535

The doctor drove up to the automobile repair shop with a flat tire, and the man in charge recognized him as the physician he had consulted the day before. When the car stopped, he said:

"Doctor, I diagnose this case as flatulency of the periphery. My fee is five dollars for the advice and fifty cents if you wish it treated."

1536

A girl from one of the mountain districts of Georgia made a trip to Atlanta to have her teeth filled.

After drilling a tooth the dentist used compressed air to blow out the cavity. The girl jumped and let out a yelp.

"Do you feel that air?" the dentist inquired.

"That air what?" asked the girl.

1537

From the wife of one of his patients a doctor inquired:

"Has your husband followed my prescription—a pill before each meal and a drink of whiskey after?"

"Pretty well, Doctor," she replied. "He may be a few tablets behind, but he's months ahead on the whiskey."

1538

A man called at a doctor's office and the door was opened by a colored maid.

"Is the doctor in?" the man asked.

"No suh," the maid answered.

"Will he be in soon?" the man continued.

"Prob'ly not," said the maid; "he went out on an eternity case."

1539

At three o'clock in the morning the doctor was called out of bed by the loud ringing of the telephone bell.

"What is it?" he asked.

"Oh Doctor," said a woman's wailing voice, "I can't sleep."

"Well, it's going to be all right now," answered the doctor. "Just hold the wire for a minute or two and I'll sing you a lullaby."

1540

A precise little man had been consulting his physician. "You see," he said optimistically, "I want to live to be a hundred. Just what do you think my chances are?"

"How old were you on your last birthday?" the doctor asked.

"Just fifty," the patient replied.

"Do you smoke, drink or—"

"No indeed!" the man exclaimed in a shocked tone of voice.

"Then," the doctor said, "why the heck should you want to live another half-century!"

1541

Doctor MacGregor's boy and a son of one of the neighbors were playing, without permission, in the doctor's office.

Suddenly, with a dramatic gesture, Dickie MacGregor flung open a door and showed up a human skeleton. The young visitor was horrified. Said Dickie:

"Pop's awful proud of that skeleton."

"Why?" asked the other lad.

"I don't really know," was the answer; "maybe it was his first patient."

1542

Here's to the doctor and dentist—
  Neither one nor the other's a faker.
But the doctor's work fills six feet of ground,
  While the dentist's fills only an acher.

1543

A woman was being psychoanalyzed by a famous specialist. She explained that her family thought there was something the matter with her simply because she liked buckwheat cakes.

"I can't see anything wrong with liking buckwheat cakes," the doctor said; "I like them myself."

His patient was delighted.

"Oh, goody," she said. "You must come over some day. I have seven trunkfuls."

1544

Back in the old days before the radio took over the medicine show business, there was a quack who peddled an elixir of life. His line was very convincing:

"Have a look at me, my friends; I am all of 300 years old. How do I do it? Why it's the simplest thing on earth. I take this elixir every day, and it keeps me hale and hearty."

"Can he really be as old as that?" a skeptical woman asked the peddler's young assistant.

"You kin search me," the youth replied; "I've only been working for him a hundred years."

1545

At the home of Dr. Robert A. Millikan, the famous physicist, the telephone rang and the maid answered the telephone. Said she: "Yes, this is the residence of Dr. Millikan, but he ain't the kind of doctor that does anybody any good."

1546

"I've had nearly all the childhood diseases," said the chatty young man, "but the only time I've been troubled by diphtheria has been when I've tried to spell it."

1547

He had been complaining about his sinus trouble.

"What do you take for it?" his friend asked.

"Just make me an offer," the sufferer answered.

1548

A steamship passenger was suffering acutely from seasickness, and the steward tried to console him.

"Don't despair, sir," he said. "No one ever died of seasickness."

"Don't tell me that," the sick man groaned. "It's only the hope of dying that is keeping me alive."

1549

If the palm of your hand itches, you're going to get something; if your head itches, you've got it.

1550

A story is not necessarily un-funny simply because it is untrue. For instance, when Adolf Hitler was ill his doctors could not find out what was the matter with him. Finally a specialist from Vienna was summoned. After examining the Fuehrer carefully, he said:

"The only cure is bathing."

Hitler's physicians asked him to specify exactly the kind of bathing, and the specialist replied:

"The patient should be entirely submerged in the bath twice—and taken out once."

1551

She had finished her First Aid training and was awaiting an opportunity to apply her knowledge. When the opportunity came, quite unexpectedly, she told her friends:

"I was crossing Fifth Avenue at 42nd Street when I heard a dreadful crash. I turned and saw a poor woman who had been knocked down by a taxicab. She had a compound fracture of the leg, was bleeding profusely, was unconscious, and seemed to have a fractured skull. I was so glad of my First Aid training. I stooped right down and put my head between my legs and prevented myself from fainting!"

1552

There was an old man of Calcutta,
Who coated his tonsils with butta,
Thus converting his snore
From a thunderous roar
To a soft, oleaginous mutta.

Ogden Nash

1553

Newspaper editors are infallible as to what constitutes news, so it was no surprise to the reporter when he was sent to interview the nonagenarian and find out his secret of long life. Of course that was one of the first questions that he put to the old man. And Methuselah II replied:

"Young feller, you can put it in your paper that my secret of health and long life is to eat some garlic every day."

"Migod," exclaimed the reporter, "why do you call it a secret?"

1554

Appendicitis: A modern pain that costs $500 more than the old-fashioned bellyache.

1555

The great English dramatist, Richard Brinsley Sheridan, was advised by his doctor to have an operation for a tumor. He flatly refused, saying that he had already had two operations during his life and would not undergo a third. The doctor asked him what the earlier operations were, and the playwright answered:

"I have had my hair cut and sat for my portrait."

1556

Last winter a Western hospital displayed a sign that read: "During this intense cold weather, and owing to the scarcity of coal, no unnecessary operations will be performed."

1557

A member of the French Chamber of Deputies had been a veterinarian before he became a radical politician.

One day in debate he caused his opponent, an aristocratic Conservative, to writhe under his telling arguments. The Conservative lost his temper and began to make personal remarks.

"Is it true," he sneered, "that you are really a veterinary?"

"It is indeed," the radical replied; "are you ill?"

1558

One of the classic items of vilification is attributed to that dean of newspaper gentlemen Irvin S. Cobb when he was on the staff of the New York World. The editor, Charles E. Chapin, was a slave-driver and none of his men liked him. One day when Cobb arrived at the city room, he looked around and said:

"Where's Chapin?"

"He's out sick," one of the men replied.

"Oh dear!" Cobb exclaimed; "I hope it's nothing trivial."

1559

There's only one thing worse than a giraffe with a sore throat and that's a centipede with chilblains.

1560

The worst case of insomnia on record is that of the man who couldn't sleep even when it was time to get up.

1561

Smith had hit the high places during his checkered career, but he decided to settle down and take out some life insurance. One of his friends was an agent for a big company, so he went to him and applied for a policy. There was an examination by one of the company doctors, and then Smith waited a long time. One day he met his friend the agent on the street and asked him about the life insurance policy. The friend answered:

"Well, you see, the doctor after the examination takes a chart of the applicant's body and punches a hole in it wherever he finds anything wrong."

"Did he do that in my case?" Smith asked.

"He certainly did," the agent replied. "Then he took the chart home, put it on the player-piano, and it played 'Nearer My God to Thee.' "

1562

Sydney Smith, English cleric and wit, consulted his physician about a minor ailment, and the medico said:

"You must take a walk every morning on an empty stomach."

"Gladly," Smith answered; "whose?"

1563

And the old maid whose mouth is so small that she has to use a shoehorn to take a liver pill.

1564

Victor Hugo gave this recipe for sound sleep: Courage for the great sorrows of life and patience for the small ones, and when you have laboriously accomplished your daily task, go to sleep in peace. God is awake.

1565

Most of the hospitals were very short of help during World War II, and a lot of novices were employed. One of these said to a young man just out of the operating room:

"They told me that I'm to get you ready for bed. You are my first patient. Just what am I supposed to do?"

"Don't worry, gal," said the patient; "it's quite simple. You just fluff up my pillows, then rub my back with alcohol, and finally kiss me good night."

So the tyro went ahead. The patient was quite satisfied. But as she closed the door on him, she paused and reflected:

"Now about that last part; I'd like to bet I wasn't supposed to do that at all."

1566

A man rushed into a doctor's office. The lobe of his left ear was bleeding.

"Quick, Doc," he said; "I bit myself."

"Man, that's impossible," the doctor replied; "how could you bite yourself in the ear?" And the man came back:

"I was standing on a chair."

Section 18

MONEY AND FINANCE

1575

It is better to give than to lend, and it costs about the same.

Sir Philip Gibbs

1576

There are two classes of people to whom life seems one long holiday, the very rich and the very poor, one because they need do nothing, the other because they have nothing to do.

Washington Irving

1577

Add newly filed saws: Nobody loves a flat man.

1578

"Money is not everything," said a philosopher to his son. "Money will not mend a broken heart or reassemble the fragments of a dream. Money cannot brighten the hearth nor repair the portals of a shattered home." Then he paused momentarily, and added, "I refer, of course, to Confederate money."

1579

Books have been written about the predatory careers of those two 19th century financiers, Jim Fiske and Jay Gould. Included in the booty that came their way was the elegant Hudson River steamer *Mary Powell*. Fiske and Gould had it redecorated and refitted magnificently, and included two life-size paintings of themselves in the main saloon.

Among the guests present at the unveiling party was William R. Travers, New York's most celebrated lawyer and outstanding wit. When the owners proudly exhibited the pictures, Travers turned to Fiske and said:

"You on one side and Gould on the other. But where is the picture of our Lord?"

1580

You can't win either way. As a rule, rich relatives are either distant relatives or close relatives.

1581

If you are asked to give the location of the capital of the United States, just say that it's in every country in the world.

1582

Budget: A plan for worrying before you spend instead of afterward.

1583

The fellow was down on his luck; his shoes were so thin he could step on a dime and tell whether it was heads or tails.

1584

When some men discharge an obligation you can hear the report for miles around.

Mark Twain

1585

A father suggested to his small son that he start saving his pennies and put them in a pretty yellow box.

"When you get five pennies give them to me and I'll give you a nickel and you can put it in this blue box."

"All right, Daddy," agreed the boy eagerly.

"When you get five nickels, give them to me and I'll give you a quarter and you can put it in this red box," continued the father.

Seven years later the boy discovered that the red box was the gas-meter.

1586

The broke-est man on record is the one who said, "If a trip around the world cost a nickel, I couldn't get out of sight."

1587

Two rowdies held up a Negro woman on a back road in the deep South. "Your money or your life," they shouted.

"You all can take my life," the woman answered; "I'm saving up my money for my old age."

1588

As a Government employee was walking along the street he heard screams issuing from a house and rushed in to investigate. A mother was frantic because her little boy had swallowed a quarter. The man grabbed the boy, held him upside down, and shook him by the heels, whereupon the coin dropped onto the floor. The grateful mother said:

"Well, mister, you certainly knew how to get it out. Are you a doctor?"

"No ma'am," he replied; "I'm a collector of internal revenue."

1589

"Katie, has anybody telephoned while I've been out?" asked the master of the house.

"Yes, sir," said the new maid, "but I could not make out the name. To be on the safe side, I said you would let him have something on account tomorrow."

1590

The world traveler became somewhat boresome after an hour or two, but he kept right on. Presently he arrived at a great fishing center of the Old World which he described at length.

"Over there," he said, "the fish are so plentiful that they are used as a medium of exchange; money, you know."

"No foolin'!" a listener exclaimed.

"On my honor," said the traveler.

"Well," the listener observed, "they must have a messy time playing the slot machines."

1591

"Five years ago," said Smith to his friend Jones, "I decided to quit smoking. I figured I was wasting a lot of money, so I gave up the habit."

"Very sensible," Jones observed.

"Yes, that's what I thought. I reckoned about what I had been spending each day on tobacco and put that amount in the bank."

"How did it work out?" Jones inquired.

"After five years I had $1800 in the bank."

"Good for you! Now if you could lend me—"

"But last Tuesday," Smith interrupted, "the bank failed. You haven't a cigar on you, have you?"

1592

The young fellow wasn't such a dope after all. When his dad threatened to cut him off with a shilling, he asked:

"But fawthah, where on earth will you borrow the shilling?"

1593

A thrifty Yankee—in other words, a Yankee—emigrated some years ago to Iowa and took up farming beside a river. When it became necessary he would ferry passengers across the river at five cents a head. One day a seedy looking individual came along and said:

"I want to get across the river, but I haint got a nickel for the fare."

The Yankee shifted his quid of tobacco to the other side of his mouth and replied:

"If you aint got five cents, you're just as well off on one side of the river as the other."

1594

Bank: An institution where you can borrow money if you can present sufficient evidence that you don't need it.

1595

The president of a well known Chicago bank prided himself on his conservatism, but he was equally broad-minded, a fact that was evidenced by his employing a valet who was an avowed Communist. The valet attended a party meeting each week, but that was the only evidence the banker saw of his being a red. After several months of asking permission to attend this meeting, there were no more such requests.

Finally the banker became curious and asked the reason.

"Well, it's this way, sir," the valet replied. "According to what I have heard, if the wealth of this country were divided equally, each inhabitant would receive $4,782.32."

"So what," said the banker.

"Sir," the valet explained, "I have $7,000 right now."

1596

A Scotchman was observed hunting through his pockets in a frenzy of haste. A friend stopped him and said:

"What are you doing?"

"I can't find my wallet," said Sandy; "it's disappeared."

"Have you looked through all your pockets?" the friend asked.

"All but one," Sandy replied. "If I look in there and don't find it, I'll drop dead."

1597

Francis Wilson, the well-loved actor of a generation ago, told this story of a conversation that Mark Twain had with another man:

"Your friend H. H. Rogers of the Standard Oil Company is a very good fellow. It's too bad that his money is tainted."

"It's double tainted," replied the shaggy-haired author, " 'taint yours and 'taint mine."

1598

Tipping: Paying wages to other people's hired help.

1599

Theodore Roosevelt was distinctly unpopular in Wall Street on account of his "Big Stick" methods. When he left for a hunting trip in Africa, someone posted a big sign in the New York Stock Exchange reading "Wall Street Expects Every Lion to Do Its Duty."

1601

Zeke Daniel says: "Always borrow money from a pessimist; he never expects it back anyhow."

1602

Thomas Hook, the English poet, often entertained his guests with comic song improvisations. One afternoon, when he was in the middle of an improvisation, his man entered the room and said: "Please sir, here's Mr. Winter, the tax-collector; he says he has called for the taxes."

Hook refused to be disturbed, but went right on playing as if nothing had happened, and sang the following stanza:—

"Here comes Mr. Winter, collector of taxes,
I advise you to pay him whatever he axes:

Excuses won't do; he stands no sort of flummery,
Though Winter his name is, his presence is summary."

1603

Add newly filed saws: A penny saved is a pocket burned.

1604

Debt: The only thing that doesn't grow smaller when it's contracted.

1605

Andrew Mellon was once approached by an unbalanced individual who ranted against the injustice of one man's having so much wealth. He insisted it should be more evenly distributed. Mellon cut him short by asking his secretary for a statement of his possessions and holdings, at the same time looking up the world's population. He made some notes, figured awhile and then told his secretary, "Give this gentleman sixteen cents. That's his share of my wealth."

1606

A banker, according to Mark Twain, is a man who loans you an umbrella when the sun is shining and demands its return the moment it starts to rain.

1607

When young Mark Twain was a struggling journalist in San Francisco a lady friend saw him on the street one day holding a cigar box under his arm.

"Mr. Clemens," she greeted him, "you are always carrying a cigar box with you. I'm afraid you're smoking too much."

"It isn't that," the writer answered; "I'm moving again."

1608

Money never made a fool of anybuddy; it only shows 'em up.

Abe Martin

Section 19

POLITICS

1624

Strong nations co-operate to the harmony and wealth of the world. Weak nations are a perpetual cause of disturbances and perils.

Anatole France

1625

One day Louis XIV was playing a game called trictrac with one of his courtiers, and he disputed a throw with his opponent. Bystanders were asked for their opinion, but none could decide who was right. Then the case was put up to Count Grammont. He had been at the farther end of the gallery and had not seen the play, but he immediately rendered a decision against the King. When Louis protested that he had not heard the case, Grammont said:

"Ay, Sire, but if your majesty had but a shadow of right, would these gentlemen have failed to decide immediately in your favor?"

1626

Diplomacy is to do and say
The nastiest thing in the nicest way.

Isaac Goldberg

1627

How a minority,
Reaching majority,
Seizing authority,
Hates a minority.

L. H. Robbins

1628

The Old Bromide thought he had said something when he observed:

"Well, we can at least be sure of death and taxes."

His companion yawned a little bit as he agreed.

"But," he said, "there's one advantage about death; it doesn't get worse every time Congress meets."

1629

A pup reporter was quite pleased with himself.

"I've got a perfect news story," he told his boss.

"Yeah! Man bites dog?" growled the old man.

"Nope! Bull throws Congressman!"

1630

Politicians are like horses, they cannot go properly without blinkers.

Anatole France

1631

A conservative is a man who is too cowardly to fight and too fat to run.

Elbert Hubbard

1632

Man's infinite capacity for inflicting suffering upon himself and his fellows needed an art form through which the emotions attendant to that fact could find amateur expression. Thus the party was invented.

George Bernard Shaw

1633

When Charles G. Dawes was Ambassador to Great Britain he made the statement that American diplomacy was easy on the brain but hell on the feet. Henry P. Fletcher, a fellow ambassador who heard him, said:

"I should say that it depends on which you use."

1634

At a dinner in Versailles, a British minister had toasted King George III and compared him to the sun. Then a French nobleman had toasted Louis XIV and likened him to the moon. Following these, Benjamin Franklin was called on for a toast to George Washington. And he hailed him as "a new Joshua, who commanded the sun and the moon to stand still, and they obeyed him."

1635

Was the poet John Harrington predicting modern politics and racketeering when he wrote the following couplet?

Treason doth never prosper; what's the reason?
For if it prosper, none dare call it treason.

1636

A political speaker got a laugh out of the crowd he was addressing when he said:

"If he only takes this stand when he runs, he'll have a walk-over."

1637

One man with courage makes a majority.

Andrew Jackson

1638

During the 1944 presidential campaign, Bob Hope said: "I see that Tom Dewey has his eye on a seat in the White House. But goodness me, look what Roosevelt has on it."

1639

President Coolidge and Senator Spencer were walking together one evening. They passed the White House.

"I wonder who lives there?" joked the Senator.

"Nobody," said the President. "They just come and go."

John Hiram McKee

1641

Back in the days when Benito Mussolini was the cock of the walk, it is said that he was once stranded in a small village when his armored car broke down. To pass the time away, he went to a local movie house. When his picture appeared on the screen, as it did in all movie houses in the sunny land of Italy, everyone arose but Mussolini the Great, who remained seated. The manager of the theater tapped him on the shoulder, and whispered in his ear, "I feel the same way, but you'd better stand up. It's safer."

1642

Conservatives are but men who have learned to love the new order forced upon them by radicals.

1643

When he defined *aristocracy* as "government by the best men," Ambrose Bierce added parenthetically, "In this sense the word is obsolete; so is that kind of government."

1644

An old-time political boss once defined an honest politician as one who, when he is bought, stays bought.

1645

What the five-cent cigar needs is a good country.

Ed Wynn

1646

The millennium will have arrived when this country can have a man who will be right and President at the same time.

1647

Talleyrand, in speaking of the members of the French Academy, said: "After all, it is possible that they may some day or other do something remarkable. A flock of geese saved the capitol of Rome."

1648

Depending on your politics, you may tell this either one way or the other.

The Republican candidate for Governor was making a speech in New Hampshire. In the course of his talk, he asked if there was a Democrat in the audience.

"I am a Democrat," announced a stringy-looking individual in the back of the hall.

"Why are you a Democrat?" the candidate asked.

"Well, I've always been a Democrat," was the answer. "Besides, my father was a Democrat, and my grandfather was a Democrat."

Little did he know it, but he was playing right into the speaker's hand. So the candidate said:

"Then, I suppose, if your father had been a horsethief and your grandfather had been a horsethief, you would be a horsethief."

"Not at all," was the rejoinder; "I'd be a Republican."

1649

Washington, D.C. has been characterized in a hundred or more different ways, but both Democrats and Republicans will have to admit that it is "The City Bureauful."

1650

America never lost a war or won a conference.

Will Rogers

1651

This concerns two screwball Kings—Charles II of England, 17th century, and Carol of Rumania, 20th century.

King Charles, the Merry Monarch, was beloved by his courtiers, who indeed liked him well enough to razz him occasionally. One day they hung the following rhyme on the door of his bedchamber:

Here lies our Sovereign Lord the King.
Whose word no one relies on.
He never does a foolish thing
Or ever says a wise one.

Carol of Rumania has done many foolish things, but the following shows that he has said at least one wise one.

Several years ago he told a newsman that he had selected fourteen of the brightest young fellows in Rumania for training in government service. Half were sent to England and the other half to the United States. Said Carol:

"The seven who went to England were very smart, and now each of them has an important position in Rumania."

"How about those who went to America?" he was asked.

"They were even smarter," His Majesty replied; "they stayed there."

1652

A group of Nazis were rescued from a raft in midocean by a British war vessel. The officer aboard the ship pointedly told his men that the captives were to be treated "just as if they were gentlemen."

The following morning one of the Germans showed up with a bruised and blackened eye. The British captain asked the Nazi who was responsible. Lieutenant Hawkins was named and was forthwith called to task.

"You are a disgrace to His Majesty's Navy," said the captain. "What have you to say in defense of yourself?"

"Well, Sir," the lieutenant replied, "when I came up on deck this morning, this—this blighter said to me, 'God damn the King!'

"I controlled myself, Sir, and said nothing. Then he came nearer, stuck his face close to mine, and yelled, 'To hell with the Queen.'

"That was almost impossible to bear, Sir, but still I remembered that I was a British officer and controlled myself. But then, Sir, he grinned at me contemptuously, and spat into *our ocean*. That, Sir, was too much, and I lost my temper."

1653

Washington was full of bureaucrats during World War II, and many of them were military men. One afternoon during the spring of '43 a dashing young officer was introduced to a very beautiful girl. Spring was in his blood, and that, together with three Daiquiris under his belt, impelled him to make a whispered suggestion in the girl's ear.

"Absolutely no," the young woman said decidedly.

Whereupon the officer fainted dead away. It made quite a commotion. Cold water was thrown in his face. When he came to, he found a very worried girl beside him.

"I know, of course," she said, "that you must have been disappointed by my refusal, but why did you faint?"

"It wasn't disappointment at your refusal," he answered; "but in all the ten months I have been in Washington, it was the first time I ever got a definite answer."

1654

When the idea of votes for women was suggested to the Chamber of Deputies in pre-war France, there was plenty of opposition from custom-ridden members. One of these pompous, hidebound gentlemen marshalled his anti-vote argument in a wandering but wordy hour long speech. Finally he attempted to crush all opposition with an unanswerable point.

"We must admit that nature herself did not plan to have women on the same level as men. Even the most rabid gentleman of the Left must recognize that there is a certain difference . . ."

As one man the members in the radical section leaped to their feet with the fervently Gallic shout "Vive la difference."

1655

A member of the opposition attempted to embarrass Clemenceau by stating in the Chamber of Deputies that the "Old Tiger's" son had joined the Communist Party.

The great French statesman arose and fixed his tormenter with a scathing glare. "Cher ami, my son is twenty one years old. If he hadn't joined the Communists at twenty one, I would have disowned him. If he is still a Communist at thirty, I will do it *then*."

1656

It is a well known fact that Adolf Hitler frequently consults astrologers and soothsayers. The Reich astrologer was asked by him, "On what day will I die?"

The famous astrologer consulted his charts and announced solemnly, "You will die on a Jewish Holiday."

Hitler pondered his reply a moment and then in a frenzy demanded, "Which one? I must know at once and there must be no question of a doubt."

"I cannot tell. I do not know," replied the astrologer, "because any day you die will be a Jewish Holiday."

1657

Congressman: A man who votes for all appropriations and against all taxes.

1658

"Where were you born?" asked the reporter of the great politician.

Swelling out his ample chest, the big shot replied:

"I am a native of Providence."

"Are you?" said the reporter, accenting the *are*.

"No!" bellowed the politician; "R. I."

1659

Even the British have had their fascists, with Sir Oswald Mosley as their leader. At one of their meetings Sir Oswald was escorted to the platform by a bodyguard of Black Shirts, and on the leader a spotlight was thrown. As he reached the platform, he raised his right arm in the fascist salute. There was silence, until from a remote corner of the auditorium came a voice:

"Yes, Oswald, you may leave the room."

1660

Brewster H. Ginsberg prided himself on being an individualist in every way, and so he announced his intention of going to Germany on a Nazi steamship. His friends tried to dissuade him, but he held firm and left on the *S.S. Hochzeit*. But when he was halfway across he received a radiogram that read, "If you can't get Hitler, get Goering."

1661

Epitaph for Adolf Hitler's gravestone: This is definitely my last territorial demand.

1662

Cato, Roman statesman of the pre-Christian Era, was asked why his statue was not set up along with others of the time. His reply was:

"I would rather folk would inquire why there is not a statue of Cato than why there is."

1663

In years past, President Roosevelt has frequently been a guest on Vincent Astor's luxurious yacht, the *Nourmahal,* later requisitioned by the United States Government for use in World War II.

The President, being asked to take a winter cruise with Mr. Astor, said, "Oh, don't put that big thing in commission just for me."

"But, Mr. President, the *Nourmahal* is in commission all the year round," said Mr. Astor.

"In that case," laughed the President, "I guess we'll have to raise taxes on the rich again."

1664

It is incredible how gentlemen can flay one another when they are political opponents. An outstanding example of high grade libel is the remark made by John Randolph about Edward Livingston.

"He is a man of splendid abilities, but utterly corrupt. Like a rotten mackerel by moonlight, he shines and stinks."

1665

Definition of *Genius* in Washington: The infinite capacity for taking trains.

Walter Winchell

1666

Probably the simplest and briefest statement of war aims ever made was expressed by Jan Masaryk, Foreign Minister of the Czechoslovakian government in London.

He said: "I want to go home."

1667

Harold L. Ickes, New Deal Secretary of the Interior, made the following comment when New York's young district attorney, Thomas E. Dewey, tried to obtain the Republican Presidential nomination in 1940:

"I see that Dewey has thrown his diaper into the ring."

1668

Edward Everett Hale, who wrote "The Man Without a Country," was at one time Chaplain of the United States Senate.

"Do you pray for the Senate, Dr. Hale?" someone asked.

"No," he replied, "I look at the Senators and pray for the country."

1669

Uncle Joe Cannon once met a German in Washington. They discussed world affairs at great length, ending with Uncle Joe's remark, "What we Americans need is a darned good licking." This pleased the German, who assented eagerly. But his delight was short lived, for Cannon added dryly, "The only trouble is, there ain't nobody can do it."

A. C. Edgerton

1670

Dictatorship: A system of government where everything that isn't forbidden is obligatory.

Section 20

RELIGION

1680

Two politicians were adrift in a lifeboat five days after their ship had been sunk. Down to their last morsel of bread and final swallow of water, the two men began to lose hope.

One of them decided to take extreme measures. He fell to his knees and began to pray.

"I swear that if I come out of this alive I'll stop leading the awful life I've been living. I promise that I'll never speak anything but the—"

"Hold up that prayer for a minute," said the other man. "Don't commit yourself until I can see if that's land ahead or just another mirage."

1681

A group of English scholars entertained Mark Twain at a banquet in London. Among other things they discussed the Bacon-Shakespeare controversy. One of the men on the Bacon side turned to Mark and asked if he would commit himself on the subject. Mark replied:

"I'll wait until I get to Heaven and ask Shakespeare himself."

"I don't think, Mr. Clemens," the Britisher said, "that you'll find Shakespeare in Heaven."

"Then you ask him," the humorist answered.

1682

Eddie Cantor, automobiling in Iowa, dined at a country hotel among a roomful of ministers. The ministers, who were holding a convention in the town, were amused when they saw Eddie Cantor in their midst. One of them said to him, "How does it feel, sir, to be in such reverend company as this?"

"I feel," said Cantor, rolling his eyes, "like a lion in a den of Daniels."

1683

Of course I prayed—
And did God care?
He cared as much
As on the air
A bird had stamped her foot
And cried "Give me!"

Emily Dickinson

1684

A small newspaper in Mississippi is credited with the publication of the following ad:

IMPORTANT NOTICE:—Positively no more baptizing in my pasture. Twice here in the last two months my gate has been left open by Christian people, and before I chase my heifers all over the country again, all the sinners can go to hell.

1685

Little Harold, having climbed to the pinnacle of the roof of a very steep shed, lost his footing and began to slide with terrifying swiftness toward that point where the roof swept gracefully off into space.

"O Lord, save me!" he prayed. "O Lord, save me! O Lord! . . . Never mind. I'm caught on a nail."

1686

A Jewish soldier at a training camp in the deep South wrote his dad in Boston that he had met a beautiful girl and wanted to marry her. "I hope you will make no objections," he said, "but the girl is not Jewish."

Somewhat upset, the father finally wrote his son that he would not object if they would promise to be married by a rabbi.

The son answered that both of them would agree except that there wasn't a rabbi within a hundred miles. Whereupon the father wrote that he would send a rabbi down from Boston. And so it was arranged.

The rabbi arrived at the place set for the ceremony. He was dressed in the black rabbinical coat of alpaca, wore the usual black felt hat, and had a long beard. When he stepped off the train he was spied by one of the local kids, who gazed at him in wonder. Then another kid appeared, and as the rabbi walked down the street, a dozen or more children joined the group. Finally the rabbi, incensed by all this attention, turned on them and shouted:

"Get oudt—get oudt! Hevn't you Southern kids ever seen a Yenkee before?"

1687

People would be surprised to know how much I learned about prayer from playing poker.

Robert Ingersoll

1688

The will of Stephen Girard, endowing Girard College in Philadelphia, prohibits clergymen from coming onto the grounds. One day Horace Greeley approached the campus, wearing his usual clerical-looking garb. The gatekeeper challenged him, calling out, "You can't come in here."

"The hell I can't!" roared Greeley.

"I beg your pardon, sir," replied the guard. "Pass right in."

1689

Sally Satter, she was a young teacher who taught,
And her friend, Charley Church, was a preacher who praught,
Though his enemies called him a screecher who scraught.

Phoebe Cary

1690

A speaker was introduced in high-flown words by the toastmaster, and was much concerned about his ability to live up to what was promised. When he rose, he said:

"Gentlemen, a few years ago I was driving through a New Jersey village, and on a little church I saw a sign that read: 'Big Strawberry Festival.' Then I looked closer and saw a line saying, 'On account of the depression, prunes will be served.' "

1691

EPITAPH ON PETER ROBINSON

Here lies the preacher, judge and poet, Peter,
Who broke the laws of God, and man, and metre.

Francis Jeffrey

1692

THE CHOSEN PEOPLE

How odd
Of God
To choose
The Jews.

W. N. Ewer

1693

Charles Sumner, a senator and Abolitionist, was once asked by a minister of the gospel why he did not go into the South with his anti-slavery speeches, since it was there that slavery existed. The answer was characteristic.

"You are trying to save souls from hell, aren't you?" the Senator said. "Then why," he added, "don't you go there?"

1694

One Sunday Calvin Coolidge went to church alone. When he returned to the White House, Mrs. Coolidge asked:

"Was the sermon good?"

"Yes," said the President.

"What was it about?" his wife continued.

"Sin," said the President.

"What did the minister say?" Mrs. Coolidge persisted.

"He was against it," said the President.

1695

Madame Chiang was talking with her mother, Madame Soong, about the Japanese menace and the horrors of the long war in China.

"Mother," cried Madame Chiang, "you are so powerful in prayer, why don't you pray that God will annihilate Japan by an earthquake or something?"

Looking at her daughter gravely, she replied, "When you pray, or expect me to pray, don't insult God's intelligence by asking Him to do something which would be unworthy even of you, a mortal."

1696

Sam Jones, the great Southern evangelist, preached a sermon to a large gathering of colored people. He made a tremendous impression. After the service was over an old Negro woman pushed her way toward him, grabbed his hand and said:

"Gawd bless you, Brother Jones. You sure is everybody's preacher, both black and white. You may have a white skin, Brother, but you sure has got a black heart."

1697

Nobody talks so constantly about God as those who insist that there is no God.

Heywood Broun

1698

We use religion like an omnibus—we ride on it only while it is going our way.

1699

After a sermon on free salvation, the minister of the Negro church announced that the collection would be taken by Brother Jones. In the back of the church, one of the congregation rose and said:

"Parson, you all done said that salvation was free—free as the water we drink."

"Yes, brother," the minister agreed; "salvation *is* free, but when we pipes it to you, you gotta pay for the piping."

1700

During a terrific storm at sea, a woman passenger clutched the Captain's arm and said:

"Tell me, are we in great danger?"

"Madam," replied the Captain, "we are in the hands of God."

"Oh," the woman groaned, "is it as bad as all that?"

1701

Mary Jane was given two nickels as she was about to leave for the morning service. One was for the collection plate and one for herself. As she trudged along to church she dropped one of her precious nickels and it rolled into the sewer. Mary Jane looked down through the grating and came to the sad conclusion it was lost forever.

"Well, there goes the Lord's nickel," she murmured.

1702

A small boy was saying his evening prayers in a very low voice.

"I can't hear you, dear," protested his mother.

"I wasn't talking to you," said the small boy firmly.

1703

Anne sat at the window looking up at the heavens bright with stars.

"What a lovely place Heaven must be, Mother, when its wrong side is so beautiful," she exclaimed.

1704

A group of children from the slum districts of New York were taken on their first visit to the country. One day a violent hail storm broke, and one of the little girls expressed her disapproval:

"God's gettin' awful fresh, throwing down those pieces of ice. First thing He knows, He'll hit somebody."

"Don't talk that way about God," protested one of the others. "Most everybody on our block likes Him."

1705

Religion often gets credit for curing rascals when old age is the real medicine.

1706

There is no unbelief.
Whoever plants a seed beneath the sod
And waits to see it push away the clod,
Trusts in God.

Bulwer-Lytton

1707

If there were no God, it would have been necessary to invent Him.

Voltaire

1708

Sir, my concern is not whether God is on our side; my great concern is to be on God's side, for God is always right.

Lincoln

1709

The newest recruit to the ranks of the Salvation Army was telling her experiences at a big open-air meeting.

"A great change has been wrought in me," she said. "Before I joined the Salvation Army I loved fine clothing and jewelry and luxurious furs. Then when I joined the Army I came to the knowledge that such material things would drag my soul down to hell, so I gave the whole lot of them to my sister."

1710

It is not so much God who created Man in His own Image, as every one of us who creates unto himself a God in his own Image.

1711

A friend asked Pat Casey where he was working.

"Sure I have the very best job in all the world," Pat answered. "I'm pullin' down a Protestant church, and what's more, I'm gettin' paid for doin' it."

1712

They that worship God merely from fear,
Would worship the devil too, if he appear.

1713

An old man had come a long distance to attend a reception at the White House. The guests were lined up and led past President Lincoln under the watchful eye of the ushers. No one was allowed to come very close to the President or to shake his hand. The old gentleman was very much disappointed at not having shaken the President's hand. Just before leaving, he waved his hat at the President and shouted, "Mr. President, I'm from way up in York state where we believe that God Almighty and Abraham Lincoln are going to save the country."

The President waved back at him, and cried, "My friend, you're half right."

1714

A great admirer of Mark Twain, wishing to express her enthusiasm, called upon him and effusively kissed his hand. He accepted her homage graciously and with dignity.

"How God must love you, Mr. Clemens!" she breathed reverently.

"I hope so, Madam," said the author, gently.

After she had gone he sighed and remarked just as gently and without a smile, "I guess she hasn't heard of our strained relations."

1715

At any rate, the high school boy gave his teacher something to think about when he wrote: "Science is material; religion is immaterial."

1716

When the Devil was sick, the Devil a monk would be;
When the Devil got well, the devil a monk was he.

1718

The Reverend Henry Ward Beecher
Called a hen a most elegant creature.
The hen, pleased with that,
Laid an egg in his hat,
And thus did the hen reward Beecher.

Oliver Wendell Holmes

1720

The only difference between the saint and sinner is that every saint has a past and every sinner has a future.

Oscar Wilde

1721

Some years ago there was a theological tempest over the issue of Fundamentalism versus Modernism. Dr. Harry Emerson Fosdick, of the Riverside Church in New York, was a leader in the fray.

It is said that one night he was awakened in the small hours of the morning by the ringing of his telephone. He jumped out of bed and sleepily said, "Hello."

"Ish thish Mr. Foshdack?" asked a voice over the wire.

"Yes, this is Dr. Fosdick speaking," said the minister in disgust.

"Dr. Harry Emerson Foshdock?"

"Yes, yes," was the impatient answer. "What is it you want?"

"Dr. Foshdick, I want to know the difference between Fundamentalism and Modernism."

"Good heavens, man, that's not something I can explain to you over the telephone," answered the Doctor in exasperation. "And obviously you are in no condition to hear. Come around to my study tomorrow and I'll be glad to answer your questions."

"But, Dr. Foshduck," insisted the voice, "I can't wait until tomorrow. I must know now."

Out of patience, Dr. Fosdick said, "Why can't you wait until tomorrow? Why do you have to know now?"

"Becaush," said the voice patiently, "tomorrow I won't give a damn."

1722

Governor Arthur M. Hyde of Missouri is highly regarded as a humorist among his friends and liked by the audiences of his political addresses for his favorite stories. Here is one:

Perhaps you have heard the story of Circle Bar Bill. Bill was one of the toughest of the old-school cowboys. He went to town one fall to the annual roundup, expecting to have the time of his life, but instead he fell into the tent of a traveling evangelist, and was converted. He was immediately fired with a desire to convert his companions, and he determined to do it by way of an object lesson —that is, by giving them an exhibition of the meekness and patience that a Christian is supposed to possess. He hired a hall and the cowboys flocked to hear him.

When the meeting was assembled Bill mounted the rostrum and said: "Now, fellers, I'm going to show you long-necked, leather-skinned so-and-so's the meekness and patience and long suffering that a feller gets when he is really and truly converted. I will stand up here and you fellers can heap on me any indignities that you feel like and I won't kick none, although you know that afore I was converted there warn't a cowpuncher on the range that was handier with his dukes or his gun than me, Circle Bar Bill. Here I stands before you personifyin' meekness and patience, in the hope of winnin' you unregenerate sons of the devil to the proper way of life."

Bill folded his arms and the cowboys began. They threw prairie hens, tobacco quids and other things at Bill, but he only smiled. Finally Two-gun Tommy of the Bar-10 outfit produced an old and time-worn wild turkey egg and he let Bill have it smack in the face. The egg exploded and its contents spread over and obliterated Bill's sweet smile. Whereat Bill jumped down into the audience and said:

"Boys, there's goin' to be an intermission. I ain't lost my faith in religion none, but there ain't no Scripture that forbids me from lickin' everlasting hell out of the coyote that'd throw an egg like that."

1723

A bishop went to his dentist to arrange for having a set of false teeth made. Said he:

"Are you sure you can make some that won't hurt me?"

The dentist said he was positive, and the bishop said to go ahead. When they were ready some time later, the bishop put them in his mouth.

"Christ!" he bellowed. "Jesus!"

"Why, Bishop," the red-faced dentist exclaimed, "if they hurt you that badly, take them out and I'll fix them."

The bishop looked surprised, and he said:

"The teeth are fine. This is the first time in years I have been able to say those beautiful names without whistling."

1724

One woman said to another, "Have you been to church today? We had a most beautiful sermon on training children."

"No, I was home doing it," was her friend's reply.

1725

There had been a revival meeting in a little Kansas town, and one of the partners in a coal concern joined the church. He was full of zeal and went to work on the other man to join.

"I can't do it, Bill," he replied; "if I joined, who'd do the weighing?"

1726

In an Arkansas village there was a preacher who, in the middle of his sermon, would always take off his coat and vest and wrestle with the Devil in his shirtsleeves. One Sunday a United States Senator attended the service, and one of the deacons warned the minister to be more formal in view of their guest. In spite of the warning, the parson followed his usual custom. After the service one of the congregation went to him and said:

"I'm sorry to criticize you, sir, but I reckon you forgot we had a United States Senator with us today."

"No I didn't," the minister retorted. "Anyway, I don't believe he's as bad as he's painted; and besides, I laid my coat and vest right beside me on a chair where I could keep my eye on it all the time."

1727

A crabbed old Quaker died. At the funeral services the few who had gathered were standing silently by, waiting, as was the custom, to pay a tribute to the departed if they so wished. No one spoke. Finally an old man said, "Well, I can say one good thing about Thomas. He wasn't always as mean as he was sometimes."

1728

Bobbie was perplexed.

"Say, Dad, the teacher in Sunday School told us about the evil spirits entering the swine."

"Yes, Bobbie? What do you wish to know?"

"I want to know, Dad, if that was the way we got the first deviled ham?"

1729

A New York street urchin, maybe seven years old, walked up to a church dignitary on the lower East Side and said:

"Say, guvnor, what time is it?"

"It's half-past five, my boy," was the reply.

"Okay, boss," the urchin continued, "at half-past six you can go to hell." Then he beat it as fast as he could.

The cleric, nettled by the kid's effrontery, went after him. While he was giving chase, he ran smack into his bishop, a portly gentleman with a twinkle in his eye.

"My dear fellow," he exclaimed, "why this unseemly haste?"

When the minister caught his breath he explained:

"That little rapscallion had the impudence to tell me that at half-past six I could go to hell!"

"I still see no reason for the unseemly haste," the bishop persisted; "you still have almost an hour."

1730

Grandma thought it was high time she gave her four-year-old grandson some religious instruction. Getting down the great family Bible, she began by reading the story of the Creation. She read: "And the Lord God formed man of the dust of the ground and breathed into his nostrils the breath of life." At this point little

Bobbie became interested and cried out excitedly, "Oh, Granny! Superman!"

1731

A cowboy blew in town one Sabbath morning, found things a mite slow, and wandered into a church. He got quite wrought up by the service and, under its spell, put a five-dollar bill in the collection plate. The minister was at the door as he went out, and he said:

"I trust that you liked the service."

"You bet I did, parson," the cowboy replied; "so much I put five dollars in the plate, and you know that's a hell of a lot of money."

The minister smiled:

"Yes, but then I'm a hell of a good preacher."

1732

A Vermont farmer, walking home from the village, was accosted by a sanctimonious individual with a stern countenance.

"Stranger," the sourpuss burst out, "have you made your peace with God?"

The tiller of the rockbound soil stopped and looked at his interrogator for a moment. Then he shifted his quid to the other cheek and answered:

"We ain't come to no open break yet."

1733

When visitors came to the Sunday school, the teacher asked one of the lads to recite a verse from the Bible. The boy promptly obliged, saying:

" 'And Judas went out and hanged himself.' "

The teacher had a pained expression. One of the visitors said:

"Maybe you can give us a different verse."

"Yessir," the boy agreed. " 'Go thou and do likewise.' "

1734

A Sunday School teacher had been giving her class a talk on behavior and what had to be done about it in order to go to heaven. When she had finished, she said to one of the boys:

"Horace, what must we do before we can expect forgiveness of sin?"

Horace squirmed in his seat, scratched his head, and finally replied:

"We gotta sin."

1735

Old Aunt Matilda was a spinster. Her niece came in just as a visitor was leaving, and Aunt Matilda asked her:

"What did you say was the name of that new minister?"

"That wasn't the minister, Auntie," said the girl; "he was the specialist from the city."

"Well!" exclaimed the old lady; "I thought he was a little mite familiar even for a minister."

1736

The speaker turned to the chairman of the meeting and said, "Please let me know if I talk too long. It would embarrass me to feel like the long-winded preacher who paused to say to his congregation:

" 'Now it's all right for you to consult your watches to see what time it is, but I am very much annoyed when you hold them to your ears to find out whether they are still running.' "

1737

When Tommy came home from Sunday school, his mother asked him if anything happened. Tommy said:

"I met the minister outside the church, and he asked me if I ever went fishing on Sunday."

"And what did you say, darling?" asked his mother.

"Well," said Tommy, "I said, 'Get thee behind me, Satan,' and ran right away from him."

1738

Someone overheard a young woman say to another: "The attendance at our church is so small that every time the rector says 'Dearly Beloved' you feel as though you had had a proposal."

1739

A revivalist was warning his congregation to flee the wrath to come.

"In that awful day," he shouted, "there will be weeping and wailing and gnashing of teeth."

There was a pause, during which came the voice of an old lady in the back:

"Sir, I have no teeth."

"Madam," the evangelist roared, "teeth will be provided."

1740

On one of his calls, the pastor was being entertained by six-year-old Mary. There came a lull in their conversation and the pastor tried to draw the little girl out on theological matters.

"What are the sins of omission?" he asked.

"I know," Mary answered; "they're the sins we ought to have committed, but haven't."

1741

An elderly Negro applied for membership in an exclusive metropolitan church, and the pastor, while not saying no, tried to discourage him by giving an evasive answer. Finally the colored man sensed that he wasn't wanted, and said:

"I reckon I'll sleep on it and maybe the Lord'll tell me what to do."

In a few days he came back and the minister asked him if the Lord sent him a message.

"Yes, Reverend," the Negro replied, "He sho did. Said there wasn't no use a-tall. Said He'd been trying for years to get into this church but He couldn't make it."

1742

Like most ministers' families, they were as poor as church mice. The little girl was the youngest of ten children until her father explained to her that a baby sister had come in the night.

"Well," she said, after due thought, "I s'pose it's all right, papa, but there's many a thing we needed worse."

1743

The telephone at the parsonage rang so constantly that the minister in desperation had his name omitted from the telephone book.

It happened that there was a plumber of the same name in the neighborhood, and forthwith he began to be pestered by requests to officiate at marriages, christenings and such. He went to the minister and asked him to have his name reinstated in the phone book. But the minister refused.

So the next time the plumber got a phone call to address the Ladies' Aid Society, he answered:

"Can't do it. I'm too blankety-blank busy writing my sermon."

1744

Two young schoolboys, one of Irish and the other of Italian parentage, saw an Episcopalian minister on the street.

"Good afternoon, Father," said the Italian boy politely.

The clergyman replied to the greeting and passed on, whereupon the other lad said:

"Shucks, he ain't no Father. He's got a wife and four kids."

1745

Just to show how broad-minded he was, an Episcopalian minister went to a Negro barber to be shaved. The barber was known to indulge in the cup that cheers. On this particular occasion he had a decidedly alcoholic breath. Suddenly the razor slipped and cut the parson's face.

"Now you see, Sam. That comes from drinking."

"Yessir," the barber returned genially; "it certainly do make the skin tender for a fact."

1746

It was unprecedented. The sermon was only ten minutes long. When the minister finished he said:

"I am sorry to say that my dog, who seems to be very fond of paper, ate the remaining portion of my sermon. Let us pray."

After the service a parishioner met the clergyman at the door, and said to him:

"Doctor, when that dog of yours has pups, I'd like to give one to each of several preachers that I know."

1747

In Louis Nizer's introduction for a well known Catholic prelate was the following:

"If you could get religion like a Baptist—experience it like a Methodist—be loyal to it like a Catholic—sacrifice for it like a Jew—be proud of it like an Episcopalian—pay for it like a Presbyterian—and enjoy it like a Negro what a great religion you'd have!"

1748

There was a well attended baptism service on the bank of a Southern river. One man seemed to be holding back, and the minister said to him:

"Are you baptized, brother?"

"Yessir," was the reply.

"Who baptized you, brother?" the preacher persisted.

"I was baptized," he said, "by the 'Piscopal minister."

"Humph!" the preacher exclaimed; "that wasn't no baptism; that was just dry cleanin'."

1749

The Negro preacher said to the bride, "Does you take this here man for better or for worse?"

And the bride replied:

"I'm a gonna take him jest as he is. If he gets any better, I'm afraid he'll die, but if he gets any worse, I'll kill him myself."

1750

Johnny was busy with a paper and pencil, and his teacher asked him what he was doing.

"I'm drawing a picture of God."

"You mustn't try to do that, Johnny; nobody knows what God looks like."

Johnny smiled complacently as he replied:

"Well, they will when I finish this picture."

1751

One Sunday morning Reverend Pettit arrived at church and suddenly discovered that he had left the manuscript of his sermon at home. It was too late to send for it, so when he went into the pulpit he addressed the congregation thus:

"Inasmuch as I have forgotten my notes, I shall have to rely on the Lord for guidance. Tonight I will come better prepared."

1752

Little Bobbie was entertaining the visiting minister, who also did his part in keeping up the conversation. He said to the boy:

"You're a bright young man. How high can you count?" And the boy answered:

"One, two, three, four, five, six, seven, eight, nine, ten, Jack, Queen, King."

1753

A certain very dignified bishop was advised by his physician to take up golf. He took a few lessons and then one day he went out on the course to practice. He was alone except for the boy who carried his clubs.

When the caddie had teed up the ball, the bishop took a vigorous swing at it, but missed by a bare ten inches. Then he tried again and tore up a divot about a foot behind the ball.

Whereupon he lost his patience and exclaimed, "Tut-tut."

"Mister," said the caddie in disgust, "you'll never learn to play golf with words like that."

1754

There was a new sexton in the Scottish church, and when Mrs. MacTavish, who was very hard of hearing, appeared with her large ear-trumpet, he became excited.

Finally he tiptoed over to her pew and admonished:

"One toot and you're oot!"

1755

The vicar of an English church wrote as follows to his bishop:

"My Lord: I am sorry to tell you of the death of my wife. Can you arrange to send me a substitute for the week-end?"

1756

There was a visiting pastor who preached the sermon during the absence of the regular minister. An old deacon of the church passed the plate. Just before he handed the collection to the pastor, he extracted a fifty-cent piece from it.

After the service was over, the new pastor said:

"By the way, Deacon, what was the idea in taking that half-dollar from the collection plate?"

The deacon chuckled and said:

"Oh, you mean that counterfeit half-dollar?"

"Counterfeit?" the pastor exclaimed.

"Sure it's a counterfeit," said the deacon. "I've been using that as a decoy for twenty years."

1757

This one isn't any good for a person who is unaware of the intense rivalry that exists between the cities of Minneapolis and St. Paul. The conversation was between two members of different churches.

"I heard that your pastor was to have a call from a Minneapolis church."

"He expected it, all right, but he went over there to preach a trial sermon and he showed bad judgment."

"How come?"

"He chose a text from St. Paul. It's all off."

1758

There was a mild-mannered preacher of the gospel walking along a country road when from around a bend he heard many words of blasphemy uttered most feelingly. A few steps more and he came upon a man who was trying to change a tire on his automobile.

"Oh my friend," exclaimed the minister, "I beg of you do not use such language. Please realize that it is only by prayer that you will do yourself any good."

"Well," said the motorist, "maybe you're right; I've tried everything else to get that wheel off."

So the parson and the motorist prayed silently for a while. Then the motorist went back to the wheel, and it came off with the greatest of ease. The men looked at each other in silence for a minute. And then the parson said:

"Well, I'll be a son of a ——!"

1759

The five-year-old daughter in the minister's family had been, as she thought, unjustly disciplined. When at last it came bedtime she knelt as usual for prayer at her mother's knee. Earnestly she prayed:

"O Lord, please make all the bad people good; and, Lord, if it's possible, please make all the good people nice."

1760

Converted to religion at a revival service, Henry Smithers went after it in a big way. At the first prayer meeting following he offered himself for service, saying:

"I'm ready to do anything the Lord asks me, as long as it's honorable."

1762

The pastor of a New York church was trying to calm the fears of a nervous woman parishioner at a Civilian Defense meeting during the war. "Perhaps," he said, "New York won't be bombed at all."

"What!" she exclaimed in wrath; "after all the expense we've been put to!"

1763

No great respect these days is shown to the word Hell. A Negro preacher, however, believed in the place firmly and sought to impress his congregation with its terrors. His sermon on the subject was a wow.

"Brethren and sistern, has any of you ever been through the big steel works in Birmingham, Alabama?"

"Yes, Parson, I've been there," answered one of the congregation.

"Has you ever seen the molten steel as it comes out of the furnaces?" continued the preacher.

"Yes indeed, Parson, I've seen it."

"Then you know, brother; then you know. You know it's hot; it's white hot; it's sizzlin' hot. Real warm is what I mean. In fact, it's so hot that a person shrivels when he gets anywheres near it."

The preacher paused impressively; and then he concluded:

"Well, brethren and sistern, in Hell they uses that there stuff for ice-cream."

1764

A visiting archbishop had preached an eloquent sermon on the beauties of married life. Two Irish women, as they came out of church, were heard to comment on the discourse.

"Sure 'tis a fine sermon his riverence is after givin' us."

"Indeed it is," said the other, "and I wish I knew as little about the subject as he does."

1765

The following might be hung on any one of a dozen different denominations.

A minister in a —— Church preached a sermon on the subject "Recognition of Friends in Heaven." During the following week someone put this note in the suggestion box in the lobby:

"Reverend Sir: Could you make it convenient to preach on 'Recognition of Friends on Earth'? I have been coming to your church for six months, and nobody has ever taken any notice of me."

1766

The young minister's father was rather deaf. One day he was walking along the street and met his parson son in the company of another man. They all stopped, and the minister said:

"Father, this is our new deacon, Mr. Smith." The old man sniffed and replied:

"So he's a New Dealer!"

"No, no, Father; he's the son of a bishop."

The deaf man made a wry face.

"They all are," he said.

1767

A Rochester Negro evangelist was in the habit of building up spectacular endings for his revival meetings. Coming to the church one Sunday, he arranged for his usual finale by hiding in the rafters of the ceiling a small Negro boy with a caged dove. At the appropriate moment moment the parson would shout for the Holy Ghost to come down, whereupon the dove was to be released to fly about. The moment came, and devoutly the preacher called out "Holy Ghost, come down!" Nothing happened. Again he raised his voice and arms heavenward, saying, "Holy Ghost, come down!" Nothing happened; and then in the expectant silence the boy poked his head out and called: "A yaller cat done et the Holy Ghost; shall I throw down de yaller cat?"

1768

After the service, a close friend of the minister asked him why he became so disconcerted during the sermon.

"Well, it was this way," said the cleric. "An elderly lady who had a quite determined look on her countenance took a seat in the front pew. When I began my sermon, she opened a wooden box and took out an elaborate hearing device. Carefully she put the parts together and adjusted something to her ear. In about five minutes, she removed the earpiece, disassembled the mechanism, and packed the parts away in the box." The minister paused, gulped, and added, "Wouldn't that get *your* goat?"

1769

Mrs. Evans hurried to her neighbor's house with the latest news.

"Have you heard the news, Mrs. Adams? Our minister's son has decided to become a jockey. Of course you know he was planning to go to the Theological Seminary this year; that is, his father planned it so."

Mrs. Adams, more worldly wise than her neighbor, replied drily, "Well, I guess he'll bring a lot more people to repentance that way than he would as a minister."

1770

Not long after the new clergyman had been called to the little town, he was taken ill and consulted the local physician, who was an irregular attender of the church. The medical treatment was prolonged, and the young pastor, became worried, fearing a mounting bill. He spoke to the doctor concerning the bill.

"I tell what I'll do, Pastor," said the doctor, "I am told you are a very good preacher and you seem to think I'm a fair doctor. We'll make a bargain. I'll do all I can to keep you out of Heaven, and you do all you can to keep me out of Hell, and it won't cost either of us a cent."

1771

A young girl came to the confessional, saying she feared she had incurred the sin of vanity.

"What makes you think that?" asked the father confessor.

"Because every morning when I look into the mirror I think how lovely I am."

"Don't worry, my girl," was the reassuring reply. "That isn't a sin, it's a mistake."

1773

The big shot of a town in the Northwest had an argument with the local preacher and was getting nowhere. Pro and con the argument went. Finally the big shot lost his temper and said:

"If I had a son who was an idiot, I'd make him a parson."

"Evidently," the dominie replied, "your father had other ideas."

1774

A fresh young guy out of college once was thrown with a well known clergyman and began to express himself on the subject of religion. Finally he said:

"Maybe you've noticed, parson, that I never go to church."

"Yes indeed," the clergyman said.

"The reason I don't go," the brash young man continued, "is that there are so many hypocrites in church."

"Don't let that bother you," replied the clergyman, "there's always room for one more."

1775

"Today," said the minister, "I shall preach on the subject of liars. Now I should like to know who in this congregation has read the 17th chapter of Mark."

About three-quarters of the hands in the church were raised. Whereat the minister sighed and said:

"Certainly most of us need this sermon. There isn't any 17th chapter of Mark."

1776

Maybe these two fellows were both right. One was a theologian, who said that a philosopher was like a blind man in a dark room searching for a black cat that wasn't there.

The other was a philosopher, whose retort was:

"But a theologian would have found it."

1777

A minister was calling on one of his women parishioners one afternoon when suddenly the lady's little boy rushed in holding a rat by the tail.

"Don't be scared, Mother," he reassured her; "he's dead. We whacked him and slammed him and busted him until—"

Then the boy noticed that the minister was there and continued:

"—until God called him home."

1778

A traveling evangelist in a small Western city stopped a newsboy and inquired the way to the postoffice. He received an intelligent answer, thanked the boy and then said:

"You're a bright lad. Do you know who I am?"

"Nope," was the reply.

"Well, I'm the preacher who is holding revival meetings in the tabernacle. If you come to my service tonight, I'll show you the way to Heaven."

"Nuts!" the newsboy exclaimed; "you don't even know the way to the postoffice."

1780

A young Sunday school teacher had asked each child to commit to memory a verse from the Bible.

Johnnie's memory stood by him but when he came to the thee's and thou's, he hesitated, preferring to use his own vernacular.

"But, Johnnie," remonstrated his teacher, "the words used in the Bible, are thee, and thou, and ye."

"Aw," said Johnnie, "I can't get on to all that Bible slang."

1781

A frail little old lady, bonneted and shawled for the Sabbath service, sat next to a little boy. As the collection plate was passed, he noticed the little old lady couldn't open her bag. Moving closer to her, he whispered reassuringly, "Here, lady, you take my penny. I can hide under the seat."

1782

It was suggested at a church meeting that a drive be launched to raise funds with which to buy a chandelier for the church. The suggestion met with the unanimous approval of all present with the exception of a sour-faced old deacon who arose and said, "It's all a lot of nonsense and showoff extravagance. It'll cost a pile of money to buy the dern contraption and install it, and next thing we know we'll have to hire some upstart to play it."

1783

An ingenious minister in a southern town contrived an original way to omit the annual Church bazaars. He sent to all the members of the congregation the following bill: "Bus fare . . . admission . . . wear and tear on clothes and tempers . . . ice cream . . . useless articles . . . total . . . Please remit."

The amount received was far in excess of any previously raised.

1784

The old bishop took his job very seriously, and he took himself very seriously as well. One evening he was at a dinner party, and the hostess had considerately seated him between two charming women. Things were off to a good start.

Presently the lady at his right inquired about his health. The bishop sighed and said:

"When I came here this evening I felt in the best of health, but right at this moment I have been strangely afflicted with a paralysis of my lower limbs. I've been pinching my left leg and there is absolutely no sensation in it."

"Don't worry about that, Bishop," said the lady on his left. "It's been my leg that you have been pinching."

1785

There was once a minister who couldn't remember people's names. So if he was called upon for an address and it became necessary to use names, he would write them on a small piece of paper, which he would pin on the under side of his four-in-hand necktie. Then he would casually glance at it from time to time.

One day when he had occasion to deliver a funeral sermon he said:

"Dearly beloved friends, we are gathered to pay the last tribute to our late lamented (glancing at the under side of his tie) William Smith. I remember well back in 1899 when he came to our midst and married (pause) Mary Brown. Now, after many years spent in noble works and as a model husband and father, our brother rests in the arms of his blessed Savior (again a look at his notes) Jesus Christ."

1786

The Sunday school lesson had been on how Samson had slain the Philistines, and the children were much interested. When she had finished, the teacher asked various questions. Then she said to the class:

"What did Samson slay the Philistines with?"

There was no answer. In order to give them a clue, the teacher put her hand up to her cheek and said:

"What is this?"

"I know," a little boy exclaimed. "It's the jawbone of an ass!"

1787

As most people are aware, George Bernard Shaw has always appreciated himself. Another British writer, Israel Zangwill, commented that "The way Shaw believes in himself is very refreshing in these atheistic days when so many believe in no God at all."

Section 21

SCIENCE AND PSYCHOLOGY

1790

At one of our great observatories on a starry night a distinguished astronomer was looking through the monster telescope. Suddenly, without turning away from the eyepiece, he said to one of his colleagues:

"I think it's going to rain."

"Why do you think so, Doctor?" the other scientist asked.

"Because," the astronomer answered, "my corns hurt."

1791

Relativity

There was a young lady named Bright
Who would travel much faster than light.
  She started one day
  In the relative way,
And came back the previous night.

Anonymous

1792

I

Nature, and Nature's laws, lay hid in night:
God said, *Let Newton be!* and all was light.

Alexander Pope

II

It did not last: the Devil, howling *Ho!*
Let Einstein be! restored the status quo.

J. C. Squire

1793

Edgar Bergen was talking to his protégé Charlie McCarthy one day, telling him of some of the wonders of the solar system.

"Light from the sun travels at the rate of 186,000 miles a second, Charlie. Isn't that a remarkable speed?"

"Oh, I don't know," chipped in Charlie. "It's down hill all the way."

1794

Mrs. Brown had attended a lecture on psychology as applied to children. She was terribly enthusiastic about the whole subject and forthwith took her six-year-old daughter to a psychologist for examination. The great mental expert said to the child:

"What are you, a boy or a girl?"

"A boy," the little lassie answered.

The psychologist was somewhat stumped by this reply, but he kept on.

"When you grow up," he asked, "will you be a woman or a man?"

"A man," said the little girl promptly.

On their way home, the mother said:

"Why did you give such strange answers to the man's questions?"

"The old silly!" the child exclaimed. "If he was going to ask me nutty questions, I was going to give him nutty answers. He couldn't kid me."

1795

The eight-year-old son of a professor of psychology from a western university was visiting New York with his father. The lad was amazed at the shop windows. He stopped before the shop window of a famous jeweler, where invisible glass makes it appear that nothing but air separates the passer-by from the glittering display. The boy stared for a while and then turned away, saying sadly,

"If I were not so well adjusted, I would reach in there and grab some of those jewels."

1796

A six-year-old boy was taken to the toy shop of a large New York department store late one afternoon. The child was bored until he saw a rocking-horse, when his joy knew no bounds. He leaped on its back and began to rock vigorously. This continued for five minutes or so while his mother looked and beamed. Presently a clerk came up and said:

"I'm sorry, madam, but we're about to close up, and I'm afraid we'll have to ask the boy to postpone his riding until another day."

"Sir," the mother replied, "I wouldn't think of taking him off the horse. He has never been crossed in anything he wants to do."

That stumped the clerk and he moved away. The boy continued to rock. In a few minutes the department manager appeared.

"Madam," he said, "you must realize that your son cannot continue, since we are right on the point of closing. I must therefore ask you to take him off the horse."

"Certainly not," said the adamant woman. Whereupon the department manager got an inspiration. In his most suave manner he said:

"I wonder if you would mind if I asked our store psychologist to speak to your son?"

The mother was flattered that such a dignified person as a psychologist was to be brought into consultation.

"Not at all," she replied.

In a few moments a studious looking man with a beard stepped up to the boy and whispered something in his ear. The boy jumped off the rocking-horse, took his mother's hand, and went out with her. When they reached the street, the mother asked:

"What did the nice man say to you?"

To which the boy replied:

"He said, 'Get off that rocking-horse, you little so-and-so, or I'll beat your brains out with a baseball bat!' "

1797

The president of the firm asked for a new secretary. A psychological test was decided upon and three girls from the agency were brought in to be examined by a psychologist.

"Now, give me your undivided attention. Listen carefully," said the psychologist. "What do three and three make?"

"Six," was the quick reply.

"Thank you," he said. "Will you please wait in the next room?"

To the second applicant he said, "What do three and three make?"

The girl hesitated, suspecting something was afoot. "Well, it might be thirty-three," she said, archly.

"Thank you. Will you wait in the next room?"

To the third girl he said, "What do three and three make?"

She took her time and answered slowly. "Might be thirty-three, or it might add up to six."

"Thank you," the psychologist said, and turned well pleased to the president. "There you are, sir. The first girl gave the obvious answer. The second suspected me of tricking her. The third had it going both ways. Now, sir, which girl will you have?"

"Oh, I'll have the blonde with the beautiful blue eyes," said the president without hesitation.

Section 22

SPEAKING, WRITING AND LANGUAGE

1800

Frank Harris, whom some people liked and others tolerated, was in a group that included Oscar Wilde. You know about Oscar; if he had not been clever, he would have been impossible in any man's language.

Harris was given to plagiarizing the good things that he had read, and on this occasion he related a story that nearly everyone present recognized as having originated with Anatole France. It was met by a more than momentary silence. Finally Wilde said in an unctuous tone of voice:

"You know, Frank, Anatole France would have spoiled that story."

1801

One orator in a family, nay even in a city, is enough.

Cicero

1802

President Coolidge was asked to turn a spadeful of earth at the laying of a cornerstone. He complied, and then remained silent, spade in hand. The master of ceremonies, expecting him to speak to the gathering, suggested that he say a few fitting words.

Mr. Coolidge looked over the upturned earth, saying, "That's a fine fishworm."

1803

On his American lecture tour, Oscar Wilde said to one of his audiences:

"You are Philistines who have invaded the sacred temple of art."

He paused to let that sink in. Then came a voice saying:

"And you're trying to drive us forth with the jawbone of an ass."

1804

Reverend E. Williston Phipps was being congratulated by one of his parishioners on the fact that he did not preach overlong sermons.

"I never liked them myself," said Dr. Phipps, "and especially since I went to fill my first pulpit in Oklahoma. Before the service the deacon came to me and said, 'Young man, we don't set a time limit on sermons, but we don't believe any souls are saved after the first twenty minutes.' "

1805

His voice was as intimate as the rustle of sheets.

Dorothy Parker

1806

Then there's the deaf mute who wears mittens to bed so he won't talk in his sleep.

1807

There comes a time in the affairs of gentlemen when no amount of cursing will suffice. Let us merely observe a moment of silence, like a deaf-mute who has just hit his fingers with a hammer.

John Barrymore

1808

Convincing Talker: A man who can explain to his high school age son wherein algebra is going to be any use to him after he's out of school.

1809

You can hang this gag on a man just as well: That woman talks so much, I'm hoarse listening to her.

1810

Sidney Franklin, the American bullfighter, was once cornered at a party by a dowager who took him to task for the alleged cruelty of his art. She refused to hear his explanations, but talked on endlessly about the "poor, defenseless bulls." After about fifteen minutes of this, Franklin could no longer restrain himself.

"Madam," he protested, "I can't agree with you. I have killed many bulls in my day, but I have always spared them the ultimate cruelty—not one did I ever bore to death!"

1811

To prove how little attention people pay to actual words, a hostess said smilingly as she passed the cakes at a tea:

"These green ones are colored with Paris green, the pink have strychnine in them." Everyone present unconcernedly took a cake and thanked her.

1812

Will Rogers, of blessed memory, some years ago introduced a well known aviator at a dinner. The flyer was continually announcing his proposed trip across the Atlantic Ocean and just as often postponing it. In his introduction, the humorist said:

"I want to introduce this intrepid flyer—here today and here tomorrow."

1813

Chauncey M. Depew, ace after-dinner speaker of the 1900's, played a trick on Mark Twain on an occasion when they were both to speak at a banquet. Mark spoke first for thirty minutes and was received enthusiastically. When Depew's turn came, he said, "Mr. Toastmaster, ladies and gentlemen, before this dinner, Mark Twain and I made an agreement to trade speeches. He has just delivered mine and I'm grateful for the reception you have accorded it. I regret that I have lost his speech and cannot remember a thing he had to say."

Then he sat down while the rafters rang with applause.

1814

Often a speaker is handicapped by a eulogistic or flowery introduction. Here are two examples of how he has gotten off to a good start after being unduly praised:

"An introduction is like perfume; it smells something beautiful, but it shouldn't be swallowed." Also:

"That sure was a swell obituary."

1815

Novelist, politician and ranchman, Clarence Budington Kelland is even better known to his friends for his slightly outrageous wit. As a master of ceremonies, he shines, scintillates and sparkles.

He found himself in this capacity one evening at a large dinner. There was a large number of speakers. Kelland rose from his seat and began:

"Ladies and gentlemen: the tactful toastmaster feels that it is his duty to be so infernally dull that the speakers who follow will appear to be brilliant by contrast."

There was a self-conscious titter among the speakers. Then Kelland continued:

"But I have looked over this list and I don't believe I can do it."

1816

A good story teller is a person who has a good memory and hopes other people haven't.

Irvin Cobb

1817

On one occasion when William Howard Taft was campaigning in unfriendly territory, someone threw a cabbage at him. It rolled to a stop at Taft's feet.

"I see," was his comment, "that one of my adversaries has lost his head."

1818

A guest at a dinner was called on for a few remarks. He rose from his seat and talked for a solid hour. When he was through he apologized for talking so long because he had no watch. Somebody in his audience, however, sang out:

"Yeh, but there's a calendar back of you."

1819

A big, heavy-set man, somewhat dour in appearance, asked a little fellow on the street, "C-c-can you t-tell me how to g-g-get to C-c-city Hall?"

The small man paled and, turning on his heel, ran down the street. Angry at his not answering, the big man ran after him. They ran for several blocks until the little fellow's breath gave out and he was overtaken and cornered. The big man grasped his arm and cried angrily, "W-w-what do you m-m-mean by running away w-w-when I ask you a c-c-civil question?"

The little man looked up and gasped, "D-d-do you t-t-think I w-w-wanted my block knocked off?"

1820

The audience was swell. They were so polite, they covered their mouths when they yawned.

Bob Hope

1821

At the end of a banquet given by Marshal Stalin at the Russian Embassy in Teheran, after Churchill, Roosevelt, Stalin, the Armies, the Navies, and the Air Forces had all been toasted, Marshal Stalin rose.

He spoke quickly and eloquently, and with humor, judging from the smiles on the faces of the Russians present. The British and

Americans sat with their fingers around their glasses, ready to get to their feet, but waiting for an interpreter to translate.

Marshal Stalin sat down. The interpreter rose and said:

"Gentlemen, Marshal Stalin says the men's room is on the right."

1822

Alexander Black, novelist and newspaper editor, was one of four speakers at an open-table dinner at the National Arts Club. Much to his surprise, he was called on first. When he rose from his chair, he began drily:

"I am reminded of an epitaph on an old tombstone in a Rhode Island cemetery. It said, 'I expected this, but not so soon!' "

1823

Dr. George E. Vincent, then president of the University of Minnesota, was said to have delivered his addresses at the remarkable rate of 300 words per minute.

He was introduced to a New York audience by Chauncey M. Depew, who referred to him as the "Cyclone of the Northwest." When Dr. Vincent responded, he said with his accustomed urbanity:

"I appreciate the designation that has been given me by the most eminent wind authority of the East."

1824

Edmund Burke, the British statesman who protested vigorously against England's treatment of the American colonies, was making his famous speech against Warren Hastings. Suddenly he stopped in the middle of an idea. At this juncture he raised his hand slowly and pointed his finger impressively at Hastings. He stood that way for almost a minute while the audience held its breath.

When the speech was over, one of the opposing advocates approached him and said:

"Mr. Burke, that was one of the most effective pauses I have ever seen. We held our breaths, wondering what you were going to say next."

Burke's Irish eyes twinkled as he replied:

"That's exactly the way I was feeling."

1825

A verbose and boresome speaker finally approached his summing up.

"Well," he said, "to make a long story short—"

"It's too late," shouted a man at a distant table.

1826

Henry Guy Carleton, wit, journalist, and playwright, had an impediment in his speech. One day he met Nat Goodwin, the comedian and asked: "G-Goodwin, c-c-can you g-g-give m-me f-f-fifteen m-minutes?"

"Certainly," answered the comedian, "what is it?"

"I w-w-want to have a f-f-five minutes' c-c-conversation with you."

1827

Artemus Ward used to do a lot of talking to audiences. Sometimes he would stop in the middle of a lecture and say:

"Owing to a slight indisposition, I am now going to declare a brief intermission," and then he would add: "but to pass the time away, I shall continue to talk."

1828

Mark Twain, years ago, gave a dinner in honor of Major Edward Bowes. There were some thirty distinguished guests present.

"Don't you feel well?" asked Mr. Clemens of the Major.

"I'm scared to death," said the Major. "I know I shall be called upon to speak, and I'm sure I shan't be able to rise from my chair. When I stand up, my mind sits down."

"Eddie," said his host, "it may help you if you keep one thing in mind—just remember they don't expect much."

1829

The political speaker ranted on. "I want reform . . . I want land reform . . . I want housing reform . . . I want educational reform . . . I want . . ."

And from a tired-looking man in the audience came:

"Chloroform."

1830

An Irish agitator was arrested in the midst of a political speech. A year later upon his release, he went back to the scene of his arrest, opening a harangue with these words, "As I was saying when I was interrupted—"

1831

Gladstone always had his hooks out for Disraeli, and vice-versa. The former had finished a long speech attacking Disraeli's policies, and an equally long reply was expected. But all that "Dizzy" said was:

"The man needs no reply. He is inebriated by the exuberance of his own verbosity."

1832

Franklin D. Roosevelt's advice to his son James on the subject of speech-making:

"Be sincere; be brief; be seated."

1833

Abie Ginsburg was coming back from Europe, and the steward placed him at a table for two. At dinner he was joined by a very polite Frenchman who, before he sat down, bowed and said:

"Bon appetit!"

The American was not to be outdone. He rose from his seat, bowed, and said:

"Ginsburg."

1834

"My wife," said the boastful party, "speaks ten different languages."

"Does she speak Esperanto?" asked the bystander.

"She speaks it like a native," was the rejoinder.

1835

The best way of answering a bad argument is to let it go on.

Sydney Smith

1836

"I often quote myself," Bernard Shaw once said; "it adds spice to my conversation."

1837

If all the people who have to listen to after-dinner speeches were laid end to end, they would stretch—*period.*

1838

A man went into a butcher shop and gave an order as follows:

"Give me two pounds of kidleys."

"I don't quite get you," said the butcher. Then he thought a moment or two. Finally he said, "Oh, you mean kidneys."

"Well," said the man, "that's what I said, diddle I?"

1839

I do not agree with a word you say, but I will defend to the death your right to say it.

Voltaire

1840

The political speaker found it hard going. When there was a pause in the heckling, he shouted:

"There are so many interruptions that I cannot hear myself speaking."

"Cheer up," said a voice in the audience; "you ain't missing anything."

1841

Strickland Gillilan, equally well known as a poet and a lecturer, was billed to speak one night in a small Pennsylvania town. On reaching the platform he discovered that the usual pitcher of water was missing. So he asked for it.

"What's the water for—to drink?" asked the chairman.

"No," Gillilan replied; "I do a high-diving act."

1842

When angry, count four; when very angry, swear.

Mark Twain

1843

A speaker may be made by force of circumstances, but an orator —that's something else again. The best definition of oratory was given by a Negro who said:

"If you says black am white, dat's foolish. But if you says black *am* white, an' bellers like a bull an' pounds de table with bof' fists, dat's oratory."

1844

When Carter Glass was still a member of the House of Representatives, he was heckled over and over again while he was giving a talk. Glass's patience was sorely tried, but he kept on talking. Finally a sympathizer exclaimed:

"Give him hell, Carter!"

"Why waste dynamite," Glass retorted, "when insect powder will work just as well?"

1845

Applause is the echo of a platitude, if Ambrose Bierce is correct in defining it.

1846

In dinner talk it is perhaps allowable to fling on any faggot rather than let the fire go out.

J. M. Barrie

1847

A hotel page was walking through the hotel lobby calling:

"Telegram for Mr. Papadiamentopulos; telegram for Mr. Papadiamentopulos!"

Presently a guest rushed up to him and inquired:

"What are the initials, please?"

1848

One may tell the following on his favorite toastmaster; and it will probably apply.

Mr. Blank rapped on the table with his gavel and said: "I am not going to stand here and tell you a lot of ancient jokes, but I will introduce speakers tonight who will."

1849

William Jennings Bryan, three times Democratic candidate for the Presidency, once arrived in a town to deliver a speech and was met by a large crowd. There was no platform available, so he climbed up on a manure-spreader.

"Ladies and gentlemen," he began, "this is the first time I have ever talked to an audience from a Republican platform."

1850

We often forgive those who bore us but we cannot forgive those whom we bore.

La Rochefoucauld

1851

A sharp tongue is the only edged tool that grows keener with constant use.

Washington Irving

1852

At a banquet in Paris given in honor of the Wright brothers' first demonstration of an airplane flight in France, Wilbur Wright spoke as follows:

"I am no hand at public speaking, so I will say only a few words. In listening to the speakers who preceded me I have heard comparisons made to the eagle, with the swallow and the hawk as being types of skill and speed in the air. But somehow or other, I couldn't help but think of another bird, which of all the feathered kingdom is the poorest flier and the best talker. I refer to the parrot."

1853

Two Rotary Club members were discussing a well known man who was being considered as a guest for one of their luncheons.

"What do you think of him as a speaker?" asked one of them.

Said the other: "He reminds me of the Erie Railroad."

"How come?" asked the first.

"Efficient in the long run, but very poor terminal facilities."

1854

Congressman Fred Landis of Indiana made a reputation for himself as an orator. Speaking at the unveiling of a monument to President Lincoln, he said: "Abraham Lincoln—that mystic mingling of star and clod." His words were loudly applauded.

After the speech a friend repeated the phrase and asked him what it meant.

"I don't know, really," Landis replied, "but it gets 'em every time."

1855

Before Andrew Jackson became President of the United States, he was making a stump speech in a small village. A friend sitting near him whispered, 'Tip 'em a little Latin, General; they won't be contented without it."

Jackson recalled the few phrases he knew, and in a voice of thunder ended his speech with, "E pluribus unum, sine qua non, ne plus ultra, multum in parvo." The shouts of the Hoosiers could be heard for miles.

1856

There are plenty of people who don't believe everything they hear, but mighty few who won't repeat it.

1857

After World War I, Oliver Herford and Major General "Jack" O'Ryan were joint guests of honor at a banquet. The toastmaster, acting on what he believed to be an inspiration, announced that:

"Mr. Oliver Herford will now improvise a poem in honor of this occasion."

Herford shuddered.

"No, no, no," he expostulated; "have the General fire a cannon."

1858

After dinner speaking is the art of saying nothing briefly.

1859

During one of Theodore Roosevelt's political campaigns, he was repeatedly heckled by a man who was slightly inebriated.

He was interrupted by the heckler's shouting again and again, "I'm a Democrat."

Roosevelt was usually a dangerous man to heckle. Now, howere, pausing in his speech, he smiled, leaned forward, and said, "May I ask the gentleman why he is a Democrat?"

The man replied, "My grandfather was a Democrat, my father was a Democrat, and I'm a Democrat."

"My friend," said Roosevelt, "suppose your grandfather had been a jackass, and your father had been a jackass, what would you be?"

Instantly the reply came back, "A Republican."

1860

A speaker who does not strike oil in ten minutes should stop boring.

Louis Nizer

1861

As the poet says, out of the mouths of babes and suckers cometh wisdom, and it was doubtless one of these who was called upon to tell the difference between *climate* and *weather*.

"Climate," he said, "lasts all the time, while weather lasts only a few days."

1862

During the time of the French Revolution, when the months in France were named, Thermidor, Floreal, Nivose, etc.—it was proposed to extend the innovation to the English language, beginning with January, as—"Freezy, Sneezy, Breezy, Wheezy, Showery, Lowery, Flowery, Bowery, Flowy, Glowy, Blowy, and Snowy."

1863

Sir Ronald Storrs, who in his time, was noted as a diplomat, was one day strolling through a Cairo bazaar when an idler said to him in Arabic:

"God curse your father, O Englishman!"

Storrs was a young man, but even then he understood and spoke perfect Arabic. He couldn't resist the temptation to retort that God would also curse the Arab's father—that is, if the Arab would tell Him which of his mother's ninety-two admirers his father had been.

Then the young man remembered Lord Cromer's belief that it was an unforgivable sin for a British civil servant to have an altercation with a native, so he immediately walked on after speaking his mind. In a few moments he heard footsteps behind him. It was the Arab, who said:

"Return, O Brother, and drink coffee with us, I pray you. I did not think your worship knew Arabic—still less, correct Arabic abuse—and we would fain benefit by your important thoughts."

1864

There is a Mrs. Malaprop of some description in every era. The other day she was discussing her daughter with a friend, who made the comment, "I take it that your daughter is a delicate girl."

"No indeed," said Mrs. Malaprop, "she's the most indelicate girl you ever saw."

1865

Damn: A feminine expression of annoyance.

Oliver Herford

1866

The poet Wordsworth on one occasion remarked to Charles Lamb:

"I believe I could write like Shakespeare if I had a mind to try it."

"Y-yes," stuttered Lamb, "n-nothing is w-wanting b-but the m-mind."

1867

Many authorities claim that a pun can occasionally be justified. Whether the following is one of that kind or not must be determined by the reader.

The king's jester made puns until the ruler could stand him no longer and sentenced him to be hanged. As the jester stood on the gallows with the rope around his neck, the king relented to the extent of saying that if he'd promise never to make another pun, his life would be spared. But the jester just couldn't help exclaiming:

"No noose is good news!" So they went ahead and hanged him.

1868

It was Woodrow Wilson's wont to designate his mark of approval on the margin of a paper by writing "Okeh, W. W."

When asked why he didn't use the simpler "O.K." he answered, "Because it is wrong. "Okeh" is a Choctaw word meaning "It is so."

1869

Belladonna means, in Italian, a beautiful lady; in English, a deadly poison. "A striking example," says Ambrose Bierce, "of the essential identity of the two languages."

1870

A mid-westerner asked a San Franciscan if it were true that everyone in California slept under two blankets.

"That's a slight overstatement," was the reply. "No doubt it comes from Los Angeles. The truth is, I doubt if all the people of California could get under two blankets."

1871

A proverb is a short sentence based on long experience.

Cervantes

1872

An American girl was wandering about the London zoo when an excited keeper rushed up to her and said:

"There's a moose loose!"

"Oh!" the girl yelped. Then she recovered sufficiently to ask: "Are you a Scotchman or an Englishman?"

1873

Henry James considered the English language a game of chance; he would pick up a word from his mental storehouse, drop it, substitute another, then another, and so on until he had built up a veritable tower of synonyms. This word-malady came upon him once while giving an order to a waiter in a café:

"Bring me . . . fetch me . . . carry me . . . supply me . . . in other words (I hope you are following me) give me, when it is cooked . . . scorched . . . grilled, I should say, a large . . . considerable . . . meaty (as opposed to fatty) . . . chop."

1874

H. C. Bunner, humorist of the 90's, said a very ample mouthful when he wrote:

"Shakespeare was a dramatist of note;
He lived by writing things to quote."

1875

The following sentences, culled from several sources, prove that English may be grammatical and at the same time far from good; and that rhetoric may sway off its base and still be amusing:

The major was shot in the ticket-office.
A red-headed man was injured in the suburbs.
He kissed her with passion upon her return.
The mother spanked her child on his reappearance.
The Negro was cut in the fracas.

1876

The reception was to be something special, and Mrs. Grand was instructing her old servant.

"Now Maggie, for the first half-hour you are to stand at the drawing-room door and call the guests' names as they arrive."

"Thank you very much, ma'am," she replied with fervor; "it's what I've been wanting to do to some of your friends for the last ten years."

1877

Six-year old Horace was at the circus with his mother. He made no remarks until the aerial performer stood on his head on the trapeze bar, then he exclaimed:

"Ma, ain't he a damn fool!"

She was deeply shocked.

"Horace," she admonished, "how many times have I told you not to say ain't!"

1878

There are still some extremely dainty people who persist in calling legs limbs. One of these was a spinster who asked her maid if she had given the canary bird its bath.

"Yes," the girl replied decorously, "you may come in now."

1879

On the bus going from New York to Boston, the man next to the window said to the one sitting beside him:

"It just struck me that the word *reviver* is spelled the same either forward or backward. Can you think of another?"

"Tut-tut," replied his seat mate.

1880

Plural: It's the same thing as *singular,* only more of it.

1881

A father once said to his son,
"The next time you get off a pun,
Go out in the yard
And kick yourself—hard,
And then I'll begin when you're done."

1882

Only presidents, editors, and people with tapeworm have the right to use the editorial "we."

Mark Twain

1883

And then there are times when a soft answer does not turn away wrath.

There was a traffic jam at a busy street intersection, and one truck driver got in another's way. His remarks gave evidence that he didn't like it:

"Look where you're going, you big stiff. Who taught you to drive, you dirty, crosseyed runt; you bowlegged, fat-headed galoot!"

The other man looked tough enough to come back in kind, but he just smiled and said:

"You're a pretty handsome guy yourself."

1884

Some years ago the noted French author André Maurois came to America and gave a series of lectures in French before a group of club women. The women attended regularly and made copious notes. Maurois was pleased with the response to his talks.

One afternoon, the women arrived at the club only to find Monsieur Maurois was not there. They waited an hour or so and then phoned his secretary to ask if he were ill or simply delayed.

"Monsieur Maurois will not be there this afternoon," the surprised secretary answered. "He announced that very clearly at last week's talk!"

1885

Most after-dinner repartee may be classed under the head of chestnut dressing.

1886

Joseph H. Choate was a thorough gentleman as well as a distinguished lawyer. He was likewise quick on the trigger. Someone asked:

"Mr. Choate, if you were not yourself, who would you rather be?"

And immediately he answered:

"Mrs. Choate's second husband."

1887

The chairman replied in a few appropriated words.

Cecil Hunt

1888

Bostonian: An American, broadly speaking.

1889

Many stories are told of the embarrassing predicaments that confront public speakers at one time or another. One speaker tells of consenting to address a banquet at a nudist colony. Upon his arrival at the colony, he was greeted by a number of men and women sans habiliment. He was shown the guest room and it was suggested that he might like to prepare for dinner.

He felt called upon to do as the Romans do, so, feeling like a fool, he divested himself of his clothes, suffering extreme mental anguish. Hearing the dinner bell, he walked down the stairs, to discover, to his amazement, that the colonists had all assumed formal dress in deference to him.

1890

Speeches are a good deal like the horns on a healthy Texas steer —a point here and a point there, with a lot of bull in between.

1891

I have never been hurt by anything I didn't say.

Calvin Coolidge

1892

Not that the story need be long, but it will take a long while to make it short.

Thoreau

1893

W. S. Gilbert the witty librettist and side-partner of the composer Sullivan, was once making light of Shakespeare, to the horror of guests at the Garrick Club in London.

"Take this passage for example," said Gilbert in answer to their protests:

" 'I would as lief be thrust through a quickset hedge,
As cry, "Plosh," to a callow throstle.' "

"That is perfectly clear," insisted one of his hearers, rising to the defense of the Bard. "It means that a bird-lover would rather get himself scratched up in the thorny bush than disturb the bird's song. What play is the passage from?"

"No play," said Gilbert, laughing heartily; "I made it up—and jolly good Shakespeare it is too."

1894

We like a speech to be like a woman's dress: long enough to cover the subject yet short enough to make it interesting.

1895

Abraham Lincoln could turn a neat gag on occasion. The governor of a middle Western state was describing a small stream named Weeping Water. For Mr. Lincoln the name had humorous possibilities.

"No doubt," he said, "the Indians out there call it Minneboohoo."

"Why?" the governor asked.

"Well," said Lincoln, "isn't it logical when they call Laughing Water, Minnehaha?"

1896

The Reverend Doctor was pleased to learn that his guide on the fishing trip was once hired by Harry Emerson Fosdick. They spoke of his many noble traits and estimable character.

"Yes," said the guide. "He was a good man except for his swearing."

"But my good fellow," exclaimed the parson, "surely you don't mean to say Doctor Fosdick was profane."

"Oh, but he was, sir," protested the guide. "Once he caught a fine bass. Just as he was about to land him in the boat, the fish wiggled off the hook. So I said to the Doctor, 'That's a damned shame,' and the Doc come right back and said, 'Yes, it is.' But that's the only time I ever heard him use such language."

1897

The boy who afterward became General Wood was told by his teacher of grammar:

"Leonard, I will give you a sentence, and I want you to change it into the imperative mood. Here is the sentence: The horse draws the cart."

"Giddap," young Wood replied.

1898

Albert Smith once wrote an article in "Blackwood's," signed "A. S."

"Tut," said Douglas Jerrold, on reading the initials, "what a pity Smith will tell only two-thirds of the truth."

1899

When the late Hendrik Willem Van Loon visited Cambridge the first time he showed great interest in the venerable buildings. "That," said the guide who was showing him about the university, "is Miss Jones," pointing to a scholarly looking woman striding along before them. "She's the mistress of Ridsley Hall."

"And who," inquired the urbane Dutch-American, "might Ridsley Hall be?"

1900

There was a spelling lesson in process and the teacher called on one of the students:

"Horace, spell 'weather'."

The boy rose slowly to his feet and drawled:

"W-e-t-t-h-e-r."

"Sit down," said the teacher; "and I'd like to say that is the worst spell of weather we have had in some time."

1901

"Mother! Mother!" called Richard, from Back Bay, Boston. "The baby has fell out of the window!"

"Fallen, you mean, dear," corrected his mother.

1902

Nero proclaimed a Roman holiday at the Coliseum. He had made a rather decent collection of Christians, the imperial lions were hungry, and his publicity department had been busy. When the day arrived, the S.R.O. sign was hung out fully an hour before the show started.

The first victim was one who had been no end of trouble to the Roman Emperor. There was a hush of expectancy as he was led to the center of the arena. Then the lions, roaring and, in a manner of speaking, champing at the bite, rushed in—nine slavering brutes eager for blood.

In the vanguard was the ugliest lion of all. He hotfooted it over to the Christian, who merely stooped down and whispered something in his ear. Whereupon the lion, tail between his legs (his hand legs, mind you), slunk away.

The scene was repeated with each of the lions. The show went plop. Nero was disgusted, but he was curious as well. So he sent for the Christian and told him that if he would give him the low-down on the situation, freedom would be his. And the martyr replied:

"It's really quite elementary. I simply whispered to each lion: 'Just remember this, you'll be expected to say a few words after dinner.' "

1903

Even if Henry Clay had not had a cigar named after him, he should have earned undying fame for one remark he made when a public speaker after continuing far beyond his allotted time said:

"I speak, not only for today, but for posterity."

Clay, tried beyond further endurance, shouted:

"But it isn't necessary to keep on talking until the arrival of your audience."

1904

An epigram is a half truth so stated as to irritate the person who believes the other half.

Mathews

1905

Lisp: To call a spade a thpade.

Oliver Herford

1906

A woman returning from California by train was discussing her trip with the man across the aisle. In reply to his query she said she had been in San Jose, which she pronounced *San Josie.*

"That is pronounced *San Hosay,*" the man corrected. "In California you pronounce J's like H's. By the way, when were you there?"

"It was in Hune and Huly," the woman replied meekly.

1907

Synonym: A word you use when you can't spell the other one.

1908

Alas: Early Victorian for OH, HELL.

Oliver Herford

1909

"An epigram," says Hiram the Hired Man, "is a lot like ipecac; a little is good for you, but too much makes you sick."

SECTION 23

SPORTS

1931

Two farmers went fishing one day, and when they got home, they compared their experiences. One said he had caught a 200-pound salmon. The other called his attention to the fact that salmon never weigh 200 pounds, but the first stuck to what he claimed. Then he asked:

"What did *you* catch?"

"Well," was the reply, "all I got was a rusty old lantern bearing the inscription 'Captain Kidd, 1756', and, would you believe it, there was a lighted candle inside it."

The first fisherman gulped, cleared his throat, and said:

"Looka here. Let's get together on our fish stories. I'll take 100 pounds off my salmon if you'll put out the candle in that there lantern."

1932

This is a fish story, so it must be added to the list of 'taint-so yarns.

A fisherman was having no luck at all. After a while he spied a frog and thought it would make good bait. He grabbed it just before a snake got it. That snake was plumb disappointed and looked so reproachful that the man took pity on him and poured a drink of whiskey down the reptile's throat.

Then he went back to his fishing, having baited his hook with the frog. Presently he felt a gentle tapping at his right leg. He looked, down, and there was the snake with another frog in his mouth.

1933

This fish story emerged from this year's creel:

The old cronies were getting out their line and tackle and limbering up their memories of last year's catches.

"Man—you've never seen such a fish as I caught from that stream!" said the angler.

"About the size of a whale, wasn't it?" grinned his companion.

"Shucks, I was baitin' with whales," came the prompt reply.

1934

A butler in an English country house came to his master and announced:

"Pardon, milord; there's a burglar downstairs."

"Quite so, Parkins," said his lordship. "Bring me my fowling piece and sports suit—the heather mixture."

1935

An Iowa fisherman has developed a new technique. He cuts chewing tobacco into small pieces and sprinkles them on the water. The fish come and gobble the chunks and dive to the bottom. The fisherman waits until the fish have to come to the surface to spit, and then he hits them on the head with a club.

1936

Two refugees, not long in this country, went out hunting for pheasants. A nice cock pheasant flew up in front of them and perched on a large bush.

"Don't shoot yet, Herman," one of them shouted; "the gun isn't loaded."

"Can't help it," the other replied; "the bird won't wait."

1937

This story has been told as coming from various African explorers, but that doesn't matter.

It seems that a jungle hunter came up with an elephant that was limping badly. He followed it for some distance, when he saw the great pachyderm wobble and fall to the ground. The hunter rushed up and looked it over. On one of his feet there was a big thorn, which he removed and then went back to camp.

Five years elapsed. To kill time, the hunter went to a circus and bought a cheap seat. When a group of performing elephants came into the arena, one of them looked about, spied the erstwhile hunter, reached over with his trunk, grabbed him, and lifted him from his cheap seat and placed him gently into a private box.

1938

When a man wants to murder a tiger he calls it sport: when the tiger wants to murder him he calls it ferocity.

G. B. Shaw

1939

Among the Marx Brothers' famous routines which delight the memory was Groucho's query "Did I ever tell you how I shot a wild rhinoceros in my pajamas? How he got into my pajamas I'll never know."

1940

One of our more unsavory nouveau riche decided to break into Southern society by joining in the bird hunting activities. To assure his success the fellow paid five thousand dollars for a famous bird dog and proceeded on his first shoot.

But something went wrong because at the end of the day he returned empty handed while all other members of the group, in spite of their less valuable dogs, had shot the full quota of birds they were permitted.

"How could you do so badly with such a famous dog?" he was asked.

"Famous dog!" he scoffed bitterly. "That blamed idiot didn't do a darned thing but stand still with his tail sticking out behind him and his head stuck out in front. It took the whole morning to kick that habit out of him."

1941

I bought a gun and learned to shoot.
I bought a flute and learned to toot.
Now I'm a shooter and a tooter.
I wonder could anything be cuter.

1942

The world traveler was holding forth among a group at a house-party. He, incidentally, was the only one who was not bored. He told of the continents one by one, finally reaching India by a circuitous route.

"It was there," he said impressively, "that I first saw a man-eating tiger."

"That's nothing at all," exclaimed an impatient looking man. "Only the other day I saw a man eating rabbit."

1943

Definition of fox-hunting by Oscar Wilde: "The unspeakable after the uneatable."

1944

A twosome were searching for their golf balls that seemed to have disappeared in the rough. About to give up, they were approached by an interested lady spectator, who had been watching them sympathetically from the green.

"I don't know a blessed thing about the game of golf, gentlemen," the woman said, "but would it be cheating if I were to tell you where the balls are?"

1945

Two golfers in the smart set of the Country Club Section were discussing social matters as they teed up. Said one:

"Is your wife entertaining this Fall?"

The other made a swipe at his ball and replied:

"Not very."

1946

The golfer was in an awful hurry to begin playing.

"Take it easy, take it easy," his opponent counseled; "you know that the more haste, the less teed."

1947

On a Scottish golf course there is a sign that reads: "Members will kindly refrain from picking up lost balls until they have stopped rolling."

1948

Casey poured another drink and observed to his companion:

"Well, Houlihan certainly got rich quick, didn't he?"

"He sure did," Sweeney answered; "he got rich so quick that he can't swing a golf club without spitting on his hands."

1949

A young member of a country club went out alone one day to play a few holes of golf. He was a personable young fellow, but he had an impediment in his speech that made conversation embarrassing.

However, when he approached the second green he became very much interested to see a beautiful young woman who was also playing alone. He thought he should introduce himself, so he smiled and said:

"M-my n-name is P-P-Paul." Then he added, with a twinkle in his eye, "B-But I'm n-no s-s-saint!"

The girl smiled back at him and answered:

"M-m-my n-n-name is M-Mary; b-b-but I'm n-not a v-v-v-very good p-player."

1950

One Sunday Eddie Cantor took on Champion Gene Sarazen for a round of golf at the Bonnie Brae Country Club. Finally when they sat down at the 19th hole, the comedian said:

"Gene, what do you think of my game?"

The champion shrugged and replied:

"Oh, I suppose it's all right, but I still prefer golf."

1951

A really fat man is no good at the game of golf because if he tees the ball where he can hit it, he can't see it; and if he puts the ball where he can see it, he can't hit it.

1952

The late Henry P. Davidson, then a partner of J. P. Morgan, told this story at a convention of social service workers some years ago in Kansas City.

An Army sergeant was transferred from one camp to another and his captain sent along a note to the commanding officer that he was a good soldier but that he was an inveterate gambler. "I wish you would cure him of this vice," he added.

When the sergeant arrived, the C.O. said:

"Young man, I understand that you have one besetting sin—gambling. I don't approve of it. It's a bad habit. What do you bet on?"

"Anything, sir," the sergeant replied. "For example, I'll bet twenty-five dollars you have a mole on your right shoulder."

"Maybe it'll cure you if I take that bet. Put down your money." The captain thereupon took off his blouse and shirt and proved that there wasn't a mole in sight.

So the sergeant paid up, and the C.O. hastened to write the captain how he had taught the sergeant a lesson.

In two or three days came a reply: "*Still* the sergeant wins. Just before he left he bet me a hundred dollars that he'd have the shirt off your back five minutes after he reported."

1953

Animals are superior to human beings. If there are thirty horses in a race, fifty thousand people will go to see it, but put thirty people in a race and not one horse would go to see it.

1954

One of Abraham Lincoln's early neighbors was a boaster on every occasion. One day when the future president was in a crowd the man stepped up to him and bragged:

"I have the best horse in the whole country. Yesterday I ran him nine miles in three minutes flat, and he never fetched a long breath."

"But," Abe observed, "I imagine he fetched a good many short ones."

1955

In a racing stable an old horse was talking with a much younger horse about a race in which they both were going to run. The older horse asked the younger if, as a special favor, he would let him win the race, because if he did, he would then be put out to pasture for the rest of his life. Otherwise he would be sent to the boneyard.

Then a dog that was in the stable spoke up. "Oh go ahead," he said to the young horse, "be a sport and let him win the race."

At that the two horses looked at each other, and the young horse said:

"Great Scott, here's a dog that can talk!"

1956

A prim old New England lady was visited by a nephew who induced her to go to a horserace. More than that, he persuaded her, much against her principles, to make a bet at 20 to 1.

It just happened that the horse won. She had put up a dollar, and the old girl was handed a twenty-dollar bill and a one.

"What—what—what's all this?" she exclaimed.

"Why, that the money you won on the race, Auntie," said her nephew.

"Do you mean to say, Horace, that I am getting back twenty-one dollars for the one I put in?" the old lady asked.

"You sure do," the boy answered.

"Well!" she exclaimed. "I should like to know how long this thing has been goin' on."

1957

"Hear no evil, see no evil, speak no evil," and you'll never be a success at a bridge party.

1958

Bridge: A card game in which a good deal depends on a good deal.

1959

After this happened, the authorities at a middle-western college banned minstrel shows:

The interlocutor was asked the difference between an amateur and a professional athlete. He didn't know the answer, so he said:

"What *is* the difference, Mr. Bones?"

"The difference," the end-man returned, "is that the professional is paid by check."

1960

All hula-hula dancers have to do is to stand around and twiddle their tums.

1961

A man and his eighteen-year old grandaughter stood watching a group of young people dance.

"Bet you never saw any dancing like that back in the 1880's," said the girl.

"Yes I did too," said gramp, "but the place was raided."

1962

An Englishman, on his first visit to this country discovered that a jitterbug is not an insect, but a human being acting like one.

1963

"How do you like it, Kid?" asked a fond uncle to the six-year-old boy he was taking for his first ride on a roller-coaster.

"Great," was the answer; "just like they had laid the tracks over Mae West."

1964

After the big football game a new stadium employee was being told of his duties in cleaning up the litter. The field was strewn with programs, bottles, and what not, and the new man looked them over.

"So you pick all them up and take 'em away," said his instructor.

"Okay," the other replied. "By the way, what are all those grapes doing on the field?"

"Nuts," was the contemptuous answer; "them ain't grapes; them's eyeballs.'

1965

The young man had just received a last-minute invitation to the picnic, but he turned it down. He said there wouldn't be any use; he'd already prayed for a hard thunder storm.

1966

Up at the Associated Press radio room, Bob Harlow, the celebrated sporting writer, told of a radio announcer who was broadcasting a play-by-play account of a World's Series game.

"The fellow got excited when a popular batter was up. At one thrilling point the announcer shouted, 'He swang at it!'

"And do you know," Harlow continued; "seven hundred and fifty sets in Boston burned out."

1967

The members of the local Athletic Club considered themselves pretty good, but none had a higher estimate of his physical prowess than Tim Seward. A new member got fed up on his boasting and blustering about, and he made up his mind he would cure him once and for all.

"Tim," he said, "I'll bet I can wheel something in a wheelbarrow from the clubhouse to the street, and you can't wheel it back again,"

Tim looked at the little fellow and laughed.

"I'll take you up on that," he agreed.

A wheelbarrow was brought to the clubhouse and the new member grasped the handles of the barrow, motioned to Tim, and said:

"All right, get in."

1968

The physical culture fan was boasting of his prowess.

"Why," he said, "when I was a boy I thought nothing of a ten-mile walk."

"Humph!" exclaimed his listener, "I still don't think much of it."

1969

Five-year-old Sammie had just seen his first football game, and the excitement and cheering made a great impression on him. That night after he had said the Lord's Prayer, he added:

"God bless Mummie,
God bless Daddy,
God bless Mary Lou.
Rah! Rah! Rah!"

1970

Max Baer, the wise-cracking and frequently unsuccessful pugilist, was training out of doors one summer at a New Jersey resort. He told his manager that he was trying to get a good sun tan so that spectators wouldn't be able to tell him from Joe Louis when they got into the ring.

"Don't let that worry you," the manager answered. "They'll be able to tell. The one standing up will be Joe Louis."

1971

"Courage and strength run in our family," boasted the man as he downed his fourth highball. "Why, my brother walked right up to Joe Louis and socked him on the nose."

"Holy Smoke!" gasped a listener. "I'd like to shake hands with your brother."

"Don't be silly," was the reply; "do you think we're going to disinter him just to shake hands with YOU?"

1972

There is an authenticated story of Dr. Charles W. Eliot, late President of Harvard University, being on his way to a Yale-Harvard football game with Edward Everett Hale. A friend stopped them and asked Eliot where he was going. To which he replied:

"To yell with Hale."

1973

The drama of the racetrack has seldom been better illustrated than in the yarn about two honeymooners at Saratoga, both of whom were sincere gamblers. But they had tough luck consistently for nearly a week. On the last day of the meet they had only two dollars left between them. After taking stock of the situation, the young man said:

"Looka here, sweet; let me go out to the track alone today; I've got a hunch."

His wife agreed, and he won a 40-to-1 shot on the first race. He followed this up with such success that toward the end of the afternoon he had won $10,000. Later he stopped in a gambling house and ran the amount up to $30,000. He had about decided to quit when he stopped at a roulette wheel and put the entire roll on "red."

The wheel spun, the ball bounced, and ever so slowly finally settled to a standstill in "black."

The young fellow walked slowly back to the hotel, where he met his wife waiting on the porch.

"How did you make out?" she asked eagerly.

The boy lit a cigarette, inhaled, and answered:

"Lost the two dollars."

1974

The Chinese are a philosophical and gentle race as the following story proves:

A Chinaman visiting America for the first time, was taken to the races. Along about the third race the Chinaman got up and started out, when his host said, "Here, where are you going? It isn't nearly finished yet."

"In our country," replied the Chinese gentleman, "it was proved thirty centuries ago that one horse can run faster than another."

1975

"Why do you want a divorce?" asked the judge before whom the suit was being tried.

"It's this way, Judge," the woman answered; "my husband is a no-good loafer. All he thinks about is gambling and horse racing. Why, he doesn't even remember our wedding day."

At this, the husband jumped to his feet and shouted:

"That's a lie! We were married the day that Twenty Grand won the Kentucky Derby."

SECTION 24

THE THEATRE AND THE MOVIES

1999

Now that John Barrymore is gone—rest his soul—he will be the central figure in many a story he never heard of. At any rate, this is typed for him.

Years ago, when he was with a stock company, there came an evening when he was unable to remember his lines. He stalled for time by faking a piece of business and slid over to the side of the stage to get his cue from the prompter.

"What's the line, what's the line?" he asked in a hoarse whisper.

"Damned if I know," the prompter sighed; "what's the play?"

2000

W. S. Gilbert, whose name is even more quickly recognized in connection with his composer-partner Sullivan, said of an acquaintance: "No one can have a higher opinion of him than I have—and I think he's a dirty little beast." When he heard a theatrical manager lauding an actress, he observed: "That fellow is blowing his own strumpet."

2001

Percy Hammond, who used to be dramatic critic for the New York Herald Tribune, was famous for being both caustic and readable. He could pan a play so that both actors and producers would enjoy reading his review. On one occasion his review of an opening night ended as follows:

"Upon looking over this report, I find that I have knocked everything but the chorus girls' legs—but nature has anticipated me there."

2002

Heywood Broun was one of the few radicals who, on many occasions, gave a humorous twist to what he wrote and said. One evening he attended the first performance of a play with the author, a woman. He said nothing about it until half way through the second act. Then he nudged the lady and whispered:

"Don't look now, but your show is slipping."

2003

It is said that once William Randolph Hearst invited Will Rogers to come to San Simeon, his California estate, for a weekend. Hearst had a large house party, and Rogers was the star guest whom Hearst did not fail to show off. A few days later Hearst received from Rogers a bill for several thousand dollars for services as a professional entertainer. He called Rogers on the phone and protested, saying, "I didn't engage you to come as an entertainer. I invited you as my guest."

"When people invite me as a guest," Will answered, "they invite Mrs. Rogers too. When they ask me to come alone, I go as a professional entertainer."

2004

Cornelia Otis Skinner, one of America's greatest actresses and daughter of Otis Skinner, one of America's greatest actors, tells this story on herself.

When she was a child and her distinguished father was on tour, she kept up a steady correspondence with him. Her letters from him would be addressed "Cornelia Otis Skinner," so she would carefully cut the "Otis Skinner" from them and sell it as her father's autograph.

"Sometimes," she said, "it would bring ten cents; at other times as much as a quarter."

2005

Bob Hope would have told this old one on himself, and thereby made it a lot funnier. It seems that a well-known French actor was discussing his latest triumph. He said:

"When I came to my big scene, the audience was sitting there open-mouthed."

"That's a lot of hooey," exclaimed a rival. "They simply couldn't *all* be yawning at once."

2006

Alfred Lunt and Lynn Fontanne are recognized as a devoted husband and wife. When they started rehearsing "At Mrs. Bean's," the script called for Miss Fontanne to strike Mr. Lunt in the face. She found she couldn't do it. She pulled her hand back—and then stopped before she struck. Lunt begged her to hit him, but after a half hour she still couldn't. Finally Mr. Lunt shouted in desperation: "For God's sake, Lynn, you're the lousiest actress I've ever played opposite!"

Lynn let fly a resounding smack. Mr. Lunt yelped with pain, then grinned. But when they put on the show he had to whisper, "Don't be lousy, dear," each time before she would hit him.

2007

One day a down-at-heel individual came to Billy Rose and made him a startling proposition.

"I'll do an act in your show that will be the greatest sensation ever presented. You can advertise it in advance, and get $100 a ticket. If you'll put $25,000 in the bank for my wife, I'll then commit suicide in the full view of your audience."

"It's a natural!" said Rose, appearing enthusiastic, "but just a minute. What will you do for an encore?"

2008

There are not too many of the old-school actors and actresses on the stage and screen today, but among the dwindling few is Helen

Westley. She is well-loved not only for her acting but for her sense of humor. One day on a movie set an extra rushed up to her and exclaimed:

"Dear Miss Westley, what are you doing in this picture?"

"Oh, hadn't you heard?" the gray-haired actress replied. "I'm supplying the sexagenarian appeal."

2009

It was a pleasant little family dinner party, and among those present was a magician. The main dish was stewed rabbit, and the magician partook rather copiously of it. Then suddenly he left the table, apparently in great discomfort.

"Very unusual," observed one of the guests.

"What do you mean?" inquired another.

"Because," came the reply, "it's probably the first time on record that a rabbit made a magician disappear."

2011

If anyone believes the radio will replace the newspaper, just let him try to wrap up last winter's suit in a radio.

2012

Dorothy Parker, in reviewing a play, said of the leading lady, "She runs the gamut of emotions from A to B."

2013

Before W. C. Fields made his enviable reputation as a screen comedian he was the best juggler on the vaudeville stage, and this, in combination with his sense of comedy, gave him top billing wherever he appeared.

One evening, after he had gone through most of his routine, he came to the most difficult stunt of all. The orchestra stopped playing, and the house was hushed as the climax was approached. Suddenly there came a crash from backstage, as if a stagehand had dropped a case of cannon balls. Fields threw up both hands, smiled at the audience, and said:

"Mice!"

2014

As the young man and his girl left the movie theater after a performance, the young woman said:

"It's perfectly marvelous what progress the films have made in just the last few years."

"Yes," her escort agreed; "first they moved, then they talked, and now this one smells."

2015

A large sign outside a movie theater in a California town announced: Children's Matinee Today. Adults not Admitted Unless with Child.

2016

An actor's motto: Better a small role than a long loaf.

2017

Roger Kemble, father of the lovely Mrs. Siddons, once forbade the young lady to marry an actor.

She defied him, whereupon Kemble berated her not only for her disobedience but for the fact that she had married the most incompetent member of his company.

"Precisely," replied the defiant bride. "Nobody can call him an actor."

2018

I want a film that begins with an earthquake and works up to a climax.

Samuel Goldwyn

2019

Some of the greatest love affairs I've known have involved one actor—unassisted.

Wilson Mizner

2020

A well known actor was giving platform recitals of scenes from his successes. Just after his appearance the program chairman of the woman's club who presented him brought him a telegram announcing that his wife had just given birth to twins. He was overcome with delight and exclaimed joyously, "It is the first time I ever received two fees for one performance."

2021

Perhaps the all-time low in enthusiasm for dramatics was reached when one of them wrote of a performance of "Uncle Tom's Cabin": "The bloodhounds were badly supported."

2022

A well known comedian who liked his liquor strong and often appeared in the hotel dining-room one morning with a devastating hangover.

The waiter was understanding and sympathetic.

"Shall I fix you a Bromo-Seltzer?" he asked.

"Ye gods, no!" the actor groaned. "I couldn't stand the noise."

2023

A movie actress was told of a rumor that she was going to divorce her latest husband. She denied it vigorously, and added:

"Why, I hardly know him!"

2024

A hopeful young actor was turned down time and again by the Hollywood casting directors. In a desperate last attempt, he approached one of the film directors and said, "It's now or never, if you want me in one of your pictures. I now have many companies after me."

"Have you!" said the director, his interest aroused by this statement. "What companies are considering you?"

"Well," said the actor solemnly, "there's the telephone company, the electric and gas company, the milk company . . ."

The director laughed; the actor got the job.

2025

A well known actor, called on to testify in a lawsuit, was put on the stand and asked to identify himself. In a dignified manner he said:

"I am the greatest actor in the world."

Later one of his friends asked him if he hadn't laid it on a bit thick by making such a statement. The actor replied:

"I always avoid self praise, but you must remember that they had me under oath."

2026

During World War II somebody commented to a well-known screen actor that the draft was taking a lot of Hollywood's popular leading men.

"True enough," said the actor. "Now the chances are that many of our leading ladies will be playing opposite men of their own age."

2027

A theatrical group were discussing the marriage of a famous actress, whose pre-marital life had been the subject of much comment.

"She has made a very good match, they say," one of the group observed. "And they say she made her husband a full confession of all her past liaisons."

"What honesty she must have had," another remarked. "What courage!"

"Yes," said a former admirer, "and what a memory!"

2028

One of the members of the well known Singer's Midget troupe got on a Pullman sleeper between Chicago and New York. He had a good dinner in the dining car, during the course of which he drank several cups of black coffee. Then he went to bed in an upper berth.

In the morning the man who had occupied the lower berth appeared in the washroom at an early hour. The porter asked him how he had slept.

"Not a wink," the man replied; "all night somebody was pacing up and down in the upper berth."

2029

The night that a certain gangrenous play opened in New York one of the drama critics was on his way home to write his piece when a friend asked him how the show was.

"Dirtiest show I ever saw," said the critic.

"How dirty?" asked the friend.

"Well," said the critic, "one character says to another, 'You ——— — —— — ———.' " (The speaker fills in the blanks)

"That's not so bad," said the friend. "I've heard worse on the stage."

"But that," snapped the reviewer, "was the only clean line in the play."

2030

It was a perfectly hateful critic who wrote of a well-known actress:

"Her performance belongs in a sandwich rather than on the stage."

2031

When he was one of New York's leading drama critics, Lieut.-Com. John Mason Brown was invited to lecture on the theater to the soldiers in a Long Island training camp. Before he began his lecture, the critic suggested to the men that they write out any questions and hand them in. He would answer them later. A flock of slips was handed to him as he finished, and he disposed of the first few without any trouble. Then came one that stumped him. "Will Commander Brown," it said, "be kind enough to give me Betty Grable's telephone number?"

2032

Genius, stage and screen were represented at a cocktail party given in a swank East Side apartment. The lion of the afternoon was a distinguished writer, and women were vying with each other for his attention. He seemed, however, to be definitely intrigued with a beautiful but vapid movie actress. One of the brilliant women present complained to the hostess, saying:

"I don't understand how those two can spend so much of their time together; what can they have in common?"

"The only thing they have in common," the hostess replied, "is difference in sex."

2033

At the end of a slightly devastating play review, a dramatic critic wrote:

"But I saw the play under adverse conditions; the curtain was up."

2034

A movie magnate (*or* an Army Chief of Staff, *or* the editor-in-chief of a publishing house) was conferring with a group of script writers (*or* under officers, *or* sub-editors).

He had not been talking long when he was about to be interrupted by one of the men present. Banging the table with his fist, he shouted:

"Don't say yes until I'm through!"

2035

A certain motion picture producer with social pretensions is said to have spent $25,000 in connection with his genealogy. He paid $5,000 to have it looked up, and $20,000 to have it hushed up.

2036

Two chorus girls were discussing the party they had been invited to.

"Are you going?" asked Maisie.

"No," replied Dot, "and if you ask me the reason why, I'll tell. Every girl is supposed to go dressed to match the color of her boy friend's hair. And my boy friend is bald."

2037

A vaudeville actor, alone on the stage, was entertaining the audience with funny stories and gags when a cat walked out from the wings.

"Get out of here," the actor shouted. "This is a monologue, not a catalogue."

2038

Mr. Jones was in the dog-house again. "What's wrong now?" he asked his wife on their way home from a performance of *Hamlet*.

"Nothing, Henry, nothing," she replied, "except that at the final curtain you insisted on calling out, 'Author!' "

2039

The rich old bird who married a popular actress got even with the flighty young thing when he died. He left her half a million dollars payable at the age of thirty-five.

2040

The advance agent of a touring dramatic troupe visited the manager of a small-town theater where the company was to appear.

"We'll want to rehearse next Wednesday afternoon at two o'clock, so please have your stage manager, carpenter, property man and electrician present at that time."

"Okay, Chief," said the manager. "He'll be here."

2041

As a stuttering comedian, Joe Frisco, the great vaudeville performer, made an early beginning. When he was a small boy at school, his teacher asked him what a cocoon was; and Joe answered:

"A cocoon is a c-colored person."

2042

If you don't remember Lola Montez—and if you did, it would date you badly—you must remember her name. She had *it*. In spite of her Spanish name, Lola was an Irish gal.

She wowed 'em, laid 'em in the aisles with her charms, both in Europe and America. She wasn't satisfied, though, for she hadn't appeared in Paris. So she laid siege to the French capital. First, a barrage of publicity—then her appearance.

But Lola Montez couldn't sing and she couldn't dance, and she was booed and jeered by the Parisian audience.

Then she got her Irish up. She looked around for a convenient weapon to throw. There wasn't anything handy, so she took off a slipper and hurled it into the audience. The other slipper followed along with some rather neat Billingsgate. Still not satisfied, she removed her garters, both with heavy buckles, and slammed them down on a bald head in the front row.

Whereat thunderous applause shook the house. Lola Montez had won the heart of Paris. . . .

Gentlemen, I shall stop short of nothing to win your approval.

2043

That actor is so conceited that every time he hears a clap of thunder, he goes to the window and takes a bow.

2044

Late one evening Oscar Wilde returned to his club after attending the first performance of one of his plays that was a complete flop. A friend inquired of him how the play went.

"The play," Oscar replied loftily, "was a great success, but the audience was a failure."

2045

A stage magician was doing his stuff at an entertainment on shipboard. He completely mystified his audience, which included the captain's pet parrot. The specialty of this sleight-of-hand expert was making things disappear—a pack of cards, a lighted cigar, and electric lamp, all in quick succession. The mystified parrot couldn't keep his eyes off the proceedings. Finally the magician said:

"And now, ladies and gentlemen, I will demonstrate a feat that has never been accomplished by anyone else in the history of magical art."

At that moment a terrific explosion occurred. Every light went out, women shrieked and whistles blew. There was panic. The ship sank.

Later, the parrot was sitting on a piece of floating driftwood. The magician came to the surface, shouted "Help," and disappeared. Again he came up, called for help, and went under. After his third appearance he disappeared for good.

The parrot pondered what had happened, and exclaimed, "Amazing!"

Section 25

TRAVEL

2060

Add this to conversations that could have happened but never did. It begins with a traffic officer who said:

"So you didn't see me signal you to stop?"

"No, sir."

"And you didn't hear me whistle?"

"No, sir."

"And you didn't notice the red light?"

"No, sir."

"Dearie me! I guess I'd better go home. I don't seem to be any use around here."

2061

A Pullman passenger poked his head out between the curtains and said: "Porter, what about my shoes? One shoe is black and the other tan!" To which the porter replied:

"Well, sah, if it don't beat all! Dis is de second time dat's happened dis mawnin'."

2062

A Pullman passenger, nearing his destination, said to the porter:

"What's the average tip you get from passengers on this run?"

When the porter said, "One dollar, suh," the traveler gave him a dollar bill, and the porter showed extreme gratefulness.

"Suh," he said with enthusiasm, "you're the first gentleman who has ever come up to my average."

2063

The garage man charged the motorist ten dollars for towing him two miles, but the motorist got his money's worth; he kept his brakes on all the time.

2064

A hook-and-ladder came screaming down the avenue and swung into a side street. When it had passed, one woman was heard to say to another:

"I don't see why they have a man steering from the rear of that fire truck."

And her companion answered:

"Neither do I; it's woman's work."

2065

The hitch-hiking annoyance didn't bother Mr. Smithers. As soon as he got out of town he put a sign on his windshield reading TAXI.

2066

The collision had occurred. The cop was bawling out the man.

"Didn't you see this lady driving toward you? Why didn't you give her the road?"

"I was going to, officer, as soon as I could find out which half of the road she wanted."

2067

A car with a flat tire was stalled alongside the curb, and a loquacious passerby said to the motorist:

"Have a puncture?" The motorist took a drag at his cigarette and replied:

"No thanks, I just had one."

2068

A woman may be said to have learned the rudiments of driving a car when the road begins to turn when she does.

2069

This might have happened to a man, but it was a girl who was driving her new car when something went wrong with the engine. The traffic light changed from red to green and then back to red, and she could not get the automobile started. Finally the traffic officer approached her and asked:

"What's the matter, lady? Ain't we got colors to suit you?"

2070

A man was taking a driver's test for his license. He was asked:

"If the driver of a car ahead held a hand out straight, what would you do?"

The applicant thought hard and then inquired:

"Man or woman?"

2071

A motorist stopped his car on a country road and asked a native-looking individual how far it was to Millerstown. The reply was:

"It's 24,999 miles the way you're headed, but if you just turn around it ain't but four."

2072

One advantage enjoyed by the fellow who sits at the wheel of a hearse is that he never has a backseat driver.

2073

Ten seconds after the crash occurred, there was a motorcycle cop on the scene. Of the man who seemed to be at fault he asked:

"What was the cause of the accident?"

And the man replied:

"My wife fell asleep in the back seat."

2074

A man limped into an automobile agency and said to the salesman:

"I think you claimed when you sold me this car that you would replace anything that was broken or was missing."

"That is entirely correct, sir."

"Well, I want three front teeth and a collar bone."

2075

A traffic cop stopped a pretty young thing who was going at a good clip.

"Whaddye mean, goin' fifty miles an hour?"

"Oh dear," the girl said. "My brakes don't work and I was hurrying to get home before I had an accident."

2076

A young married woman drove her car into a garage and asked the proprietor if he could straighten the right-hand fender so it wouldn't be noticed.

The garage man wasn't too hopeful, but he had an idea.

"I don't know as I could do that, Madam," he said, "but I could fix it so's you could wait a few days and then ask your husband how he happened to get it all dented up."

2077

There was the usual argument after the automobile crash. The lady, as usual, was talking:

"I turned the way I signaled," she averred.

To which the man retorted:

"Yes, I know it; that's what fooled me."

2078

With the change from horse-drawn vehicles to those propelled by gasoline, the following story loses a part of its vigor, but it still remains one of the American classics.

When Joseph H. Choate was American Ambassador to the Court of St. James, he attended a diplomatic reception in the plain black evening dress usual for Americans, while other countries' representatives wore resplendent gold-braided uniforms.

It was therefore not surprising that a ranking British official took Choate for one of the waiters, and said:

"Call me a cab."

"You're a cab," said Mr. Choate tartly.

It puzzled the Britisher no end, and he went to his host about it.

"Good God," the man exclaimed; "that wasn't a waiter. He was the American Ambassador."

"Oh, really, really," said the Britisher. "Do take me to Mr. Choate so that I may apologize."

Of course Choate was big about the affair. He smiled pleasantly when the man explained, and said:

"You asked me to call you a cab. I did so." Then he added with a twinkle: "If you had been better looking, I would have called you a hansom cab."

2080

A friend met John Godfrey Saxe, the poet, in a railroad station. He was carrying two large pieces of luggage and seemed in a hurry.

"Where are you going, John?" asked his friend.

"To Boston, Deo volente."

"What route is that?" the man asked.

"By way of Providence, of course," replied Saxe, running for his train.

2081

A little jack can lift up an automobile, but it takes a lot of jack to keep it up.

2082

There was a young man of Ostend
Who vowed he'd hold out to the end;
  But when halfway over
  From Calais to Dover,
He done what he didn't intend.

2083

Here lies till Gabriel's trumpet peal
The bones of Shelby Sharp.
He dozed while holding a steering wheel
And woke up holding a harp.

2084

The perfect epitaph for a motorist:

Here lies the body of William Jay,
Who died maintaining his right of way;
He was right, dead right, as he sped along,
But he's just as dead as if he'd been dead wrong.

Section 26

WRITERS AND BOOKS

2100

Even novelist-playwright-actor Sinclair Lewis must have been flabbergasted when he received a fan letter from a middle-western young lady who said that she was crazy to meet him and, with her mind on a secretary's job, to do anything for him. "And when I say anything," she wrote him, "I mean anything."

The novelist turned the letter over to his wife and she answered it. She said that her husband was provided with a competent secretary and that she herself did everything else. "And," she added, "when I say everything, I mean *everything*."

2101

Clarence Budington Kelland, always the master of situations, was listening one day to a young writer commenting on his own productions.

"I'm not at all satisfied with my later work," said the youthful fictionist. "My books are selling better than ever, but the writing doesn't seem to me to be nearly as good as it was."

"That's a lot of nonsense," Kelland replied. "Your writing is just as good as it ever was. Probably your taste is improving."

2102

William McFee, the novelist, told this story at a dinner given by a group of literary friends:

A certain sea captain and his chief engineer were tired of debating which one of them the ship could the better dispense with.

Finally they decided to swap places for a day. The engineer went up to the bridge and the skipper dived into the engine-room. After a couple of hours at most the captain suddenly appeared on deck covered with oil and soot, and with a bruised eye.

"Chief!" he called, wildly beckoning with a monkey-wrench, "You'll have to come down here at once. I can't seem to make the ship go."

"Of course you can't," said the chief, calmly removing his pipe from his mouth, "she's ashore."

2103

A well known American novelist got a bright idea that he could make more money by raising chickens than by writing, so he started a poultry ranch. He became pretty interested in the project; so much so that he was calling his chickens after his literary friends.

One day Dorothy Parker visited him, and asked:

"Well, how is little Kathleen Norris getting along?"

"Now here's a strange thing," the novelist replied; "the remarkable thing about Kathleen Norris is that she turned out to be Ernest Hemingway."

2104

Bernard Shaw was swimming in a pool during his stay in South Africa. Some small boys who did not know his identity dared the youngest to duck the old man for a shilling. The little lad accepted, but when he swam close to Mr. Shaw, he became panic stricken. Shaw turned, and asked him what he wanted. The boy told of the plot and of the shilling bet.

Shaw looked sternly at the youngster and said, "If you'll wait a moment while I get my breath, I'll let you push my head under water."

2105

A ghost writer, it is said, who had been doing a series of articles purported to be by Sam Goldwyn, movie magnifico, became sick, and one of the pieces was written by a substitute ghost. Upon reading this article, Mr. Goldwyn expressed considerable dismay, saying, "This is not up to my usual standard."

2106

Manuscript: Something that is submitted in haste and returned at leisure.

Oliver Herford

2107

Publishing a volume of verse is like dropping a rose petal down the Grand Canyon and waiting for an echo.

Don Marquis

2108

The difference between the dime novel of yesterday and the best seller of today is about $2.40.

2109

One of the most muriatic book reviews of the present century was of Margot Asquith's autobiography. It was written by Dorothy Parker and contained the line: "The affair between Margot Asquith and Margot Asquith will rank as one of the prettiest love affairs in literature."

2110

In refusing to autograph his books, George Bernard Shaw sometimes gives the following story as his reason. During his travels in the United States he painstakingly autographed many books for his hostesses.

While browsing in a small Manhattan bookshop he noticed a copy of Pygmalion which bore his signature. "What's the price of this book?" he inquired. "It's usually $2.98 but some illiterate has scribbled all over the frontispiece so I'll sell it for $.98" came the answer.

2111

When Spenser had completed the "Faërie Queen," he took it to the Earl of Southampton, patron of the poets of that day. The Earl read a few pages of the manuscript, and then ordered his servant to give the writer twenty pounds. Reading further, he cried out in rapture, "Carry that man another twenty pounds!"

Continuing the perusal of the manuscript, he said, "Give him twenty pounds more." At length he lost patience and shouted, "Go turn that fellow out of the house, for if I read on, I shall be ruined."

2112

Mark Twain was traveling by train through the lovely countryside of southern France when he was startled to hear an Englishman sitting near by, say: "Mr. Clemens, I would give five pounds not to have read your 'Huckleberry Finn!' "

Twain turned to him in amazement, awaiting an explanation. The Englishman smiled and added: "So that I could have again the pleasure of reading it for the first time."

2113

Ambrose Bierce, author of "The Devil's Dictionary," once wrote a book review consisting of one short sentence. "The covers of this book," he wrote, "are too far apart."

2114

A young man wanted to buy a gift for his girl friend, and he asked her if she was interested in book ends.

"Yes," she answered, "that's the part I always read first."

2115

Jack London was late in delivering a story to a fiction magazine. His friend the editor wrote him:

"Dear Jack: If I don't receive that story within twenty-four hours, I'll come up to your room and kick you downstairs—and *I* always keep my promises."

Jack's reply, at least, was prompt. He wrote:

"Dear Dick: If I did all my work with my feet, I'd keep my promises too."

2116

No man but a blockhead ever wrote except for money.

Johnson

2117

The following is stolen from Wilson Mizner: If you steal from one author, it's plagiarism; if you steal from many, it's research.

2118

You write with ease to show your breeding,
But easy writing's curst hard reading.

Sheridan

2119

Jean Baptiste Rousseau wrote "An Ode to Posterity." When Voltaire read it, he observed: "This poem won't reach its destination."

2120

Mark Twain once asked a neighbor to lend him a set of books. The neighbor wasn't enthusiastic, and said:

"I make it a rule never to let one of my books leave the house, but you may read them in my library if you wish."

The following month this neighbor asked Mark Twain if he might borrow his lawnmower. And Mr. Clemens replied:

"Sure, but you must use it on my premises."

2121

A rare book is a borrowed volume that is returned to its owner.

2122

Sir, I admit your general rule,
That every poet is a fool:
But you yourself may serve to show it,
That every fool is not a poet.

Matthew Prior

2123

The librarian was approached one afternoon by a spinsterish looking dame who said:

"Can you recommend a good book for me?"

"Here's one about a cardinal," the librarian replied.

"Too religious," snapped the dame.

"But this," the librarian persisted, "is a bird."

"Young man," the woman said, "I'm not interested in his private life either."

2124

A banker may write a bad poem and get away with it; but just let a poet try writing a bad check.

2125

Browsing in a second-hand bookstore, George Bernard Shaw ran across a volume of his plays that he had inscribed to an acquaintance with his compliments. He bought the book and wrote another inscription under the first: "With renewed compliments, George Bernard Shaw." Then he sent it back to the original recipient.

2126

After a highly successful performance of one of his early plays, there were cries for the author to take a curtain call. Shaw stepped on the stage, but as he did so, he heard a loud "Boo" from the audience. Shaw bowed in the direction of the critic and said:

"My friend, I quite agree with you; but what are we two against so many?"

2127

An ambitious but rather dull poet once complained to Oscar Wilde that book reviewers neglected to write about his work.

"There's a conspiracy against me," he said; "a conspiracy of silence. What should I do about it, Oscar?"

"Join it by all means," Wilde replied.

2128

Many thanks; I shall lose no time in reading your book.

Disraeli, to an author who had sent him a book

2129

The most truthful part of a newspaper is the advertisements.

Jefferson

2130

In Riverside Park a young poet who had just sold his first verses was walking walking dejectedly along a path. A friend met him and said, "What on earth is the matter with you?" The poet heaved a long sigh and replied:

"Shakespeare is dead. Keats, Shelley, Byron—all are dead. The responsibility on my shoulders is almost more than I can bear."

2131

It was at a party where a celebrated literary man was being lionized. A gusher type of woman had the guest of honor at her mercy for a time, and she asked:

"Do clever men make good husbands?"

"Clever men," the writer answered, "do not become husbands."

2132

Even a book reviewer has his moments, as when Charles Poore, of the New York Times, wrote: "It might be said of this author that not only does he wear his heart on his sleeve, but his glands as well."

2133

Louis Untermeyer, poet and anthologist, went to a fancy dress party one evening and apparently enjoyed himself. He checked his dignity at the door, wore a colored paper hat, tooted a horn, and in general let loose. At length a teen-age college girl walked up to him and looked him over. Then she exclaimed:

"Well for gossakes—and you're required reading!"

SECTION 27

WOMAN

2150

The lady of the house was doing the marketing as it was the maid's day off. On her way home she met the girl wheeling a baby carriage. She stopped in surprise and asked the girl whose baby she was tending.

"Mine, ma'am," said the girl proudly.

"Yours, Mandy! I thought you were an old maid?"

"I is, ma'am. But I ain't a fussy old maid."

2151

A well-dressed woman got on a New York bus and handed the driver a ten-dollar bill. She said:

"I'm sorry, but I have no nickels."

As the driver took the money he replied:

"That's all right, lady; in a minute you're going to have 199 nickels."

2152

John Smithers was explaining why he always got up for a lady standing in a bus. Said he:

"Ever since I was a kid I've had a lot of respect for a woman with a strap in her hand."

2153

Twins were born to a Negro woman Mark Twain used to know, and one day the humorist stopped in to look them over.

"This one is a little girl, isn't it?" he observed.

"Yas indeed, sir."

"And is the other one of the contrary sex?"

"Oh yas sir, yas sir; she's a girl too."

2154

Then there was the girl who was a real photograph of her father and a pretty fair phonograph of her mother.

2155

No woman is to blame for not being beautiful at sixteen, but she has herself to blame if she is not beautiful at forty.

Fra Uppo

2156

Only the men who do not care about women are interested in women's dresses. And the men who like them never notice what they wear.

Anatole France

2157

She is intolerable, but that is her only fault.

Talleyrand, of a young lady of the Court

2158

Every line in her face is the line of least resistance.

Irvin S. Cobb

2159

You know what a woman's curiosity is. Almost as great as a man's!

Oscar Wilde

2160

It has been noted many times that women can be catty to each other. Let it be stated here that they can be downright mean and ornery. They not only stick an umbrella down a sister's throat, but they open it. Listen to these two women:

"I didn't accept Billy the first time he proposed."

"No indeed, darling; you weren't there."

2161

When asked if he liked bathing beauties, Mr. Bingle looked over at his better half and said apprehensively:

"Really, I don't know; I never bathed one."

2162

No woman, says a philosopher, really makes a fool out of a man, but she sure can give him an opportunity to develop his natural capacities.

2163

Women are wiser than men because they know less and understand more.

James Stephens

2164

There was a little girl
And she had a little curl
Right in the middle of her forehead;
And when she was good
She was very, very good,
And when she was bad she was—interesting.

2165

A well known composer of popular songs spent considerable time in Hollywood and became acquainted with celebrities in the motion-picture industry. One morning at a studio he noticed a rather spectacular young blonde arriving in a very sumptuous limousine, and in a kidding spirit he made it apparent that he was much impressed. So the actress tossed her head, and exclaimed disdainfully:

"Just for that, I'll come tomorrow in a Rolls Royce."

"Maybe, maybe," the song writer returned, "but not just for that."

2166

For every woman who makes a fool out of a man there is another woman who makes a man out of a fool.

2167

When you ask her a question, its like taking your finger out of a dike.

Frank Case

2168

She'd fight a rattlesnake and give it the first two bites.

Harry Leon Wilson

2169

Sure, deck your lower limbs in pants;
Yours are the limbs, my sweeting.
You look divine as you advance—
Have you seen yourself retreating?

Ogden Nash

2170

Sophisticated Girl: One who knows how to refuse a kiss without being deprived of it.

2171

To find out a girl's faults, praise her to her girl friends.

Benjamin Franklin

2172

At a Hollywood party the guests were asked to write their own epitaph. An oft-married glamour girl was sitting next to Robert Benchley and she confessed she didn't know what to write about herself. Benchley said, "I'll write it for you."

He wrote and passed in the slip with his own, to be read aloud by the hostess. The epitaph read, "At last she sleeps alone."

2173

If you wish you may hang this one on Confucius: Mirrors reflect without speaking; women speak without reflecting.

2174

Add newly filed saws: A little woman is a dangerous thing.

2175

The ambitious girl had made up her mind to put up a good front or bust.

2176

Why the heck should men in their dotage twit women about their ages? While you are figuring out this, I'll tell you how a man answered the question: "How old is she?"

"Well, I don't rightly know," he said, "but everyone at her last birthday party was overcome by the heat from the candles on the cake."

2177

Ladies, to this advice give heed:
  In controlling men,
If at first you don't succeed,
  Just cry, cry again.

2178

SOCIETY

Ermined and minked and Persian-lambed,
  Be-puffed (be-painted, too, alas!)
Be-decked, be-diamonded—be damned!
  The Women of the Better Class.

Oliver Herford

2179

The yeggman was confessing his almost perfect crime. He had disguised himself as a woman and was making a getaway.

"Den," he said, "I made my big mistake. When I got on de street car, I had de right change ready."

2180

Mary had a bathing suit,
The latest style, no doubt;
And when she got inside it, she
Was more than halfway out.

2181

"If all the women were taken out of circulation," said the feminist orator, "what kind of a nation would this be?"

"Stag-nation," came the reply from a gallant young man in the back row.

2182

The modern girl on the bathing beach was aptly characterized by a photographer as "over-exposed and under-developed."

2183

The adventurer type, which includes a great many insufferable bores, is sometimes subject to insufferable boredom when he is in a group that insists on his telling of his wonderful exploits.

One of these, an explorer, was persuaded to tell a story at a cocktail party where most of the guests were career women.

"Well," he began, "it was back in 1899. I was shipwrecked on a particularly lonely strand of the Gold Coast. No one but me was saved. For days I subsisted on clams and raw fish. Then I came upon a tribe of wild women who, strangely enough, had no tongues."

"No tongues!" exclaimed one of the spinsters present. "Then how could they talk?"

"They couldn't," the adventurer replied; "that's what made 'em wild."

2184

Lady Montague told me, and in her own house,
"I do not care for you three skips of a louse."
I forgive her, for women, however well-bred,
Will still talk of that which runs most in their head.

Henry Fox

2185

A woman's advice to man: Don't look for home atmosphere in a hotel or hotel service at home.

2186

It is perhaps superfluous to mention the fact that feminists are extremely conscious of their sex, but probably the outstanding example of this is evidenced by the following story:

During the suffragist movement during pre-voting days for females, two lady hell-raisers were arrested and put in jail. One of them was an old-stager, but the other was a tender young thing to whom the experience was poignant and degrading. She moaned, sobbed and cried with youthful vigor.

From the next cell, the old-stager called encouragement to her: "Don't take on so, dearie; put your trust in God—*she* will help you."

2187

Women carry their wealth around in their stockings because they want to bank it where it will draw the most interest.

2188

A young lady who suffered with hay fever took with her to a cocktail party two handkerchiefs, one of which she stuck in the bosom of her frock. At the earliest possible moment she began to rummage right and left in her bosom for the fresh handkerchiefs.

Engrossed in her search, she suddenly realized that conversation had stopped and people were watching her.

Perturbed, she murmured, "I *know* I had two when I came."

2189

Men may begin with a speaking acquaintance with a young lady, but usually they end up with a listening acquaintance.

2190

When Sam Smith was asked if he believed in clubs for women, he said, "I certainly do, but only when kindness fails."

2191

Women are like men because they like money. Women are like money because if you don't keep them busy, they lose interest.

2193

The young woman was thoroughly unselfish; she didn't ask anything for herself. But she prayed, "O Lord, please send Mother a son-in-law."

2194

A spinster rang the fire alarm, and then discovered there was no fire. Then twenty fireman arrived, and she announced:

"There isn't any fire after all. Nineteen of you may go back."

2195

A man who won't lie to a woman has very little consideration for her feelings.

Olin Miller

2196

Short-story beginning: Two old maids went for a tramp.

2197

They called the girl Easter Egg because she is hand painted on the outside and hard-boiled in the inside.

2199

Overheard at a bridge party: "I don't like that woman; she can't be trusted. Confidentially, she slinks."

2200

A straight line may be the shortest distance between two points, but a good looking gal can get there quicker with curves.

2201

And the prim old lady who asked the conductor if her ticket allowed her a hangover in St. Louis.

2202

A man who has a birthday is likely to take a day off, but when a woman has a birthday, the chances are that she will take a year off.

2203

Girls at bridge parties are apt to be smarties. The other day one of them said to another:

"I wonder what men talk about when there are no ladies present."

"Oh, probably the same things we do," was the reply.

Another of the girls piped up and exclaimed:

"They ought to be ashamed of themselves."

2204

Many a girl who looks as if she had been poured into her dress evidently forgot to say "when."

2205

Lady: A woman who makes it easy for a man to be a gentleman.

Walter Winchell

2206

"Well anyway," said one chorus girl to another, "whatever you may say about Mary Jane, she has a clean mind."

"Bless my shriveled soul!" the other exclaimed. "She ought to have a clean mind; she sure changes it often enough."

2207

In the good old days before women had the vote, Dr. Samuel Johnson observed that "Nature has given women so much power that the law has very wisely given them little."

2208

The ultimate in tactfulness was displayed by the obstetrician who told the new mother that she and the child looked more like sisters than mother and daughter.

2209

It is told that Great Britain's Foreign Secretary, Lord Halifax, once shared a railway compartment with two prim-looking spinsters. A few moments before reaching his destination the train passed through a tunnel, and in the utter darkness Halifax kissed his own hand noisily several times. When the train drew into the station, he rose, lifted his hat, and in a truly gentlemanly fashion said:

"May I ask to which of you two ladies I am indebted for the charming incident in the tunnel?" He then got out in a hurry and left the two females glaring at each other.

2210

Jade: A semi-precious stone.
A semi-precious woman.

Oliver Herford

2211

"See that dizzy looking blonde over there?" asked the Hollywood guide to a group of Iowa tourists. They looked, of course. "Well," the guide continued, "she's had her face lifted so many times that finally the plastic surgeon ran out of skin and had to take some off her right thumb. He grafted it onto her nose, and now every time she goes hitch-hiking her nose waggles over to the right."

2212

It is said that a certain young lady reproached Henry Clay for not remembering her name. The statesman answered in his most gallant manner:

"Is it to be wondered at, my dear? When we last met I was sure your beauty and accomplishments would soon compel you to change it."

2213

Marie Dressler, of blessed memory, was of a build as ample as her genius as an actress and as a friend. On her first visit to Paris, when her acquaintance with the French language was somewhat sketchy, she tried to find the house of a friend. The taxi driver tried to explain to her that the house was just behind the Hotel Continental, where Miss Dressler was stopping. He said:

"C'est derrière L'Hôtel Continental."

The actress understood everything except the "derrière." So she asked:

"Que signifie derrière?"

The cabby raised his eybrows and shrugged his shoulders. Said he:

"If Madame does not know the meaning of derrière, then nobody does."

2214

Of a well known screen actress a mad wag said:

"How should I know how old she is? All I know is that she knew the big dipper when it was only a drinking cup."

2215

A bejewelled dowager with several chins gushed, "I just love nature!"

"That's loyalty," commented Groucho Marx to his companion, "after what nature did to her."

2216

A modern young miss and an old-fashioned woman were waiting for a bus. The girl took out a pack of cigarettes and offered one to her elder, who said:

"What! Smoke a cigarette? Why, I'd rather kiss the first man who comes along."

"So would I," the girl answered, taking a long drag; "but have a cigarette while you're waiting."

2217

Intuition: The strange instinct that tells a woman she is right, whether she is or not.

2218

Here's to women: once our superior—now our equal.

2219

"There ought to be a law against it," spluttered Mr. Blank. "I'm speaking about women's wearing pants. They've lost their femininity, even their identity. If you see a man and woman walking down the street, both dressed practically alike, how are you going to tell the difference?"

"Easy enough," was the answer; "the one who is listening is the man."

2220

The most efficient water power in the world—women's tears.

Wilson Mizner

2221

Women are not always consistent. There's a young woman we know who, when she goes out walking, always wears walking clothes; when she rides horseback, she wears riding clothes; when she goes out in the evening, she wears evening clothes. But when we invited her to a birthday party, we were distinctly disappointed.

2222

In London, the A.R.P. wardens sent out a health questionnaire to employes to find out if they could withstand prolonged imprisonment in the narrow, crowded air-raid shelters. One question was: "Do you suffer from claustrophobia?"

To their astonishment, 95 percent of the women employees answered, "Yes." Calling in the Chief of the women's division, the A.R.P. organizers asked her if she had told the girls exactly what "claustrophobia" meant.

"Oh, yes," said she. "I told them it meant being afraid of confinement."

2223

Here lies Nolly Goldsmith, for shortness called Noll,
Who wrote like an angel, but talked like poor Poll.

David Garrick

2224

A lady is one who never shows her underwear unintentionally.

Lillian Day

2225

A man is as old as he feels, and a woman is as old as she feels like admitting.

2226

A woman's beauty is not a gift to man; it's a bribe.

2227

After the death of Nelson, English ladies were fond of wearing the Trafalgar garter, on which was inscribed the memorable signal: "England expects every man to do his duty."

INDEX

(All references are made to individual entries, not pages.)

A

Abash, 368
Ability, 1664
Aborigines, 1717
Absentmindedness, 277, 278
Abstainer, 861
Abstention, 861
Accidents, 268, 476, 604, 1291, 1320, 1377, 1551, 2073, 2075
Acid, 196
Acquaintances, 93, 203, 207, 2189
Act, 2007
Activity, 595
Actor, 1474, 2016, 2017, 2019, 2020, 2024, 2025, 2026, 2037, 2043
Actress, 2023, 2027, 2030, 2032, 2039, 2214
Adam, 67, 308, 507, 676, 718, 916, 1368, 1386
Ade, George, 1143, 1393
Ad infinitum, 27
Adolescence, 304
Adult, 826
Adultery, 298, 304
Advertisement, 643, 1321, 2129
Advertising, 610, 616
Age, 238, 326, 538, 595, 699, 705, 733, 1242, 2176, 2214
Agitator, 1830
Aida, 91
Air, 473, 753, 1452, 1536
Airplanes, 781, 1852
Alamo, 715
Alas, 1908
Alaska, 753
Alcohol, 866
Algebra, 1808
Alimony, 1401, 1481
Allowance, 1301
Altar, 1480
Ambition, 1347, 2175
American, 544, 851, 875
American Legion, 1015
Ammunition, 227
Amphibian corps, 1055
Anarchist, 413
Anatomy, 1489
Ancestors, 541, 548, 549, 550, 552, 553
Ancestry, 95, 543, 544
Anecdote, 67
Anesthetic, 662, 1503
Angels, 455, 722, 1474
Animals, 37, 458, 540, 1484, 1953
Anniversary, 1298, 1410
Ankle, 1291
Answer, 1653
Antheil, George, 113
Anthony, 950
Antiques, 611, 614
Apartment, 375, 1379, 1392
Apology, 366, 1440
Appendicitis, 1554
Appendix, 1508
Appetite, 815, 840
Applause, 1845
Apples, 13
Apple tree, 1262
Appointment, 1524
Appreciation, 187
April fool, 501
Arabic, 1863
Archbishop, 1764
Architect, 675
Argument, 1206, 1297, 1835
Aristocracy, 1643
Arithmetic, 951
Arizona, 161
Arkansas, 754
Armor, 786

Army, 1021, 1034, 1037, 1046, 1067, 1075, 1303
Arnold, Matthew, 145
Art, 77, 1803
Art critic, 80
Art gallery, 71
Artist, 80
Asafoetida, 681
Ashes, 263, 740, 857, 1469
Asiatic, 192
Asquith, Margot, 2109
Asset, 457
Associated Press, 78, 1966
Astor, Vincent, 1663
Astrologers, 1656
Astronomer, 1790
Athletics, 1959
Auctioneer, 666
Audience, 217, 1820, 2005, 2044
Author, 529, 1346, 2002, 2117, 2126, 2132
Autobiography, 503, 2109
Autograph, 2004, 2110
Automat, 871
Automatic, 1074
Automobile, 418, 655, 960, 1377, 2060, 2067, 2068, 2069, 2070, 2071, 2073, 2074, 2075, 2076, 2077, 2081, 2084
Average man, 596
Aviator, 1812

B

Baby, 318, 502, 505, 509, 512, 513, 514, 521, 692, 698, 722, 730, 734, 737, 837, 984, 1461, 1475, 1482, 1516, 1640, 1742, 1900
Baby carriage, 2150
Bach, 98
Bachelor, 913, 1229, 1284, 1393, 1398, 1438, 1447
Back, 208, 290, 372, 723, 1223, 1335
Backbone, 162
Back seat, 1442
Back-seat driver, 2073
Back slapping, 719
Bad man, 1258
Baer, Max, 1970
Bag, 26
Baker, 605, 670
Ballads, 94
Bananas, 179
Bandage, 660
Bank, 661, 1133, 1591, 1594, 2187
Banker, 627, 1595, 1606, 2124
Bank robbery, 1478
Banquet, 969
Baptism, 1684, 1748
Bar, 902, 903, 909
Barbed wire, 171, 256
Barber, 1745
Bargain, 624, 1770
Barrel, 13, 165, 731
Barrymore, Ethel, 359
Barrymore, John, 241, 359, 1409, 1999
Baseball, 410, 789, 1071, 1132, 1339
Bass drum, 1063
Bassos, 106
Bathing, 1371, 1550, 1878
Bathing beauties, 2161
Bathing suit, 778, 2180
Battle, 452, 1001, 1064
Bazaars, 1783
Beach, 553, 629, 2182
Bean, Roy, 1147, 1148
Beans, 329, 812
Bear, 31, 644
Beauty, 547, 658, 1221, 2155, 2212
Beauty parlor, 1062
Beebe, Lucius, 674
Beecher, Henry Ward, 1718
Beefsteak, 1334
Beer, 540, 897, 899, 908
Beggars, 464, 551
Belief, 338, 466, 1856
Bell, 517, 977
Belladonna, 1869
Benchley, Robert, 2172
Bender, 105
Benedict, 1284
Bergen, Edgar, 1261, 1793
Best seller, 2108
Bet, 170, 452, 1058, 1956, 1967, 2104
Better Business Bureau, 640
Better half, 1483, 2161
Bible, 1129, 1779
Bicycle, 14
Bierce, Ambrose, 207, 366, 666, 786, 861, 1400, 1643, 1845, 2113
Bigamy, 1400

Big Dipper, 2214
"Big stick," 1599
Bills, 660, 1358, 1512, 1770, 1783, 2003
Billboards, 623
Billiards, 360, 860
Billiard tables, 648
Billings, Josh, 724
Biology, 995
Bird dog, 1940
Birds, 39, 817, 1219, 1683, 1878
Birthday, 286, 558, 652, 736, 1365, 1406, 2176, 2202
Births, 506, 517, 530, 1101, 1108, 1382, 1653
Biscuits, 1352
Bishop, 1723, 1729, 1753, 1755, 1766, 1784
Biting, 33, 453, 1105, 1399, 1566, 2168
Black, Alexander, 1822
Black crepe, 515
Black eye, 1389
Black-eyed Susan, 1229
Blacksmith, 232
Blankets, 1870
Blasphemy, 1758
Blessing, 1114, 1383
Blind man, 1776
Blockhead, 2116
Blonde hair, 1370
Blondes, 997, 1217, 1797, 2165, 2211
Blood donor, 1035
Bloodhounds, 2021
Blood transfusions, 405
Boastfulness, 1954, 1967, 1968, 1971
Body, 290, 529, 557, 792
Boer War, 1077
Bomb, 413, 1070
Bombing, 1761
Book ends, 2114
Book reviewer, 2113, 2127, 2132
Books, 219, 529, 990, 1281, 1346, 1450, 2108, 2113, 2120, 2121, 2123, 2125, 2128
Border, 5
Boredom, 31, 1423
Bores, 373, 1525, 1590, 1810, 1850, 1860
Borglum, Gutzon, 78
Borrowing, 207, 1301, 1592, 1601, 2121
Bosom, 2188
Boston, 329, 542, 755, 812, 1900, 1966, 2080
Bostonian, 1888
Bottles, 328, 1003, 1243
Bottoms, 30
Bourget, Paul, 544
Bowes, Edward, 1828
Boxes, 1585
Boy, 174, 181, 184, 232, 444, 503, 506, 512, 627, 645, 652, 681, 695, 697, 699, 729, 766, 979, 990, 1061, 1154, 1206, 1702, 1715, 1750, 1778, 1781, 1794
Brahms, 102
Brains, 547, 933, 941, 988, 1633
Brake, 2063, 2075
Bravery, 1014, 1425
Breakfast, 619
Breeding, 376, 542, 1019, 2118
Bride, 824, 1289, 1310, 1352, 1361, 1389, 1395, 1420, 1444, 1490, 1749
Bridegroom, 284, 1287, 1361, 1420, 1491
Bridesmaids, 1361
Bridge, 152, 891, 948, 1204, 1366, 1433, 1957, 1958, 2203
British, 1024
Britisher, 752, 755, 1652
Broadcast, 98
Broadway, New York, 392, 765, 1259
Bromo-Seltzer, 2022
Broun, Heywood, 2002
Brown, Arthur William, 245
Brown, Lieut. Comm. John Mason, 2031
Bryan, William Jennings, 1849
Buckwheat cakes, 1543
Budget, 1582
Buffalo, 160
Building, 948
Bull, 644, 1629, 1890
Buller, General, 1077
Bullfighter, 1810
Bum, 365, 1433
Bunker Hill, 755
Bunyan, Paul, 10
Burglar, 1934
Burke, Edmund, 1824
Burns, John, 527
Burr, 260
Bus, 268, 636, 2151, 2152, 2216

Bus driver, 636
Business man, 601, 613, 632
Bust, 72, 2175
Butcher, 668, 1289, 1838
Butler, 230, 686, 687, 1348, 1934
Butter churn, 600
Buttons, 723, 1229

C

Cabbage, 1817
Cabots, 329, 542
Cactus Pete, 161
Caddie, 407, 1753
Café, 1305
Cafeteria, 340, 630
Cairo, 1056
Cake, 670, 726, 824, 1811, 2176
Calais, 2082
Calamity, 243
Calendar, 1818
California, 352, 691, 772, 1382, 2015
Cambridge, 1899
Camp, 731, 1009, 1016, 1039, 1041, 1044, 1085, 2031
Campbell, Mrs. Patrick, 387
Candle, 1931, 2176
Cannibal, 1030
Cannon, Joseph, 1669
Canoe, 412, 1038
Cantor, Eddie, 1682, 1950
Capital, 1581
Captain, 146, 165, 1004, 1038, 1040, 1200, 2102
Car, 263, 270, 287, 395, 635, 787, 1081, 1248, 1369, 1388, 1416, 1641, 2069, 2071, 2074, 2076
Cards, 388
Cardinal, 2123
Career, 2183
Carefulness, 171
Caricatures, 81
Carleton, Henry Guy, 1826
Car license, 2070
Carol of Rumania, 1651
Carpenter, 675
Case, Frank, 212
Casey, Pat, 389, 1711
Cash, 664
Casino, 1001
Cat, 32, 41, 43, 63, 440, 645, 750, 1453, 1767, 1776, 2037
Cato, 1662
Cattiness, 2160
Cavities, 1524
Ceiling, 374
Celery, 827
Censor, 882
Centipede, 201, 1559
Chambermaid, 222
Champagne, 914, 921, 1409
Chances, 1028
Chandelier, 1782
Change, 652, 658, 1204, 2179, 2206
Chapin, Charles E., 1558
Chaplain, 1015, 1668
Character, 203, 719
Charity, 244
Charles II, 1651
Chart, 1515, 1561
Charwoman, 1048, 1523
Chauffeur, 1217
Cheating, 1529, 1944
Check, 411, 852, 1133, 1314, 1347, 1959, 2124
Checkers, 255
Cheering, 1969
Chemistry, 997
Chess, 48
Chest, 614
Chestnut dressing, 1885
Chiang Kai-shek, Mme., 1695
Chicago, Ill., 542
Chicken house, 434
Chickens, 46, 435, 606, 1162, 2103
Chilblains, 1559
Children, 401, 547, 694, 702, 703, 705, 708, 709, 715, 717, 1038, 1165, 1168, 1281, 1470, 1704, 1724
Chin, 238, 2215
Chinese, 363, 1974
Chloroform, 1829
Choate, Joseph H., 876, 1144, 1403, 1886, 2078
Chorus, 106, 446, 1102, 2001, 2036, 2206
Christening, 720, 1409
Christians, 1902
Christmas, 939, 1205
Church, 1380, 1480, 1694, 1711, 1731, 1738, 1741, 1774

Church fair, 1337
Churchill, Winston, 1821
Cigar box, 1607
Cigarettes, 267, 350, 671, 857, 924, 1059, 2216
Cigars, 1234, 1591
Circus, 712, 1877, 1937
Cistern, 742
Civil War, 759, 1045, 1075, 1078, 1083
Claptrap, 671
Clay, Henry, 247, 1903, 2212
Cleanliness, 174, 176, 1523, 2029, 2206
Clemenceau, Georges, 1655
Clemens, Samuel L., (*See* Twain, Mark)
Cleopatra, 950
Clergyman, 1688, 1770, 1774
Climate, 298, 1861
Climax, 2018
Clock, 9
Clock tower, 889
Clothes, 28, 718, 766, 776, 799, 800, 1371
Clothing, 473, 512
Club, 360, 388, 515, 1047, 1385, 2190
Clyde, 518
Coal, 257, 942, 1556, 1725
Coat, 49, 661, 1370
Cobb, Irvin S., 790, 1558
Cockcrow, 289
Cock pheasant, 1936
Cockroach, 35
Cocktail party, 2032, 2183, 2188
Cocktails, 875, 877, 888, 905, 913
Cocktail shaker, 720
Cod, 96, 329, 1381
Codfish, 346
Coffee, 262, 365, 393, 835, 849, 851, 1106, 1464
Cohan, George M., 217
Cold cream, 274
Colonel, 1039, 1045, 1067
Color, 2069
Color scheme, 696, 896, 1361
Collar bone, 2074
Collection, 618, 1699, 1731
Collection plate, 1701, 1756, 1781
College, 944, 1774
College degree, 609
College president, 996
Collision, 268, 2066
Colt, Colonel, 909
Comb, 1349
Comfort station, 471
Commandments, 864, 1053, 1109
Common sense, 1396
Communist, 1595, 1655
Competition, 601, 655, 1152
Composition, 973
Conceit, 286, 289, 2043
Concert, 105, 111
Conductor, 117, 118, 278, 699, 883, 2201
Confederacy, 1578
Confederates, 1025
Conference, 1650
Confessional, 1422, 1771, 2027
Congress, 980, 1628
Congressman, 432, 1629, 1657
Conscience, 1518
Conservation camp, 10
Conservative, 1557, 1631, 1642
Contempt, 709
Conversation, 1826, 1836
Cook, 684, 1442
Cookbook, 1490
Cooking, 1037, 1302, 1305, 1490
Coolidge, Calvin, 242, 287, 1639, 1694, 1802
Coolidge, Mrs. Calvin, 345
Co-operation, 319
Corn plaster, 406
Corns, 1790
Corpse, 284
Corset, 626
Costs, 342
Cotton picker, 11
Coughing, 1504
Coulter, Ernest, 689
Counting, 1752, 1797
Counterfeit, 1756
Courage, 162, 1564, 1637
Court, 1126, 1130, 1131, 1264
Court of St. James, 2078
Courtroom, 1129, 1135
Courtship, 1211, 1220
Cow, 3, 14, 272, 443, 974, 987, 1078
Coward, 163
Cowboy, 604, 1722, 1731
Cow puncher, 393, 751, 752, 901
Cows, 231
Crackers, 35, 710
Craps, 1036

Crash, 2073, 2077
Cream, 842, 1106
Creation, 1730
Cremation, 1469
Cripple, 900
Critic, 1027, 1102
Crosby, Bing, 1069
Crosses, 1347
Croupier, 441
Crowns, 961
Crow reservation, 276
Crying, 734, 2177
Cub reporter, 1629
Cuckoo clock, 1462
Cue, 1999
Cuff link, 622
Cure, 1550
Curiosity, 1443, 2159
Curl, 2164
Cursing, 526, 1114, 1807, 1863, 1896
Curtain call, 2136
Curves, 2200
Cushion, 285, 659
Customers, 255, 603, 637, 658, 669
Cyclone, 1117, 1823
Cynic, 396, 1257
Cynicism, 1485

D

Dam, 322
Damn, 1865
Dancing, 244, 450, 1203, 1210, 1961
Dandelions, 150
Danger, 628, 1700, 2174
Daniel, Zeke, 170, 1601
Dardenelles, 1029
Darling, 686, 963, 1208, 1318
Darrow, Clarence, 556
Daughter, 690, 905, 1373
Davis, Richard Harding, 282
Davison, Henry P., 1952
Dawes, Charles G., 1633
Day, 314, 2202
Deacon, 1756, 1776, 1782
Deafness, 1159, 1485, 1487, 1754, 1766
Deaf-mute, 1806, 1807
Death rate, 534
Deaths, 517, 518, 530, 620, 729, 1101, 1108, 1628, 1656, 1755, 2084
Debt, 1604
Decomposition, 98
Decoy, 1756
Defense, 1839
Definitions, 649, 970
Degrees, 937, 944, 945, 1380
Delicacy, 532, 1864
Delicatessen, 606
Delusion, 1257
Democrats, 1648, 1649, 1859
Dentist, 1505, 1524, 1528, 1536, 1542, 1723
Department store, 626
Depew, Chauncey M., 1813, 1823
Depression, 644
Desertion, 1167
Desire, 185
Detective, 676
Detour, 315
Devil, 207, 327, 711, 1712, 1716, 1726, 1792
Deviled ham, 1728
Dewey, Thomas E., 1638, 1667
Diabetes, 1529
Diary, 1515
Dice, 1036
Dictatorship, 1670
Difference, 1654
Dignity, 12
Dike, 2167
Dime novel, 2108
Dimes, 365, 669, 1583
Dinner, 821, 832
Dionne, Oliva, 701
Diploma, 609
Diplomacy, 1626
Diplomats, 363, 1410
Director, 2024
Dirt, 175, 2029
Disappointment, 712, 1443
Discharge, 1011
Diseases, 239, 1546
Dishwater, 860, 1052
Disraeli, 239, 243, 1831
Divorce, 1162, 1163, 1165, 1169, 1396, 1416, 1472, 1517, 1975
Doctor, 1291, 1500, 1501, 1503, 1504, 1506, 1507, 1509, 1511, 1512, 1513, 1514, 1515, 1517, 1518, 1520, 1521, 1523, 1525, 1527, 1530, 1531, 1532,

Doctor (*continued*)
1533, 1534, 1537, 1538, 1539, 1540, 1541, 1542, 1545, 1550, 1561, 1562, 1566, 1753, 1770
Doctor of Divinity, 945
Dog, 32, 33, 48, 260, 453, 729, 750, 754, 1129, 1453, 1746
Dog-house, 2038
Dollars, 8, 115, 264, 957, 1433
Dominoes, 116
Don Marquis, 2107
Doorbell, 230
Dope, 330, 996
Doughnuts, 605
Dove, 39, 1767
Dover, 2082
Dowager, 685, 686, 1810, 2215
Doyle, Conan, 225
Draft, 1042, 2026
Drake, Anthony, 1293
Dramatic critic, 2029, 2030, 2033
Drawers, 626
Dreams, 538, 985, 988, 1292
Dresses, 325, 723, 780, 789, 1296, 1312, 1446, 1894, 2156, 2204
Dressler, Marie, 2213
Drinking, 450, 839, 899, 929, 1319, 1345, 1373, 1376, 1457, 1540, 1745
Driver, 1369, 1442
Drowning, 408, 739, 1397
Drugs, 196
Drug store, 534, 653, 681
Drunkenness, 882, 910, 1171, 1200
Drunks, 865, 867, 868, 879, 880, 884, 886, 889, 891, 892, 894, 896, 898, 900, 907, 911, 1258, 1371
Dry cleaning, 1748
Duchess, 222, 838, 1242
Duck, 30, 2104
Dumas, Alexander, 537
Dumbness, 417, 418, 420, 421
Duncan, Isadora, 547
Dust Bowl, 1037

E

Earache, 1521, 1566
Ears, 176, 798, 1353
Earth, 15, 456, 673, 1765
Earthquake, 1695, 2018
Ear trumpet, 1754, 1768
Easter egg, 2197
Edibleness, 828
Editor, 599, 1101, 1103, 1104, 1105, 1110, 1111, 1116, 1117, 2115
Editorial "we," 1882
Education, 933, 936, 941, 946, 954
Educator, 955
Eggs, 36, 183, 211, 276, 474, 810, 849, 951, 1718, 1722
Eiffel Tower, 758
Einstein, 1792
Electric fan, 183
Electrician, 660, 2040
Electric sign, 641
Elephant, 698, 896, 970, 1937
Eliot, Dr. Charles W., 856, 1972
Elixir, 1544
Elman, Mischa, 95
Elopement, 1227, 1310
El Paso, Tex., 763
Emerson, Ralph Waldo, 72
Emotions, 2012
Emperor Augustus, 716
Empire State Building, 249, 862
Encouragement, 1245
Enemies, 203, 204, 1689
Enemy, 200, 702, 1528
Energy, 182
Engagement, 1298
Engineer, 533, 958, 2102
English, 851, 986, 1032, 1047, 1071, 1076, 1081, 1875
Englishmen, 641, 887, 894, 2112
Entertainment, 1945, 2003
Epigram, 1904, 1909
Epitaph, 527, 531, 1661, 1822, 2084, 2172
Erie Railroad, 1853
Ermine, 49, 2178
Eskimo, 390
Esperanto, 1834
Ethics, 649
Etiquette, 357, 362, 378
Evangelist, 1045, 1696, 1722, 1767, 1778
Eve, 67, 308, 507, 780, 1368, 1386
Evening gown, 773
Evil, 1728, 1957
Exaggeration, 1479
Examination, 673
Exercise, 258

Existence, 559, 1526
Expectation, 1205
Expert, 594
Explorer, 390
Explosion, 268
Extravagance, 1324
Eyeballs, 1964
Eyeful, 848
Eyes, 321, 382, 631, 796, 1354, 1485

F

Facetious, 218
Faerie Queen, 2111
Faints, 355, 1000, 1551, 1653
Fairy tale, 1362
Faith healer, 310
Falseness, 708
Familiarity, 709, 1735
Family, 551, 620, 1008, 1281, 1357, 1448, 1801
Fanatic, 182
Fare, 636, 1023, 1227, 1593
Farmer, 1, 4, 7, 8, 9, 10, 14, 17, 47, 385, 860, 960, 1016, 1407, 1732, 1931
Fascists, 1659
Fashions, 378, 782, 783
Father, 351, 504, 690, 721, 732, 733, 766, 899, 967, 1061, 1227, 1233, 1240, 1283, 1308, 1418, 1425, 1461, 1744, 2154
Fatherhood, 505, 506
Fat people, 1951
Faults, 296, 2171
Fee, 108, 1510, 1534
Feed, 8
Feet, 257, 381, 728, 1168, 1332, 1633, 2115
Feminists, 2186
Fender, 1332, 2076
Fermentation, 864
Ferocity, 1938
Ferry, 867, 1593
Fertility, 1230
Fidelity, 654
Field, 12, 385
Field, Eugene, 325
Fields, James T., 837
Fields, W. C., 664, 2013
Fight, 1018, 1126, 1631
Fig tree, 772
Film, 2014, 2018
Financier, 436
Fingernails, 166
Fire, 233, 340, 625, 646, 740, 1116, 1455, 1846
Fire alarm, 621, 2194
Fireplace, 1332, 1453
Fire truck, 2064
First aid, 1551
Fish, 814, 1590
Fisherman, 346, 1935
Fishing, 1737, 1896, 1931
Fish story, 1932, 1933
Fishworm, 1802
Fiske, Jim, 1579
Five cent cigar, 1645
Fjord, 418
Flagg, James Montgomery, 245
Flagpole sitter, 532
Flat tire, 1534
Flea, 27, 34, 38, 45, 1241
Flea circus, 34
Flies, 994
Flirtation, 1209
Flirting, 450
Floors, 374, 672, 879
Floorwalker, 637
Flue, 38
Flunkey, 775
Flute, 1941
Fly, 36, 38
Flypaper, 634
Fontanne, Lynn, 2006
Food, 473, 874, 1021, 1043, 1455
Fools, 193, 281, 465, 551, 721, 1427, 1439, 1608, 1877, 2122, 2162, 2166
Football, 1336, 1964, 1969, 1972
Forehead, 1247, 2164
Foreman, 10
Forgiveness, 713, 1310, 1850
Fort Dix, 1003
Fortitude, 398
Fortune, 266, 430
Fort Worth, Tex., 764
Fosdick, Harry Emerson, 1721, 1896
Fountain pen, 665, 1530
Fowling piece, 1934
Fox, Charles James, 370

Foxes, 1374, 1943
Fox-hunting, 1943
France, Anatole, 1800
Franklin, Benjamin, 529, 1634
Franklin, Sidney, 1810
Frau, 1351
Fraunces' Tavern, 926
French, 1024, 1303, 1654, 1884, 2213
French, Daniel Chester, 72
Frenchman, 164, 544, 875, 1410, 1833
Freshman, 1336
Friday, 472
Friends, 202, 203, 204, 205, 206, 209, 210, 213, 214, 216, 237, 921, 1003, 1765, 2171
Frisco, Joe, 2041
Frog, 995, 1204, 1932
Front, 724, 2175
Frugality, 1481
Fun, 450
Fundamentalism, 1721
Funeral, 556, 1727, 1785
Funeral procession, 518
Furlough, 502, 1033, 1036, 1043, 1055, 1058
Furrier, 661
Furs, 661, 778, 1484

G

Gabriel, 2083
Gallantry, 298
Gallows, 239
Gambling, 441, 1952, 1973, 1975
Garage, 1370, 2062, 2076
Gardener, 813
Garlic, 1553
Garrick Club, 1893
Garter, 320, 2042
Gas-meter, 1585
Gasoline, 2078
Gas station, 635
Geese, 1647
Genealogy, 555, 2035
General, 1000, 1047, 1052
Genius, 1665
"Gentle Art of Making Enemies," 64
Gentleman, 268, 281, 330, 372, 377, 607, 670, 703, 1224, 1652, 1713
German, 164, 1351, 1669
German officer, 1024
German prison camp, 1017
Germs, 1531
Ghost writer, 2105
Gibson, Charles Dana, 655
Gift, 2114
Gilbert, W. S., 1893, 2000
Gillilan, Strickland, 1841
Giraffe, 1559
Girard, Stephen, 1688
Girdles, 1060
Girl, 110, 258, 405, 439, 446, 450, 503, 506, 512, 514, 658, 689, 695, 706, 723, 746, 766, 774, 780, 944, 1014, 1026, 1203, 1204, 1206, 1222, 1223, 1224, 1227, 1235, 1240, 1245, 1794, 2069, 2133, 2153, 2154, 2164, 2170, 2171, 2175, 2182, 2197, 2200, 2203, 2204, 2206, 2216
Girls' school, 976, 1200
Giving, 1575
Gladstone, William E., 239, 243, 1831
Glass, 174, 621, 888, 1222, 1844
Gloves, 62
Goat, 468, 1768
Gob, 421
Goblet, 421
God, 145, 219, 329, 455, 525, 557, 674, 690, 833, 870, 930, 939, 948, 1564, 1683, 1692, 1695, 1697, 1700, 1704, 1706, 1707, 1708, 1710, 1712, 1713, 1714, 1732, 1750, 2186
Godiva, Lady, 775
Goering, Hermann, 1660
Gogarty, Oliver St. John, 886
Gold Coast, 2183
Goldfish, 65, 1287
Goldwyn, Samuel, 2105
Golf, 407, 1385, 1524, 1753, 1944, 1945, 1946, 1947, 1948, 1949, 1950, 1951
Goodwin, Nat, 1826
Gossip, 171
Gould, Jay, 1579
Governess, 682
Government, 1643, 1648
Grable, Betty, 2031
Grace, 833, 1383
Gramling, Oliver, 319

Grammar, 854, 1899
Grand Banks, 346
Grand Canyon, 288, 2107
Grandchild, 1338
Grandfather, 543, 554, 703, 1338, 1363
Grandmother, 543, 693, 703, 729, 901, 1338, 1424, 1529, 1730
Grandson, 554
Grant, U. S., 1083
Grapefruit, 848
Grapes, 311, 850, 1964
Grass, 259, 822
Graveyard, 426, 664
Gravity, 964, 967
Greeley, Horace, 432, 1688
Greenwich Village, 358
Grindstone, 958
Groom, 1295, 1395
Grocer, 444
Ground, 16, 322, 361, 1169, 1542
Guadalcanal, 1030, 1043
Guam, 522
Guest book, 387
Guest towel, 1416
Gun boat, 442
Guns, 196, 693, 1163, 1941
Gushers, 61, 694, 2131
Guts, 617

H

Haberdasher, 359
Habits, 37
Haggling, 600
Hair, 176, 521, 1244
Haircut, 521, 794, 825, 1555
Hale, Edward Everett, 1668, 1972
Half-mast, 532
Halifax, Lord, 2209
Hamlet, 2038
Hammer, 666, 1807
Hammond, Percy, 2001
Hancock, Asa, 326
Hand brake, 787
Handkerchiefs, 113, 823, 2188
Hand-me-downs, 1421
Hands, 175, 1143, 1700, 1713
Handyman, 7
Hanging, 325, 533, 743, 1131, 1133, 1733, 1867
Hangover, 619, 2022, 2201
Hansom cab, 876, 2078
Happiness, 1332
Hardware, 14, 677
Harem, 29
Harp, 2083
Harrington, John, 1635
Harris, Frank, 1800
Harvard University, 329, 1972
Harvest, 13, 15
Harvey, Fred, 393
Hastings, Warren, 1824
Hat check, 439
Hate, 459, 1166
Hats, 626, 1718
Hay-fever, 873, 2188
Head, 288, 290, 344, 370, 521, 1549, 1583, 2104
Headlight, 44
Hearing, 791, 1957
Hearse, 2072
Hearst, William Randolph, 2003
Heart, 370, 648, 1533, 1696, 2132
Heat, 750, 2176
Heaven, 106, 676, 1228, 1323, 1381, 1681, 1703, 1734, 1765, 1778
Hecklers, 1844
Heckling, 908, 1859
Heifer, 17, 1684
Heifetz, Jascha, 95
Heirs, 535
Hell, 322, 478, 759, 915, 1228, 1709, 1729, 1763
Hemingway, Ernest, 2103
Hen, 474, 999, 1718
Heredity, 545
Herford, Oliver, 183, 373, 1857, 2106
Hero, 427
Hiccoughs, 1299
Highbrow, 935
High heels, 1247
High school, 1715
Hillbilly, 260
Hindu, 788
Hippopotamus, 1212
Hired man, 9, 13
History, 1444
Hitch hiking, 2065, 2211
Hitler, 1012, 1550, 1656, 1660, 1661
Hoe, 15

Hogs, 445, 897, 1300
Holes, 1561
Holidays, 511
Hollywood, 153, 359, 1035, 2026, 2165, 2172, 2211
Holmes, Oliver Wendell, 834, 1332
Holy Cross College, 329
Holy Ghost, 1767
Homesickness, 849
Honesty, 13, 959
Honeymoon, 1302, 1426, 1464, 1481, 1973
Hook, Thomas, 1602
Hook-and-ladder, 2064
Hope, 1402, 1548
Hope, Bob, 1007, 1076, 1638, 2005
Hors d'oeuvres, 831
Horse, 43, 47, 340, 728, 974, 1044, 1399, 1464, 1630, 1955
Horse and buggy days, 2078
Horse races, 1954, 1956
Horse-sense, 228
Horse shoeing, 232
Horse's neck, 887
Horse's tail, 887
Horse thief, 1648
Hospital, 662, 1029, 1202, 1515, 1556
Hostess, 391
Hotel, 533, 2185
Hour-glass, 1469
Hours, 383, 627
House, 29, 233, 424, 643, 646, 1455
Housekeeper, 1376
Housework, 1475
Hubbard, Elbert, 282
Huckleberry Finn, 2112
Hug, 1210, 1252
Hugo, Victor, 1564
Hula-hula, 1960
Human being, 32, 37, 797, 897, 1953, 1962
Human nature, 461, 462
Humor, 7, 1449
Hurry, 1946
Husband, 446, 654, 1166, 1207, 1218, 1307, 1320, 1323, 1348, 1406, 1453, 1460, 1886, 2131
Hutchins, Dr. Robert M., 356
Hyde, Arthur M., 1722
Hydrant, 1105
Hypocrite, 952, 1774

I

Iceberg, 146
Ice cream, 325, 1763
Iceman, 271
Ickes, Harold L., 1667
Idaho, 10
Ideals, 334, 1218
Ideas, 234, 947
Idiot, 424, 1220, 1772
Ignorance, 419, 732
Illness, 93, 1557, 1558
Image, 1710
Imagination, 449
Immorality, 303
Impatience, 467
Impediment, 1826, 1949
Independence, 1307
India, 986, 1942
Indians, 276, 986
Indolence, 263
Inevitable, 319
Ingenuity, 226
Inheritance, 456
Inmate, 813
Insane asylum, 818
Insect, 1962
Insomnia, 890, 1560
Installments, 733
Insulation, 660
Insurance, 524, 646, 650, 654, 1113, 1561
Intelligence, 1695
Intelligence test, 1020
Interlocutor, 1959
Intermission, 1203, 1827
Internal revenue, 1588
Interruptions, 1830, 1840
Intolerable, 2157
Introduction, 451, 1217, 1450, 1766, 1814
Intuition, 2217
Irishmen, 1126, 1266, 1448
Italy, 345, 982
Itching, 1549

J

Jack, 593, 1752, 2081
Jackass, 1859
Jack-rabbits, 2
Jackson, Andrew, 1855
Jade, 2210
Jail, 1164, 1365, 2186
Jam, 379
James, Henry, 379, 1873
Japanese, 1049, 1060, 1695
Jawbone of an ass, 1786, 1803
Jeep, 1009
Jest, 191, 449, 528
Jewelry, 651, 685
Jewels, 1795
Jewish holiday, 1656
Jews, 620, 629, 631, 649, 1022, 1686, 1692
Jitterbug, 1962
Job, 1491
Jockey, 1769
Johnson, Samuel, 97, 1402, 2207
Jokes, 217, 450, 1848
Jones, Sam, 1696
Judas, 1733
Judge, 389, 599, 713, 893, 895, 989, 1125, 1126, 1127, 1129, 1131, 1133, 1134, 1135, 1147, 1149, 1150, 1151, 1156, 1157, 1159, 1160, 1161, 1170
Judgment, 1018, 1145, 1757
Juggling, 2013
Jury, 599, 1150, 1158, 1224
Justice, 1146, 1150, 1171

K

Kalamazoo, 845
Kangaroo, 26, 661, 710, 1299
Kansas, 763
Kelland, Clarence Budington, 1815, 2101
Kemble, Roger, 2017
Kent, 877
Kentucky, 215, 257
Kentucky Derby, 1975
Kick, 3, 1005, 1012, 1399, 1881
Kicker, 50, 477, 539
Kidneys, 1838
Kimono, 787
Kindergarten, 727
King, 552, 1171, 1752
King of England, 1050
King George V, 1427
King George VI, 1509
King's jester, 1867
Kissing, 682, 917, 1058, 1129, 1206, 1213, 1216, 1231, 1235, 1236, 1237, 1243, 1247, 1248, 1254, 1255, 1258, 1263, 1285, 1292, 1322, 1327, 1344, 1354, 1389, 1418, 1426, 1565, 1714, 2170, 2209, 2216
Kittens, 270, 739, 1503
Kitty, 28
Knaves, 551
Knit, 1304
Knockout, 16
Kreisler, Fritz, 96

L

Labor shortage, 3
Lackaye, Wilton, 622
Ladder, 1227
La Donna e Mobile, 104
Lady, 146, 153, 241, 321, 522, 626, 672, 688, 772, 815, 845, 877, 878, 906, 913, 920, 974, 1166, 1234, 1781, 1944, 1956, 2150, 2152, 2177, 2188, 2189, 2201, 2205, 2212
Lady Eden, 74
Lady-in-waiting, 972
Lamarr, Hedy, 633
Lamb, Charles, 833, 1866
Lambs, 2
Lambs Club, 622
Landlady, 65
Landlord, 665, 1379
Language, 1028, 1157, 1834
Lantern, 1931
Lap, 639, 1472
Lardner, Ring, 714
Latch key, 1307
Lateness, 353, 501, 1389, 1486, 1825
Latin, 1855
Lauder, Harry, 407
Laughter, 15, 183, 1341
Law, 1691, 2025, 2207
Lawn, 150, 259, 322
Lawnmower, 1411, 2120
Lawyers, 1129, 1132, 1136, 1137, 1141,

Lawyers (*continued*)
1142, 1143, 1144, 1146, 1147, 1152, 1154, 1158, 1162, 1166, 1168, 1169
Laziness, 256, 259, 260, 262, 264, 1207
Leacock, Stephen, 945
Leap year, 1480
Learning, 732, 940
Leatherneck, 1063
Leeds, 822
Legs, 163, 231, 267, 443, 945, 1784, 1878, 2001
Lending, 207, 1575, 1591, 2120
Letter, 240, 424, 618, 1329, 1472
Letter of introduction, 90
Lewis, Sinclair, 2100
Liar, 1153, 1381, 1775
Libertine, 295
Librarian, 2123
License, 2070
Lies, 433, 440, 446, 447, 2195
Lieutenants, 1005, 1011, 1033, 1040, 1047, 1049, 1051, 1054, 1073, 1085
Life, 194, 320, 476, 528, 1207
Life boat, 1680
Lifeguard, 603
Life insurance, 604, 613
Lightning, 551, 1006
Lightning bug, 44
Limbs, 1878, 2169
Lincoln, Abraham, 184, 219, 362, 442, 443, 973, 1073, 1075, 1078, 1128, 1145, 1600, 1713, 1854, 1895, 1954
Lincoln, Thomas, 1399
Lingerie, 680
Liniment, 1408
Linoleum, 1493
Lionizing, 380, 2131
Lions, 32, 1599, 1682, 1902
Lipstick, 504
Liquor, 539, 874, 885, 1054, 1363, 2022
Lisp, 1905
Little Willie, 728, 1329
Livingston, Edward, 1664
Lobster, 1520
Locomotive, 1116
Lodge, 675, 1456
London, 71, 116, 281, 1048
London, Jack, 2115
Lonesomeness, 200
Longevity, 540
Longfellow, Henry Wadsworth, 381
Look, 354, 361, 721, 1201, 1419
Looking-glass, 465
Lord, 1751
Lord mayor, 876
Lorgnette, 771
Los Angeles, Calif., 1069, 1870
Lot's wife, 735
Lottery, 985, 1451
Louis, Joe, 1970, 1971
Louis XIV, 1625, 1634
Louse, 2006, 2183
Louvre, 67
Love, 150, 459, 704, 870, 925, 1225, 1226, 1228, 1229, 1244, 1246, 1250, 1253, 1255, 1256, 1257, 1337, 1339, 1350, 1577, 1714, 2019
Love letters, 1224
Lovesick, 1472
Lowells, 329
Luck, 265, 1583
Luggage, 225, 2080
Lullaby, 99, 1539
Lunacy, 327
Lunch, 995
Lunchbox, 841
Lunt, Alfred, 2006
Lying, 999, 1413, 1419
Lyons, Leonard, 471
Lynching, 325

M

Mackerel, 1664
Magazines, 1513, 2115
Magician, 2009, 2045
Maid, 230, 683, 685, 688, 1236, 1325, 1538, 1545, 1589, 2150
Mailbox, 889
Mail carrier, 673
Majority, 1040, 1627
Malaprop, Mrs., 1864
Malaria, 73
Man, 33, 162, 190, 208, 222, 290, 295, 315, 330, 342, 401, 411, 421, 429, 453, 455, 457, 458, 463, 501, 533, 603, 800, 811, 870, 878, 881, 930, 1201, 1222, 1226, 1227, 1232, 1234, 1235, 1245, 1290, 1439, 1632, 1646, 1710, 2116,

Man (*continued*)
2156, 2159, 2162, 2163, 2166, 2176, 2189, 2191, 2195, 2202, 2203
Man-eating tiger, 1942
Manhole, 267
Manners, 350, 370, 817
Manuscript, 2106
Mariners, 334, 460
Marines, 846, 1026, 1043, 1062
Marriage, 16, 110, 530, 1163, 1284, 1288, 1290, 1294, 1306, 1308, 1312, 1316, 1317, 1318, 1319, 1325, 1328, 1331, 1335, 1337, 1345, 1368, 1372, 1373, 1392, 1393, 1396, 1402, 1404, 1421, 1422, 1424, 1430, 1436, 1437, 1438, 1443, 1450, 1451, 1454, 1457, 1466, 1474, 1477, 1686, 1764, 2017, 2027
Marriage license, 1288, 1336
Martin, Mary, 1246
Marx brothers, 1939
Masaryk, Jan, 1666
Massachusetts, 352, 1382
Matadors, 757
Maternity ward, 1529
Matrimony, 737, 1428
Mattress, 647
Maurois, André, 1884
Maverick, Maury, 240
Mayflower, 553
Meanness, 271, 272, 1727, 2160
Mechanics, 667, 1462
Medicine, 1510, 1526
Medium, 1323
Meek, 456
Mellon, Andrew, 1605
Memory, 276, 449, 520, 1360, 1422, 2027
Menzies, Prime Minister, 1407
Merchant, 659
Metaphors, 1048
Methuselah, 829
Metropolitan Opera, 91, 109
Mice, 32, 2013
Mileage, 2071
Milk, 43, 272, 698, 1106, 2024
Milk pail, 3, 1378
Military funeral, 1004
Millenium, 1646
Millikan, Dr. Robert A., 1545
Millionaire, 388, 850, 1347
Mind, 44, 321, 535, 602, 1455, 2206
Mind reader, 1057
Minerva, 1482
Ministers, 833, 1532, 1682, 1729, 1735, 1737, 1742, 1743, 1744, 1745, 1746, 1765, 1768, 1769, 1775, 1783, 1785
Minneapolis, Minn., 1757
Minnehaha, 1895
Minority, 1627
Minstrel show, 1959
Mirage, 1393, 1680
Mirrors, 81, 1771, 2173
Mirth, 1449
Misfortune, 243, 266, 1375
Missing persons, 1465
Mistake, 248, 336, 652, 1771
Mistletoe, 1205
Mittens, 1806
Mizner, Wilson, 441, 2117
Mob, 462
Model, 680
Modernism, 1721
Modesty, 280
Mole, 1952
Mona Lisa, 1419
Money, 392, 590, 988, 1280, 1378, 1459, 1507, 1523, 1578, 1587, 1590, 1597, 1608, 2116, 2191
Mongoose, 912
Monk, 1716
Monkey, 546
Monologue, 2037
Montez, Lola, 2042
Months, names of, 1284, 1862
Moon, 1470, 1634
Moore, Grace, 108
Moose, 1872
Morality, 303
Morality play, 981
Morgan, J. P., 1952
Mormon marriage, 1391
Moron, 423, 424
Morris, William, 758
Morrow, Dwight, 278
Morse, Samuel F. B., 73
Moses, 864
Mosley, Oswald, 1659
Moth, 421, 778
Mother, 181, 202, 286, 311, 352, 509, 513, 699, 707, 723, 738, 744, 746, 766, 924,

Mother (*continued*)
963, 975, 983, 1159, 1168, 1204, 1283, 1372, 1380, 1382, 1438, 2154, 2208
Mother-in-law, 1394, 1424
Motorist, 215, 1149, 1260, 1384, 1411, 2060, 2063, 2071, 2084
Motto, 2016
Mountaineer, 1281, 1536
Mouse, 29, 731, 1412
Mouth, 500, 840, 1353, 1563
Movies, 1107
Movie theatre, 1641, 2014, 2015
Mozart, 94
Mule, 25, 50, 1005, 1070
Mule driver, 1005
Mulvaney, Thomas, 519
Mummies, 1056
Munich, 815
Murder, 401, 1938
Museum of American History, 471
Music, 90, 97, 1210, 1296
Mussolini, Benito, 1641
Mustache, 262
Mutter, 1552
Myth, 421

Mc

McCarthy, Charlie, 1261, 1793
McClellan, General, 1075, 1078
McFee, William, 2102

N

Nail, 1685
Names, 78, 225, 359, 389, 448, 526, 700, 965, 984, 1068, 1166, 1208, 1482, 1486, 1492, 1785, 1862, 1876, 2212
Napoleon, 642
Nations, 1624
Nature, 61, 798, 1792, 2207, 2215
Navel, 676
Navy, 920, 1029, 1054
Nazis, 1012, 1022, 1652
Nearer My God To Thee, 1561
Neck, 1468
Neckties, 176, 1785
Negative, 470
Negro, 1763, 1767, 1843, 2153
Neighbor, 8, 184, 211, 375, 1280, 1285
Nero, 1902
New Deal, 1640, 1766
New England, 385, 1376, 1956
New England conscience, 297
New Hampshire, 756
New Orleans, 6, 750
News, 1105, 1769
Newspapers, 612, 1106, 1108, 1109, 1112, 1113, 1116, 1117, 1165, 1303, 1339, 1684, 2010, 2129
Newton, Sir Isaac, 964, 1792
New York Herald Tribune, 2001
New York Post, 471
New York Times, 610, 2132
Nickel, 708, 784, 862, 889, 1506, 1585, 1586, 1701, 2151
Night, 434, 714, 1330
Night gown, 725
Night rates, 1429
Nizer, Louis, 1747
Noise, 112, 328, 357, 454, 838, 992, 1330, 2022
Nonagenarian, 1553
Nonsense, 970, 1782
Noose, 196, 1867
Norris, Kathleen, 2103
Nose, 206, 823, 1011, 1500, 2211
Novelist, 2103
Nude, 340, 638
Nudist, 230, 367, 591, 659, 781, 799, 1889
Nudity, 779
Nuns, 746
Nurse, 504, 714, 725, 1202, 1515, 1565
Nut, 147, 818

O

Oakum, 1522
Obesity, 830
Obituary, 1101, 1431, 1814
Objector, 1018
Obligation, 1584
Observatory, 1790
Obstetrician, 2208
Ocean, 522, 1652
Oculist, 1528
Officer, 502, 1030, 1033, 1038, 1050, 1070, 1653
Oil, 1412, 1860
Old age, 536, 539, 558, 1201, 1587, 1705
Old maid, 1066, 1294, 1563, 2150, 2196

Olives, 1243
Omaha, 50
Omnibus, 550, 1698
OPA, 821
Opera, 116
Operations, 662, 1508, 1519, 1555, 1556
Optimist, 312, 313
Oratory, 1801, 1843
Orchestra, 90, 113, 116, 117, 464
Orchids, 1213
Organ recital, 93
Ormandy, Eugene, 90
Orphan, 401
Orthodoxy, 463
Ostend, 2082
O'Ryan, Jack, 1857
Oysters, 837, 845

P

Pail, 603
Painting, 62, 63, 79, 1579, 2197
Pants, 609, 674, 788, 796, 992, 2169
Parachutes, 1065
Parachutist, 1066
Parade, 341
Paralysis, 1528, 1784
Paratrooper, 1016
Parents, 708, 713, 1310
Paris, 67, 225, 2042
Paris green, 1811
Parishioners, 1777
Parker, Dorothy, 242, 358, 700, 880, 2010, 2103, 2109
Parrot, 1453, 1852, 2045
Partnership, 1725
Party, 183, 245, 358, 391, 558, 811, 1632, 2036, 2131, 2133, 2172
Passengers, 883, 2061, 2062
Pastor, 1740, 1756, 1757, 1761
Patent medicine, 1475
Patience, 1564
Patient, 1504, 1541, 1565
Paul, 1949
Payment, 1057, 1227, 1251, 1377, 1466, 1589
Peace, 39, 477, 1293, 1732
Pearls, 977
Peas, 557
Pencil, 1530
Penguins, 746
People, 1759
Perambulator, 733
Perfume, 628, 736, 1238, 1334, 1814
Pershing, Gen. John, 283
Pessimist, 45, 313, 461, 1601
Petticoat, 785
Phares, Dun, 78
Pharmacist, 679
Phelps, William Lyon, 939
Philistines, 1786, 1803
Philosophers, 934, 1437, 1439, 1776
Photograph, 81, 633, 1008, 2154
Physical culture, 1968
Physicist, 1545
Piano, 1446
Piccolo, 101
Pickpocket, 591, 666
Pick-up, 1259
Picture, 77, 80, 81, 1261, 1750, 2008
Pies, 688, 715
Pig, 8, 237, 878, 897, 1168
Pigeon, 1219
Pilgrims, 1403, 1717
Pilgrim Society, 1403
Pill, 1537, 1563
Pistol, 164, 1074, 1148
Pitcher, 842
Pitt, William, 1079
Pittsburgh, 176, 760
Pitts, Zazu, 1062
Plagiarism, 1800, 2117
Plaid, 696
Planter, 6, 385
Plastic surgery, 1519, 2211
Platitude, 1845
Platonic, 1249
Players Club, 373
Player piano, 1561
Plumber, 678, 1743
Plum pudding, 364
Plural, 1880
Pockets, 256, 661, 1143, 1603
Poem, 12, 1857, 2124
Poet, 1343, 2122, 2127, 2130, 2133
Poetry, 79, 971, 1110, 1343
Poker, 1032, 1687
Poland, 5
Pole, 390

Police, 153, 865, 1126, 1440
Police car, 638
Police force, 637, 1112
Policeman, 900, 1149, 2060, 2066
Policy, 625, 650, 1113
Polish-Russian border, 5
Political speaker, 1636
Politics, 333, 1630, 1635, 1644, 1653
Poore, Charles, 2132
Popularity, 428
Porter, 2061, 2062
Portrait, 64, 1555
Positive, 470
Posterity, An Ode to, 2119
Post-office, 1778
Postponement, 1108, 1435, 1456
Potatoes, 10, 549, 1104
Potato salad, 1445
Po Valley, 982
Poultry ranch, 2103
Practice, 1511
Praise, 288, 2025, 2171
Prayer, 1383, 1668, 1680, 1683, 1685, 1687, 1695, 1702, 1758, 1759, 1969, 2192
Praying mantis, 1390
Preacher, 1689, 1691, 1726, 1731, 1749, 1758, 1772
Prejudice, 330
Prepositions, 990
Preserves, 379
Prescriptions, 1300, 1507, 1512, 1537
Press agent, 642, 1102
Priam, 1236
Prices, 4, 396, 847, 850
Pride, 327
Prince, 1204
Prince of Wales, 1050
Princeton University, 609
Principles, 335
Printing press, 1114
Prison, 437
Prisoners, 1083, 1164, 1170, 1385
Private, 1040, 2123
Producer, 609, 2035
Profanity, 1127
Professor, 356, 546, 949, 956, 977, 997
Profit, 651, 1415
Progress, 980, 2014
Propaganda, 948
Prophets, 426
Proposal, 1211, 1264, 1429, 1458, 1738, 2160
Protestants, 1711
Proverb, 1871
Providence, 1653, 2080
Prunes, 898, 1690
Psalm, 522, 991
Psychiatry, 1502, 1516, 1518
Psychoanalysis, 1543
Psychologist, 998, 1794, 1797
Puberty, 304
Puddle, 30, 270
Pullman, 231, 955, 1168, 2028, 2061, 2062
Pumpkin, 285
Pun, 1867, 1881
Punctuality, 353, 371, 1041
Punctuation, 975
Puncture, 2067
Punishment, 541, 983
Pup, 645, 1746
Puritans, 993
Pussy, 32
Pygmalion, 2110

Q

Quack, 30, 1544
Quadruplets, 508
Quaker, 1727
Quart, 3
Quartette, 102
Quarrel, 164, 1159, 1238, 1306, 1458
Questioner, 352, 1372, 1430, 1457, 1794, 2031, 2167
Quintuplets, 701

R

Rabbi, 1686
Rabbits, 1374, 1942, 2009
Race (human), 12, 451, 452, 853, 1953
Racing, 1955, 1974
Raccoon, 661
Racquets, 617
Radcliffe College, 969
Radicals, 1642
Radio, 258, 464, 1392, 1966
Radio call, 638, 2010
Raffle, 663

Railroad, 151, 608
Rain, 422, 436, 691, 1265, 1790
Raisins, 311
Ranch, 2
Randolph, John, 247, 835, 1664
Rat, 1777
Ration books, 730
Rationing, 941
Rat poison, 677
Rattlesnake, 161, 604, 2168
Razor blades, 196, 504, 1493, 1745
Reality, 192, 221
Recamier, Madame, 384
Reception, 1713, 1876
Recruit, 1019, 1046, 1709
Red Cross, 1035
Red light, 989, 2060
Reducing, 843
Reference, 1600
Reform, 1829
Refrigerator, 271, 1392
Refugee, 1936
Relatives, 928, 1283, 1580
Relativity, 1791
Religion, 1162, 1698, 1705, 1715, 1730, 1747
Rembrandt, 69
Renewed compliments, 2125
Renown, 940
Rent, 342, 633, 1379
Repairs, 651
Repartée, 1885
Repertoire, 1296
Reporter, 1103, 1105, 1111, 1116, 1407, 1653
Republican, 1152, 1648, 1649, 1849, 1859
Research, 2117
Respect, 397
Responsibility, 432
Restaurant, 619, 816, 820, 825, 849
Revivalist, 1739
Revival meeting, 712, 1725, 1760, 1767, 1778
Reviver, 1879
Revolution, French, 1862
Revolving door, 1417
Rhetoric, 1875
Rheumatism, 1521
Rhinoceros, 1939
Rhubarb, 827
Rice, 1478
Rich, 592, 928, 1576, 1948
Richards, Ben, 1159
Rifle range, 1046
Rifles, 1024, 1034
Rigoletto, 104
Ring, 272, 1251, 1667
Ripley, "Believe it or not," 344
Ritz Carlton, 448
Rivalry, 656
Rivers, 196, 1748
Rivets, 737
Rocking horse, 1796
Rogers, H. H., 1597
Rogers, Will, 553, 1812, 2003
Roller coaster, 1963
Rolls Royce, 1489, 2165
Romance, 1242, 1256
Rome, 1647
Roman history, 950
Roman holiday, 1902
Rookie, 1021, 1085
Roosevelt, Eleanor, 1013
Roosevelt, F. D., 180, 948, 1638, 1663, 1821, 1832
Roosevelt, James, 1832
Roosevelt, Theodore, 596, 1072, 1599, 1859
Rope, 233, 325
Rope trick, 1076
Rose, Billy, 2007
Rose petal, 2107
Rotarian, 99
Rotary Club, 1853
Roulette wheel, 1973
Rousseau, Jean Baptiste, 2119
Rowdies, 1587
Rubinstein, Anton, 110
Rumor, 1454
Russia, 5, 962

S

Safe, 616
Safety pins, 924
Sailor, 341, 1007, 1029, 1522
Saint, 1719, 1949
Saint Francis, 261
Salary, 307, 663, 687, 1067, 1288
Salesman, 14, 647, 763, 1388

Salmon, 1931
Sales resistance, 602
Saloon, 860, 901
Salute, 1022, 1659
Salvation, 1699
Salvation Army, 1709
Samson, 1786
Sand, 761
Sandwiches, 606, 819, 871, 995, 2030
San Francisco, Calif., 111, 341, 630, 760, 1870
San Jose, Calif., 1906
San Simeon, 2003
Santa Monica, California, 153
Sarazen, Gene, 1950
Sashes, 740
Saving, 1585
Saxe, John Godfrey, 2080
Scales, 444
Scar, 191, 1508
School, 197, 965, 987
Schoolboy, 942
Schoolhouses, 1404
Schwab, Charles M., 60
Science, 1329, 1715
Scolding, 690, 704
Scotch and soda, 906
Scotchman, 404, 405, 408, 409, 410, 411, 412, 413, 852, 862, 869, 895, 910, 1069, 1221, 1415, 1429, 1596, 1872
Scoundrel, 1134
Screaming, 111
Screecher, 1689
Screw driver, 667
Script writer, 2034
Sea captain, 2102
Séance, 1323
Seasickness, 1420, 1548
Secretary, 2100
Secrets, 241, 476, 1286, 1328, 1553
Seeds, 285, 822, 1706
Self-defense, 1448
Self-made man, 431
Self-reliance, 318
Selling, 437
Semeticus, 631
Semaphores, 1048
Senate, 1668
Sentence, 198, 1131, 1161, 1170
Sentry, 1003, 1031, 1039
Sergeant, 1004, 1034, 1046, 1064
Sermons, 653, 927, 1694, 1724, 1746, 1751, 1764, 1765
Serpent, 67
Servant, 1067, 1876
Sex, 973, 1208, 1230, 1232, 2032, 2153, 2186
Sex appeal, 2032
Sexton, 517, 1754
Shad, 346
Shakespeare, William, 1681, 1866, 1874, 1893, 2038, 2130
Shampoo, 921, 1473
Shark, 522
Shaves, 521, 751, 825, 1473
Shaw, George Bernard, 81, 116, 244, 380, 547, 694, 1787, 1836, 2104, 2110, 2125, 2126
Sheep, 170
Sheep ranch, 2
Sheets, 1367, 1805
Sheridan, Gen. Philip H., 759
Sheridan, Richard Brinsley, 1555
Sheriff, 1164
Shilling, 2104
Shiner (black eye), 1389
Ship, 472, 920, 2045, 2102
Ship's log, 1200
Shipwreck, 460, 2183
Shirt, 212, 1312, 1952
Shirtsleeves, 1726
Shock, 1000
Shoehorn, 1563
Shoelaces, 277
Shoes, 257, 406, 420, 774, 784, 1583, 2061
Shooting, 894, 1036, 1434, 1440
Shortcomings, 1468
Short story, 2196
Shotgun, 385, 1478
Show, 2002, 2029
Shower, 1315
Show-off, 28
Siam, 1236
Siddons, Mrs., 2017
Sight, 791, 1586
Sign, 35, 630, 641, 668, 865, 1556, 1947, 2015
Signal, 2060, 2077
Silence, 454, 1317, 1325, 1346, 1807
Silver spoon, 500

Simile, 591
Sin, 508, 1694, 1734, 1740
Singer, 106
Singer's Midget, 2028
Singing, 283, 1516
Sink, 683, 1376
Sinner, 1684, 1719
Sinus, 1547
Sister, 1709, 2208
Six pence, 404
Skeleton, 1541
Skeptic, 1544
Skinner, Cornelia Otis, 2004
Skunk, 40
Skyscraper, 234
Slacks, 1223
Slang, 1081, 1779
Slave, 552
Slavery, 1693
Sleep, 237, 454, 943, 1072, 1231, 1322, 1386, 1501, 1506, 1516, 1539, 1564, 2028, 2172
Slip, 1527, 2002
Slot machines, 871, 1590
Slow motion pictures, 411
Slug, 249, 327
Smile, 320, 952, 1311
Smith, Abner, 1265
Smith, Sydney, 1562
Smoker, 858
Smoking, 450, 1059, 1291, 1540, 1591
Snake, 1932
Snake River, 10
Sneeze, 361
Snootiness, 362
Snoring, 1072, 1487, 1552
Snow, 691
Soap, 1315
Society, 1103
Socrates, 1437
Soda water, 927
Sodium chloride, 735
Soldier, 283, 753, 822, 846, 1000, 1006, 1007, 1008, 1010, 1011, 1014, 1023, 1027, 1031, 1032, 1034, 1036, 1037, 1041, 1044, 1049, 1052, 1053, 1055, 1057, 1058, 1059, 1067, 1068, 1071, 1073, 1076, 1080, 1081, 1084, 1303, 1686, 1952, 2031
Solomon Islands, 1062
Son, 192, 351, 360, 660, 703, 721, 733, 899, 1418, 1769
Son-in-law, 2192
Song, 100, 450, 1602, 2165
Soong, Mme., 1695
Sophistication, 2170
Sopranos, 111, 1296
Sore throat, 1559
Sorrow, 195, 595, 1244
Soul, 595, 1232, 1693
Soup, 325, 357, 818, 1015, 1037, 1052
Sourpuss, 274
Souse, 871, 912
South, 1686
Southampton, Earl of, 2111
Southerner, 330, 756, 816
Southern Pacific, 608
South Seas, 460, 464
Spaghetti, 277
Spain, 757
Spam, 226
Spanking, 738, 1475
Spare parts, 92
Speaker, 954, 1357, 1690, 1736, 1814, 1818, 1825, 1829, 1837, 1840, 1843, 1858, 1860, 1889, 1890, 2173, 2189
Specialist, 1500, 1510, 1735
Spectacles, 798, 1222
Spelling, 970, 1546, 1879
Spenser, Edmund, 1639, 2111
Spider, 612
Spinster, 514, 1453, 1735, 1878, 2123, 2194, 2209
Spit, 689, 1652, 1935, 1948
Spittoon, 902
Sport, 1938
Stagnation, 2181
Stalin, Joseph, 1821
Stamp, 653
Stars, 334, 1703, 1854
Statistics, 530, 1357, 1488
Statue, 678, 1662
Steak, 846, 847
Stealing, 1127, 1161, 2117
Steam, 1329
Steamship, 1660
Steel, 1763
Stenographer, 639, 1343
Stephens, Alexander II, 246
Sterilization, 742

Stockings, 420, 2187
Stomach, 1562
Stone, 1523
Store, 343, 620, 627
Storekeeper, 255, 620
Stork, 39, 514, 1355
Storm, 322, 1700, 1704
Story-teller, 1816, 1825, 1892
St. Paul, Minn., 1757
Stradivarius, 92
Straight line, 2200
Strained relations, 1714
Strategy, 227
Strangers, 202, 260
Strawberry festival, 1690
Street car, 355, 2179
Strychnine, 1811
Stuffing, 1331
Stuttering, 878, 1819, 2041
St. Vitus Dance, 1521
Substitute, 1755
Subway, 1441
Success, 607, 1512
Suffering, 1632
Suffragists, 2186
Suicide, 556, 2007
Suit, 365, 1160, 1421, 2010
Sulphuric acid, 823
Sullivan, 1893, 2000
Sultan, 29
Summer, 8, 750, 863
Sumner, Charles, 1693
Sun, 1634
Sun tan, 1970
Sunday School, 961, 1733, 1734, 1737, 1779, 1786
Superman, 1730
Superstition, 472
Surprise, 1371
Surveyor, 5
Swain, 1224
Swallow, 863, 1588
Swan, 107
Sweethearts, 919, 1468
Swimming, 2104
Swindle, 640
Swine, 1728
Swing, 105, 114, 1210
Swiss cheese, 819
Symphony, 94, 118
Synonym, 1873, 1907

T

Tact, 559, 2208
Tactfulness, 1406
Taft, William Howard, 938, 1817
Tag, 25
Tails, 1583
Tainted, 1597
Talent, 559
Talk, 451, 704, 1304, 1460, 2183, 2203
Talking, 1167, 1501, 1525, 1697, 1702, 1806, 1808, 1809, 1846
Talleyrand, 1080, 1647
Tarzan, 617
Taste, 2101
Tax assessor, 17
Taxes, 464, 1628, 1663
Taxi, 1221, 2065
Taxi-driver, 386, 669
Tea, 692, 834, 835, 838
Teacher, 147, 640, 715, 947, 949, 950, 951, 952, 953, 959, 961, 962, 964, 966, 970, 971, 974, 979, 980, 984, 989, 991, 992, 993, 994, 998, 999, 1689
Teeth, false, 342, 688, 841, 1485, 1505, 1723, 1739, 2074
Teething, 507
Teetotaler, 910
Teheran, 1821
Telegram, 286, 506, 722, 986, 1250, 1298, 1476, 1847, 2020
Telegraph, 73, 1326, 1429, 1471
Telephone, 654, 657, 1068, 1362, 1427, 1431, 1539, 1545, 1589, 1721, 1743, 2024, 2031
Telescope, 1790
Temperament, 273
Templeton, Alec, 98
Temptation, 299, 300, 955
Tenant, 665
Ten Commandments, 1031
Tennis, 617
Tennyson, Alfred Lord, 381
Testimony, 1135, 1475
Texas, 160, 715, 759, 762, 763, 1147, 1148
Thackeray, 837

Theatre, 734, 2040
Theologian, 1776
Thief, 435, 436
Thorn, 1937
Thoroughbreds, 195
Thumb, 1320, 2211
Thunder, 1965
Ticket, 1063, 1446
Tickle, 15
Tides, 603, 1470
Tiger, 1938
Tightwad, 1324
Time, 11, 537, 590, 706, 892, 1239, 1373, 1560, 1729
Time limit, 1804
Tips, 412, 1598, 2062
Tire, 1758, 2067
Toast, 849, 873, 926, 1821
Toastmaster, 996, 1143, 1690, 1815, 1848
Tobacco, 151, 856, 859, 1935
Toenails, 201, 1367
Tomato, 63
Tomorrow, 923, 1721
Tong, 516
Tongue, 666, 941, 1851, 2183
Tonsils, 1503, 1552
Toothache, 1344, 1521
Toothpaste, 1328
Tosca, 91
Tourists, 161, 345, 2211
Towels, 174, 448
Towing, 2063
Toy shop, 1796
Traffic, 1883, 2069
Traffic light, 2069
Traffic officer, 2060, 2069, 2075
Tragedy, 185
Train, 17, 25, 160, 912, 1059, 1258, 1724, 1970
Tramp, 2196
Transvaal, 1077
Trapeze, 1877
Traveler, 1590
Treason, 1635
Tree, 410, 557, 623, 754, 868, 948, 1016
Tricks, 743
Triplets, 1432
Trivial, 1558
Trouble, 190, 914, 968, 1341
Truck-driver, 1883
Trust, 192, 1262, 2186
Truth, 438, 708, 1153, 1543
Tsar, 962
Tsarina, 962
Trust, 2199
Truth, 433, 446
Tulip, 344
Tunnel, 1327, 1426, 2209
Turkey, 606, 1331, 1722
Turner, J. M. W., 63, 74
Turtles, 853, 1230
Twain, Mark, 62, 63, 91, 233, 433, 543, 544, 612, 1597, 1606, 1607, 1681, 1714, 1813, 1828, 2112, 2120, 2153
Twenty Grand, 1975
Twins, 724, 1479, 2020, 2153
Twin beds, 1321
Type, 1117

U

Udders, 987
Umbrella, 1606, 2160
"Uncle Tom's Cabin," 2021
Understanding, 1253, 1290, 1303, 1492, 2163
Unemployment, 464
Undertaker, 6, 664, 1469
University of Chicago, 356
Untermeyer, Louis, 2133
Untidiness, 1464
Urchin, 1729
U.S.O., 1006, 1068

V

Vacation, 658
Vagabond, 295
Valet, 282, 1595
Valise, 282
Value, 396
Vancouver, B.C., 503
Vandenberg, Arthur H., 1338
Vanity, 1771
Van Loon, Hendrick Wilhelm, 1899
Vaudeville actor, 2037
Ventriloquist, 852
Verbosity, 1831
Verdi, Guiseppe, 104

Vermin, 49
Verse, 1733, 1779, 2107
Veterinarian, 1557
Vicar, 1755
Vice, 302, 305
Victoria, 1427
Vincent, George E., 1823
Violin, 92, 194, 1246
Violinist, 90, 95
Virtue, 301, 302, 305, 306
Vocabulary, 1488
Voice, 1805
Voltaire, 248, 2119
Volunteer, 1001, 1010
Vote, 370, 1654, 2207

W

WACS, 1056
Waffle, 354
Waiter, 325, 364, 848, 852, 853, 854, 898
Waiting-room, 1513
Waitress, 393, 846, 849, 1434
Wallet, 1596
Walk, 31, 318, 451, 1562, 1968
Walnuts, 184
War, 1008, 1650, 1666
War map, 1013
Ward, Artemus, 1827
Wart, 1517
Washing, 174, 1335
Washington, D.C., 1073, 1581, 1649
Washington, George, 1381, 1634
Watches, 9, 651, 1373, 1462, 1736, 1818
Watchman, 616
Water, 43, 262, 322, 408, 603, 731, 751, 761, 874, 916, 1043, 1434, 1699, 1841, 2104
Waterloo, 642
Water wagon, 869
Wealth, 1220, 1595, 1605, 2187
Weaning, 109, 635
Weasel, 103
Weather, 249, 1861
Weather bureau, 657
Weeds, 301, 822
Wedding, 1410, 1415, 1430, 1435, 1478, 1491, 1975
Weeping, 26, 739, 1739
Weeping water, 1895
Weight, 509, 793, 903, 1477, 1725
Well, 1527
Wellington, Duke of, 281, 642
West, 761, 1234, 1258
West, Mae, 1963
Westchester County, 1144
Western Union, 506
Westley, Helen, 2008
Whales, 165, 1933
Wheat, 960
Wheelbarrow, 1967
Wheeling, 374, 2072
Whip, 270
Whipping, 717
Whiskey, 407, 409, 890, 893, 895, 906, 1043, 1537, 1932
Whistle, 271, 1723, 2060
Whistler, James McNeill, 61, 62, 64, 65, 70, 74, 200, 369, 615, 1077
White House, 1078, 1638, 1639
Widow, 524, 1136, 1323, 1421
Wife, 151, 343, 356, 502, 532, 973, 1286, 1311, 1342, 1344, 1356, 1366, 1375, 1384, 1397, 1407, 1432, 1437, 1463, 1467, 1474, 1744, 1755, 2100
Wife beating, 1151, 1365
Wilde, Oscar, 70, 1253, 1800, 1803, 1943, 2044, 2127
Will, 535, 1507, 1518, 2039
Willie, 43, 682, 693, 740, 742, 743, 1238
Wilson, Francis, 1597
Wilson, Woodrow, 937, 1868
Wind, 40, 752, 1823
Wine, 450, 540, 870, 927
Winter, 5, 634, 1484
Wire, 656, 1310
Wisdom, 475
Wise men, 198, 934
Wit, 184, 229, 1449
Witness, 1153, 1160
Women, 3, 162, 183, 238, 257, 271, 395, 444, 450, 646, 654, 672, 683, 705, 800, 843, 918, 922, 927, 930, 1160, 1169, 1171, 1201, 1225, 1226, 1253, 1290, 1363, 1370, 1377, 1440, 1654, 1809, 2151, 2155, 2156, 2157, 2159, 2160, 2162, 2163, 2166, 2173, 2174, 2176, 2178, 2179, 2181, 2183, 2185, 2187, 2190, 2191, 2192, 2195, 2199, 2202, 2207, 2216

Women's club, 1884, 2020
Wood, General Leonard, 1899
Wooden leg, 1522
Wood-wind, 101
Wooing, 1239
Woollcott, Alexander, 700
Words, 976, 1343, 1388, 1753
Wordsworth, William, 1866
Work, 11, 473, 593, 598
World Series, 1966
World War I, 283, 1050, 1070, 1856
World War II, 667, 730, 821, 1030, 1061, 1076, 1476, 1653, 2026
Worms, 16, 327, 529
Worry, 311, 703, 1292
Wright, Wilbur, 1852
Wrinkles, 311, 2158
Wrist watch, 736
Writers, 248, 680, 1107, 2032, 2101, 2118

Y

Yacht, 1409
Yale, 546, 1972
Yankee, 14, 363, 1025, 1060, 1593, 1686
Yankee Stadium, 965
Yawning, 519, 2005
Yeggman, 2179
Yessing, 1234, 1297, 1384, 1471
Yes-man, 153, 154
Yiddish, 329
Youth, 536, 694, 697, 711, 716, 766, 872

Z

Zangwill, Israel, 1787
Zero, 753
Zoo, 31, 37, 514, 853, 865, 1212, 1872